Survival

GLOBAL POLITICS AND STRATEGY

Volume 66 Number 3 | June–July 2024

'Sceptical of American exhortations not to worry about a dire alternative future, European policymakers felt compelled to start considering it.'

François Heisbourg, Planning for a Post-American Europe, p. 8.

'It took time for Western states to realise that if they wished for multilateral institutions to continue functioning, they needed to ensure that their disagreements with Russia did not result in procedural paralysis or dominate their agendas with non-Western partners.'

Hanna Notte, Russia, the Global South and the Mechanics of the Nuclear Order, p. 54.

'Gaza will be filled with angry and vengeful young men, ripe for recruitment by Hamas. Even if Hamas is militarily defeated, its theory of resistance – that the only way to create a free Palestine is through violence – remains popular.'

Daniel Byman, A War They Both Are Losing: Israel, Hamas and the Plight of Gaza, p. 70.

Survival

GLOBAL POLITICS AND STRATEGY

Volume 66 Number 3 | June–July 2024

Contents

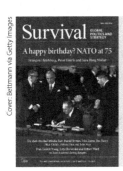

Survival
GLOBAL POLITICS AND STRATEGY

The International Institute for Strategic Studies

2121 K Street, NW | Suite 600 | Washington DC 20037 | USA
Tel +1 202 659 1490   Fax +1 202 659 1499   E-mail survival@iiss.org   Web www.iiss.org

Arundel House | 6 Temple Place | London | WC2R 2PG | UK
Tel +44 (0)20 7379 7676   Fax +44 (0)20 7836 3108   E-mail iiss@iiss.org

14th Floor, GFH Tower | Bahrain Financial Harbour | Manama | Kingdom of Bahrain
Tel +973 1718 1155   Fax +973 1710 0155   E-mail iiss-middleeast@iiss.org

9 Raffles Place | #49-01 Republic Plaza | Singapore 048619
Tel +65 6499 0055   Fax +65 6499 0059   E-mail iiss-asia@iiss.org

Pariser Platz 6A | 10117 Berlin | Germany
Tel +49 30 311 99 300   E-mail iiss-europe@iiss.org

Survival Online www.tandfonline.com/survival and www.iiss.org/publications/survival

Aims and Scope *Survival* is one of the world's leading forums for analysis and debate of international and strategic affairs. Shaped by its editors to be both timely and forward thinking, the journal encourages writers to challenge conventional wisdom and bring fresh, often controversial, perspectives to bear on the strategic issues of the moment. With a diverse range of authors, *Survival* aims to be scholarly in depth while vivid, well written and policy-relevant in approach. Through commentary, analytical articles, case studies, forums, review essays, reviews and letters to the editor, the journal promotes lively, critical debate on issues of international politics and strategy.

Editor **Dana Allin**
Managing Editor **Jonathan Stevenson**
Associate Editor **Carolyn West**
Editorial Assistant **Conor Hodges**
Production and Cartography **Alessandra Beluffi, Ravi Gopar, Jade Panganiban, James Parker, Kelly Verity**

Contributing Editors

William Alberque	**Franz-Stefan Gady**	**Nigel Inkster**	**Benjamin Rhode**	**Robert Ward**
Aaron Connelly	**Bastian Giegerich**	**Jeffrey Mazo**	**Ben Schreer**	**Marcus Willett**
James Crabtree	**Nigel Gould-Davies**	**Fenella McGerty**	**Maria Shagina**	**Lanxin Xiang**
Chester A. Crocker	**Melissa K. Griffith**	**Irene Mia**	**Karen Smith**	
Bill Emmott	**Emile Hokayem**	**Meia Nouwens**	**Angela Stent**	

Published for the IISS by
Routledge Journals, an imprint of Taylor & Francis, an Informa business.

ISBN 978-1-032-80659-4 paperback / 978-1-003-49799-8 ebook

SUBMISSIONS

To submit an article, authors are advised to follow these guidelines:

- *Survival* articles are around 4,000–10,000 words long including endnotes. A word count should be included with a draft.
- All text, including endnotes, should be double-spaced with wide margins.
- Any tables or artwork should be supplied in separate files, ideally not embedded in the document or linked to text around it.
- All *Survival* articles are expected to include endnote references. These should be complete and include first and last names of authors, titles of articles (even from newspapers), place of publication, publisher, exact publication dates, volume and issue number (if from a journal) and page numbers. Web sources should include complete URLs and DOIs if available.
- A summary of up to 150 words should be included with the article. The summary should state the main argument clearly and concisely, not simply say what the article is about.

- A short author's biography of one or two lines should also be included. This information will appear at the foot of the first page of the article.

Please note that *Survival* has a strict policy of listing multiple authors in alphabetical order.

Submissions should be made by email, in Microsoft Word format, to survival@iiss.org. Alternatively, hard copies may be sent to *Survival*, IISS–US, 2121 K Street NW, Suite 801, Washington, DC 20037, USA.

The editorial review process can take up to three months. *Survival*'s acceptance rate for unsolicited manuscripts is less than 20%. *Survival* does not normally provide referees' comments in the event of rejection. Authors are permitted to submit simultaneously elsewhere so long as this is consistent with the policy of the other publication and the Editors of *Survival* are informed of the dual submission.

Readers are encouraged to comment on articles from the previous issue. Letters should be concise, no longer than 750 words and relate directly to the argument or points made in the original article.

Survival: Global Politics and Strategy (Print ISSN 0039-6338, Online ISSN 1468-2699) is published bimonthly for a total of 6 issues per year by Taylor & Francis Group, 4 Park Square, Milton Park, Abingdon, Oxon, OX14 4RN, UK. Periodicals postage paid (Permit no. 13095) at Brooklyn, NY 11256.

Airfreight and mailing in the USA by agent named World Container Inc., c/o BBT 150-15, 183rd Street, Jamaica, NY 11413, USA.

US Postmaster: Send address changes to Survival, World Container Inc., c/o BBT 150-15, 183rd Street, Jamaica, NY 11413, USA.

Subscription records are maintained at Taylor & Francis Group, 4 Park Square, Milton Park, Abingdon, OX14 4RN, UK.

Subscription information: For more information and subscription rates, please see tandfonline.com/pricing/journal/TSUR. Taylor & Francis journals are available in a range of different packages, designed to suit every library's needs and budget. This journal is available for institutional subscriptions with online-only or print & online options. This journal may also be available as part of our libraries, subject collections or archives. For more information on our sales packages, please visit librarianresources.taylorandfrancis.com.

For support with any institutional subscription, please visit help.tandfonline.com or email our dedicated team at subscriptions@tandf.co.uk.

Subscriptions purchased at the personal rate are strictly for personal, non-commercial use only. The reselling of personal subscriptions is prohibited. Personal subscriptions must be purchased with a personal cheque, credit card or BAC/wire transfer. Proof of personal status may be requested.

Back issues: Please visit https://taylorandfrancis.com/journals/customer-services/ for more information on how to purchase back issues.

Ordering information: To subscribe to the journal, please contact T&F Customer Services, Informa UK Ltd, Sheepen Place, Colchester, Essex, CO3 3LP, UK. Tel: +44 (0) 20 8052 2030; email subscriptions@tandf.co.uk.

Taylor & Francis journals are priced in USD, GBP and EUR (as well as AUD and CAD for a limited number of journals). All subscriptions are charged depending on where the end customer is based. If you are unsure which rate applies to you, please contact Customer Services. All subscriptions are payable in advance and all rates include postage. We are required to charge applicable VAT/GST on all print and online combination subscriptions, in addition to our online-only journals. Subscriptions are entered on an annual basis, i.e., January to December. Payment may be made by sterling cheque, dollar cheque, euro cheque, international money order, National Giro or credit cards (Amex, Visa and Mastercard).

Submission information: See https://www.tandfonline.com/journals/tsur20

Advertising: See https://taylorandfrancis.com/contact/advertising/

Permissions: See help.tandfonline.com/Librarian/s/article/Permissions

All Taylor & Francis Group journals are printed on paper from renewable sources by accredited partners.

June–July 2024

Planning for a Post-American Europe

François Heisbourg

The possible return of Donald Trump as US president has again raised the spectre of the United States abandoning its central role in the European security order. NATO had a near-death experience during Trump's 2017–21 term, when he cast doubt on America's readiness to defend NATO member states such as Montenegro, kowtowed to Russian President Vladimir Putin, and considered withdrawing the US from the Alliance.[1] In the event, the US defence bureaucracy sustained and even increased the US military effort in Europe during that period. NATO assets including prepositioned US equipment and a rotational US force presence moved eastward, close to the borders of Russia and Belarus.[2] But Trump has since complained that the so-called 'deep state' had forced his hand at the time.[3]

His sentiments concerning Europe were relentlessly negative.[4] European leaders' best efforts to establish a modicum of trust fell flat, and they proved unable to work constructively with him. Despite bending over backwards, French President Emmanuel Macron never managed to establish a rapport with Trump comparable to that enjoyed by Abe Shinzo, then Japan's prime minister, or even North Korean leader Kim Jong-un. The only European figures Trump warmed to were Hungarian Prime Minister Viktor Orbán and Polish politician Jarosław Kaczyński,

François Heisbourg is IISS senior adviser for Europe. His book *Un monde sans l'Amérique* will be published by Odile Jacob in September 2024.

Survival | vol. 66 no. 3 | June–July 2024 | pp. 7–20   https://doi.org/10.1080/00396338.2024.2357473

both right-wing populists of a similar ilk who are outside the European mainstream. None of Trump's signature foreign-policy initiatives, notably the Abraham Accords between Israel and several Arab states, brought in the Europeans.

Trump has made it clear that a second term would be more disruptive than his first one, as he would be unconcerned about any subsequent term (which the US constitution bars), better sussed about how to navigate perceived political obstacles and more ruthless in doing so. He has indicated that his political appointments – informed by far-right organisations such as the America First Policy Institute, the Federalist Society and the Heritage Foundation – would be unabashedly ideological and vindictive, with an eye to eviscerating the body of civil servants and government professionals that he has branded the deep state and others call the administrative state.[5]

He has also said that he would resolve the war between Russia and Ukraine within 24 hours of taking office and might start with a peace plan carving up Ukrainian territory.[6] His supporters in Congress successfully blocked the funding of Ukraine's war effort for six months, until the end of April, causing Ukraine high casualties and substantial material and territorial losses. One statement in particular set off alarm bells in Europe and particularly in Germany. In February 2024, Trump said at a rally in South Carolina that he would encourage the Russians to do 'whatever the hell they want' to NATO members he did not consider to be pulling their weight financially.[7] Not even the most jaded Trump-watcher could simply dismiss this as muscular rhetoric about NATO's long-standing burden-sharing debate.

Sceptical of American exhortations not to worry about a dire alternative future, European policymakers felt compelled to start considering it. The content and process of full and detailed preparations for a Europe without America remain largely private, in part for reasons of common prudence. But talk in Brussels's European Union bubble is often looser than in national capitals. Vigorous public discussion has arisen on ramping up defence-industrial capabilities to help Ukraine and reduce European dependence on the US; the future of US extended nuclear deterrence; and France's readiness to give a specifically European dimension to nuclear deterrence whether in lieu of or in addition to US guarantees. Euro-American strategic intimacy –

one of the key intangible assets of the transatlantic alliance – may become an early casualty of resurgent Trumpism.

It is safe to assume that European capitals are engaging in contingency planning as to what they would do were a newly elected Trump to attempt to impose a 'dirty deal' on Ukraine. Given current divergences, notably between France and Germany, it is far from clear at this stage that such planning would produce a united response.

It's not only about Trump

While Trump may be the detonator of potential US–European estrangement, and provides strong political impetus for European preparations, it would be a mistake to assume that things will readily return to the traditional comfort zone if Joe Biden is re-elected. America overall has changed in ways that tend to narrow some of the consequences of possible presidential outcomes in November.

The COVID-19 pandemic, among other factors, has made the US body politic psychologically warier of outside exposure and commitment, economically leerier of globalisation and more comfortable with mercantilism. Biden's version of mercantilism is heavy on subsidies – the Inflation Reduction Act authorises $891 billion in new spending, the CHIPS and Science Act some $280bn – and is designed to foster not friend-shoring with European and Asian partners but rather domestic reindustrialisation and reshoring. Biden's programme doesn't preclude tariffs or straightforward protectionism: he suggests tripling duties on Chinese steel and aluminium exports (bringing them to 25%) and seeks to prevent the acquisition of U.S. Steel by Japan's Nippon Steel. Trump's plan would involve a general 10% tariff on all imports, with additional measures on specific goods or countries. Under either approach, European economies will be negatively affected.[8] China's kindred policy of massive domestic support, with $1.6 trillion to be spent on so-called 'new productive forces', will compound the effects.

In the US as in China, security issues are a central pillar of the new mercantilism. The US wants to enlist Europe in its 'high fence' policy of cutting off China's access to 'foundational technology'.[9] China, meanwhile, has been aggressively attempting to acquire such technology from Europe through intensive espionage, notably in Germany.[10] The EU countries are highly dependent on trade with both the US and China, and have found themselves whipsawed between the two. In 2019–20, for example, the US threatened to suspend the 'Five Eyes' intelligence-cooperation arrangement vis-à-vis the United Kingdom unless it removed the Chinese company Huawei, which is considered a back door for Chinese intelligence, from its 5G networks,[11] while China hinted that it would stop car imports from Germany if it refused to open the door to Huawei.[12]

The strong cultural and political links between the United States and most European countries – together they have shared democratic values, supported a rules-based international order and pursued common strategic goals vis-à-vis Russia – have so far sustained the transatlantic strategic bond. But tensions are likely to persist. If America's strategic and military commitment to NATO weakens, US leverage for co-opting Europe will diminish. While Trump 2.0 would accelerate this dynamic, it could also take hold gradually as a result of the United States' strategic rebalancing to the Indo-Pacific and increasing throw-weight in green technology, biomanufacturing, microelectronics and other critical areas advanced by the Biden administration's subsidies.

The present danger

The immediate European worry remains the future of the transatlantic strategic relationship, notably in facing the Russian threat. Biden's career has been built around the concept of the United States as the pivotal element of a mutually reinforcing 75-year-old system of set-piece alliances in Europe and East Asia, with shared values and practically unlimited security guarantees. Trump's world is about the here-and-now of the 'art of the deal', hovering between limited-liability, single-purpose, time-bounded transactions and an unabashed protection racket.

The Biden vision worked well during the Cold War. It was a more awkward fit after the Cold War ended, as NATO initially kept out of the Balkan wars and, even as NATO's Article 5 was invoked for the first time after 9/11, the US turned to a 'coalition of the willing' in undertaking the invasion and occupation of Iraq that split Europe down the middle. In a world where Russia was out and China not yet up, none of this mattered hugely for the European security order.

When Russia invaded Ukraine, the old order staged a comeback. Biden understood that transatlantic failure vis-à-vis Russia would degrade America's strategic and political position in the Indo-Pacific region. The problem is not this constructive present but the likely future. America's burden in Asia is likely to rise, especially as pressure from Beijing to resolve the Taiwan issue increases. As an increasingly recalcitrant Taiwanese population has made the peaceful approach less promising, a military confrontation has become more likely.

As the strategic centre of gravity shifts to East Asia, an analogy comes to mind. In March 1941, before the US became a belligerent in the Second World War, the so-called 'ABC-1' meeting in March 1941 involving Canada, the UK and the US produced a plan, called 'Rainbow No. 5', that if the US joined a global war in both the Atlantic and the Pacific, the former would take priority. The reasoning was that the Third Reich imperilled the entire world whereas Japan posed a more limited threat. At the time, this was a wise and difficult decision. Today, the parties would probably reach the opposite conclusion: China is clearly more pivotal than Russia. In the world of 2030, the US may no longer have its current ability to juggle emergencies in Europe and the Indo-Pacific area.

The nuclear dimension is, of course, the overwhelming factor for the future of the European security order, a dimension that did not exist during the great-power shifts of the 1930s. Since the full-scale invasion of Ukraine, Biden's Cold War formulation has made him cautious, arguably to the point of self-deterrence.

He has stated that US troops would never be deployed in Ukraine; initially was highly circumspect about transferring arguably offensive weapons, such as battle tanks, aircraft and missiles, to Ukraine; and neither supported nor abetted strikes on Russian territory.[13] The president's primary concern was to avoid uncontrolled escalation, potentially to the nuclear level. He dropped several of his reverse red lines after Russia had battered Ukraine and a consensus coalesced that Putin's actual nuclear intentions fell short of his bluster.[14] Offensive weapons were delivered from May 2022 onwards;

the release of foreign-owned F-16s was authorised in August 2023; main battle tanks were deployed by summer 2023; and extended-range Army Tactical Missile Systems (ATACMS) were transferred in spring 2024.

This sequence of unsolicited withholding and eventual release hurt Ukraine and sent mixed signals to Moscow, and presidential language that seemed to urge regime change muddled them further.[15] It also befuddled the Europeans, who didn't always share the White House's view. Eventually, some European allies either pushed hard for policy change, as Poland did on the transfer of F-16s, or simply ignored US restrictions, as the UK and France – and later Italy – did in sending Ukraine hundreds of *Storm Shadow* air-launched cruise missiles. The latter helped change the strategic picture in the Black Sea, precluding Russian warships from blocking Ukraine's critical grain exports. By February 2024, France and a number of European partners eventually moved from selected de facto breaks with US self-deterrence to a clearly stated policy of strategic ambiguity, including on issues such as an eventual European military presence in Ukraine.[16]

The day after Macron introduced this possibility on 26 February 2024, German Chancellor Olaf Scholz, apparently casting himself as the leader of both NATO and the EU, retorted that 'there will be no ground troops, no soldiers on Ukrainian soil sent there by European countries or NATO states'.[17] Since then, Macron has reiterated his suggestion: 'If the Russians were to break through the front lines, if there were a Ukrainian request – which is not the case today – we would legitimately have to ask ourselves this question.'[18] Macron has emphasised that mooting this possibility is part of calculated strategic ambiguity vis-à-vis Russia. Most EU and NATO leaders have avoided entering into the debate between Paris and Berlin.

Overall, it is clear that on an issue as critical as escalation control involving nuclear powers, there has been a parting of ways between the United States and Europe. Although the war against Ukraine has not directly implicated NATO's Article 5 and its ultimate nuclear implications, US self-deterrence on Ukraine can't help but downgrade European countries' expectations as to how the US would react to a direct attack on a NATO country and their assessments of the reliability of US extended deterrence. Were Trump to win the 2024 presidential election, those expectations would become all the more dire.

European options

For Europe, the challenge is to formulate priorities and strategies that account for these new realities. While it's not all about Trump, Trump 2.0 provides the baseline case for European preparations. Some contingencies, such as Biden's or Trump's incapacitation, would be easier to handle at least in the short run, while others, such as a reprise of the 6 January 2021 insurrection, are prohibitively difficult to plan for.

The evolved consensus in Europe is that the Russian threat is clear and paramount. Hungary stands out as an exception, with some nuisance power in terms of crafting and implementing policy, but its ability to block aid to Ukraine has proven to be less than that of Republicans in the US House of Representatives. While US military aid was suspended for close to four months in early 2024, the EU put together its €50bn aid package for Ukraine. This may change if populist parties sympathetic to Putin in France and Germany gain votes in forthcoming elections. For the time being, however, the failure of Ukraine's ground offensive in 2023 and its subsequently dismal and perilous military situation have hardened European governments' determination to raise defence budgets, which all EU and European NATO members are doing. As of early 2024, 2% of GDP was the median level of European defence spending, with countries such as Estonia, Greece and Poland reaching or exceeding 3% of GDP.[19] The UK and Sweden have stated their intent to raise defence spending to 2.5% of GDP.

The EU, and specifically the European Commission, which controls the disbursement of the EU's budget, has begun to play a more active role in the defence-industrial arena and in extending military aid to Ukraine. The European Defence Fund and related initiatives, which came on stream in 2021 with a seven-year budget of close to €8bn, is so far limited but can be viewed as a beginning. The so-called European Peace Facility has provided €11.1bn for arms transfers to Ukraine since the beginning of the war. The European Commission is thus entering into a wholly new line of business.

With more national and now EU money becoming available for defence in general and acquisition in particular, European governments are likely to be more inclined to reshore much of the defence procurement which now goes to US suppliers. Macron's call for a European preference in his Sorbonne speech of 25 April 2024 should gain greater resonance than earlier French calls of this sort, given the combination of more defence money for jobs at home and a diminished US commitment to Europe's defence. Furthermore, there is now serious talk at the European Commission of establishing a €100bn defence fund.[20] Although Germany, with its constitutional limits on public spending, will inevitably have reservations, Macron proposed doubling the EU's overall budget, which would hypothetically rise from €189bn in 2024 to some €380bn.[21]

More money and greater concentration of effort at both the EU and national levels are essential to making up for a US retreat from three-quarters of a century of 'unlimited liability' commitment to the Alliance. But money alone won't provide an answer to the strategic questions raised by such a development. As was already apparent in the German reaction last February to Trump's invitation to Russia to 'do whatever the hell what they want', the Europeans may need to seek a substitute for the United States' nuclear guarantee currently underpinning NATO's Article 5 commitment. On a number of occasions, at least three times thus far in 2024 alone, France has expressed a willingness to discuss Europeanising the nuclear dimension of deterrence.[22] Beyond inviting allied countries to follow French exercises involving the airborne component of France's nuclear forces, Paris has been short on specifics. These should emerge in discussions, as other allies will presumably have their own views on the subject and wish to make them known. The idea may begin to gain particular traction in Germany and Poland. Given the sensitive nature of the topic, however, details may not enter the public domain early on.

Russia might not find a European deterrent credible

Constructive discussion of the possibility can arise only if three very different audiences are ready to take it seriously. The first is Russia, the contemplated 'deteree' and a nuclear superpower, which might not find a European deterrent credible if it rested only on the existing French and British nuclear capabilities and postures. The second is the readiness of the putative 'deterrer' to build up a European dimension. The third consists of European nuclear countries themselves, which may prefer to stick with their putative NATO nuclear missions under US extended deterrence, however weakened, rather than adopting what they consider an untested alternative. The latter concern, however, may abate due to doubts about the future viability of Article 5. Indeed, this was the unheralded reality during the Cold War, when NATO and French tactical nuclear weapons were located in West Germany and France–NATO military agreements allowed for deconfliction.

Bolstering the European dimension of nuclear deterrence may be more feasible than ensuring extended deterrence from a United States led by a president who presumes Europe needs NATO more than the US does and separated from the continent by, as Trump put it, 'a nice big, beautiful ocean'.[23] Such concerns, of course, long predate Trump. In 1962, Charles de Gaulle famously expressed his scepticism about the United States' willingness to sacrifice Los Angeles if Stuttgart were nuked, which was one of the reasons for France's decision to go it alone in the nuclear arena at the time.[24] The advent of Trump has simply given greater weight to de Gaulle's worries.

More broadly, if the US settles into being a dormant partner within NATO, the issue of whether the Alliance will become a European-led body will probably arise. The only precedent is the US decision to play a back-seat role to France and the UK in the Libya air campaign of 2011.[25] But it is a big stretch from a limited, mission-specific operation to a continental-scale takeover. Some will no doubt support using the EU to fulfil NATO roles in facilitating force planning, inter-operability, standardisation and multinational command, though the risks in losing NATO's 'corporate culture' would be considerable. In any case, Article 5 would still come into play since the security clauses of the EU treaties are widely seen as a weak substitute. Yet Article 5 can be activated only with the agreement of all member states, which would include the US if it hasn't formally withdrawn from the Washington Treaty. In that case, the value of Article 5 as a deterrent and a source of allied reassurance would be severely compromised. An alternative would be to revive the military-assistance clause (also an Article 5) of the Brussels Treaty establishing the Western European Union – which did not include the United States – in 1948, prior to the creation of NATO.

The other key aspect of Europe's strategic conundrum is the pivot to Asia, and it is not only more complex to formulate but also trickier to execute, as it calls for an array of institutions and a skill set that are largely different from those involving the US, Europe and Russia. Until the closing years of the last decade, European trade issues did not have much of a security dimension. Europe's key player on external trade issues was and is the European Commission. As Chinese techno-pilfering and outright espionage have risen, the EU and its members have gradually built up technology-transfer monitoring and screening regimes, roughly along the lines of America's Committee on Foreign Investment in the United States.

On the basis of an idea floated by then-US secretary of state Mike Pompeo in the closing days of the Trump administration, the EU and the US have established the EU–US Trade and Technology Council. This is of some importance since the EU remains not only the largest single market but also plays an outsize regulatory and normative role, brought to bear on American and more recently Chinese tech titans.[26] But the council has been functioning at less than full potential owing to strategic anaemia on the European side – the EU hasn't yet built up the institutional machinery to effectively integrate the economic and security dimensions of trade policy and technology transfers – and strategic distance on the American side.

Whereas the United States has comprehensively embraced the Indo-Pacific as a prime area of strategic engagement, European governments have done so only piecemeal and late, such that Washington often sees them as outsiders, bit players and something of a distraction.[27] This attitude was spectacularly displayed in September 2021, when Australia abruptly cancelled its ongoing diesel-submarine procurement contract with France in favour of a closely held, Five Eyes-negotiated arrangement for the procurement of nuclear submarines with the United States and a UK that had just left the EU. The announcement of the AUKUS deal, as it is called, almost derailed the founding meeting, in Pittsburgh, of the EU–US Trade and Technology Council, and France briefly recalled its ambassadors from Washington and Canberra. Crisis was averted when it became clear that the US government's failure to brief the EU on the new development was inadvertent, as the US National Security Council coordinator for the Indo-Pacific had failed to brief his Europe-facing colleagues on the deal. Biden himself effectively apologised on camera at the October 2021 G20 summit in Italy.[28]

Improving processes will not be enough to resolve the real and likely growing conflicts of interest that mercantilism with strategic characteristics entails. A Europe caught in the middle of a superpower contest would have to count on the leverage provided by its nuisance value. That, of course, can be an effective tool when skilfully handled, as de Gaulle's political survival and eventual triumph in the Second World War supremely demonstrated. But audacity and brinkmanship don't make for a happy relationship. Although European leaders understand that their strategic role in the Indo-Pacific will remain marginal, most have also concluded that risk-sharing with the US to some meaningful degree is necessary, notably in terms of naval and air activity, and, given that European countries are seafaring and trade dependent, makes strategic sense.

*   *   *

Europe's ability to prepare constructively for a world and a continent in which America's role will substantially change, possibly sooner rather than later, will hinge on two European phenomena. First and foremost is the trend of rising authoritarian – and often eurosceptic and pro-Russian – political forces, fuelled by populism. Macron's recent reminder that the EU is mortal gives a sense of the trepidation that this trend produces.[29] US populism is a compounding factor. The turmoil that would be generated by the simultaneous election of Trump in the US and a National Rally leader in France if snap elections – which, fortunately, do not appear to be on the cards – were held in that country can hardly be overstated.

The second phenomenon is the customary difficulty France and Germany face in crafting a joint approach to strategic planning. Three-quarters of a century of European integration have shown repeatedly that substantial agreement between those two countries is a necessary (though not a sufficient) condition of progress on any major issue. Since this is well understood on both sides of the Rhine, they usually engineer a compromise, but it almost invariably takes time and considerable effort, especially if personal and political relations between top national leaders are tense.

With elections in Germany to be held by autumn 2025, inertia may increase rather than decrease in the interval as the disparate members of the current governing coalition in Berlin vie for political advantage. This sharpens the key issue: whether Europe will be ready to react effectively as the US moves inward on itself and outward to East Asia – quickly and possibly catastrophically under Trump or more slowly and less traumatically under Biden.

Notes

[1] See, for example, Julian Barnes and Helene Cooper, 'Trump Discussed Pulling U.S. from NATO, Aides Said amid New Concerns over Russia', *New York Times*, 14 January 2019, https://www.nytimes.com/2019/01/14/us/politics/nato-president-trump.html; and '"Very Aggressive": Trump Suggests Montenegro Could Cause World War Three', *Guardian*, 19 July 2018, https://www.theguardian.com/us-news/2018/jul/19/very-aggressive-trump-suggests-montenegro-could-cause-world-war-three.

[2] US funding for NATO's European Deterrence Initiative rose from $900 million in 2016 to $3.4 billion in 2017, then to $4.8bn in 2018 and 2019, and $6.5bn in 2019, dropping to $5.9bn in 2020. See Leonard August Schuette, 'Why NATO Survived Trump', *International Affairs*, vol. 97, no. 6, November 2021, pp. 1,863–81.

[3] See, for example, Jonathan Allen, 'Awaiting Possible Indictment, Trump Rallies in Waco and Vows to "Destroy the Deep State"', NBC News, 26 March 2023, https://www.nbcnews.com/politics/awaiting-possible-indictment-trump-rallies-waco-rcna75684.

[4] See, for instance, Paul Dallison, 'Trump: "Europe Treats Us Worse than China"', *Politico*, 26 June 2019, https://www.politico.eu/article/trump-europe-treats-us-worse-than-china/.

[5] See, for example, Eric Cortellessa, 'How Far Trump Would Go', *Time*, 30 April 2024, https://time.com/6972021/donald-trump-2024-election-interview/; and Maggie Haberman and Shane Goldmacher, 'Trump, Vowing "Retribution," Foretells a Second Term of Spite', *New York Times*, 7 March 2023, https://www.nytimes.com/2023/03/07/us/politics/trump-2024-president.html.

[6] See Isaac Arnsdorf, Josh Dawsey and Michael Birnbaum, 'Inside Donald Trump's Secret, Long-shot Plan to End the War in Ukraine', *Washington Post*, 7 April 2024, https://www.washingtonpost.com/politics/2024/04/05/trump-ukraine-secret-plan/; and 'Transcript of CNN's Town Hall with Former President

Donald Trump', CNN, 10 May 2023, https://www.cnn.com/2023/05/11/politics/transcript-cnn-town-hall-trump/index.html.

7 Quoted in Kate Sullivan, 'Trump Says He Would Encourage Russia to "Do Whatever the Hell They Want" to Any NATO Country that Doesn't Pay Enough', CNN, 11 February 2024, https://www.cnn.com/2024/02/10/politics/trump-russia-nato/index.html.

8 For a balanced assessment, see Nicholas Crawford, 'The Energy Transition, Protectionism and Transatlantic Relations', Survival, vol. 65, no. 2, April–May 2023, pp. 75–102.

9 See White House, 'Remarks by National Security Advisor Jake Sullivan at the Special Competitive Studies Project Global Emerging Technologies Summit', 16 September 2022, https://www.whitehouse.gov/briefing-room/speeches-remarks/2022/09/16/remarks-by-national-security-advisor-jake-sullivan-at-the-special-competitive-studies-project-global-emerging-technologies-summit/.

10 See, for instance, 'Cases of Suspected Chinese Espionage in Europe', Reuters, 23 April 2024, https://www.reuters.com/world/europe/cases-suspected-chinese-espionage-europe-2024-04-23.

11 See, for example, 'The State of Huawei in Light of the Five Eyes Partnership', TechHQ, 15 July 2020, https://techhq.com/2020/07/the-state-of-huawei-in-light-of-the-five-eyes-partnership/.

12 See Katrin Bennhold and Jack Ewing, 'In Huawei Battle, China Threatens Germany "Where It Hurts"', New York Times, 16 January 2020, https://www.nytimes.com/2020/01/16/world/europe/huawei-germany-china-5g-automakers.html.

13 See Andrew A. Michta, 'Why Is the West Self-deterring in Ukraine?', New Atlanticist, 13 April 2023, https://www.atlanticcouncil.org/blogs/new-atlanticist/why-is-the-west-self-deterring-in-ukraine/.

14 See Lawrence Freedman, 'The Russo-Ukrainian War and the Durability of Deterrence', Survival, vol. 65, no. 6, December 2023–January 2024, pp. 7–36.

15 See White House, 'Remarks by President Biden on the United Efforts of the Free World to Support the People of Ukraine', 26 March 2022, https://www.whitehouse.gov/briefing-room/speeches-remarks/2022/03/26/remarks-by-president-biden-on-the-united-efforts-of-the-free-world-to-support-the-people-of-ukraine.

16 See Sylvie Corbet, 'Macron Again Declines to Rule Out Western Troops in Ukraine but Says They're Not Needed Now', Associated Press, 24 March 2024, https://apnews.com/article/france-macron-ukraine-troops-caa788d2455dafb06dd87f79c4afe06f.

17 Quoted in Andreas Rinke and Matthias Williams, 'Germany's Scholz Rules Out Western Troops for Ukraine', Reuters, 27 February 2024, https://www.reuters.com/world/europe/germanys-scholz-rules-out-western-ground-troops-ukraine-2024-02-27/.

18 'Emmanuel Macron in His Own Words', The Economist, 2 May 2024, https://www.economist.com/europe/2024/05/02/emmanuel-macron-in-his-own-words-english.

19 As of this year, the European allies will be spending 2% of their combined

GDP on defence. Eighteen out of 30 will reach or exceed the 2% level. See NATO, 'Secretary General Welcomes Unprecedented Rise in NATO Defense Spending', 14 February 2024 (updated 15 February 2024), https://www.nato.int/cps/en/natohq/news_222664.htm.

20   Aurélie Pugnet, 'Breton Pitches €100 Billion Fund for Defence Industry Cooperation', Euractiv, 10 January 2024 (updated 5 March 2024), https://www.euractiv.com/section/defence-and-security/news/breton-pitches-e100-billion-fund-for-defence-industry-cooperation/.

21   See Emmanuel Macron, 'Europe Speech', Élysée, 25 April 2024, https://www.elysee.fr/en/emmanuel-macron/2024/04/24/europe-speech.

22   See, for example, 'Emmanuel Macron prêt à "ouvrir le débat" d'une défense européenne comprenant l'arme nucléaire', Europe1, 27 April 2024, https://www.europe1.fr/politique/emmanuel-macron-pret-a-ouvrir-le-debat-dune-defense-europeenne-comprenant-larme-nucleaire-4243948.

23   Quoted in Andrew McDonald, 'Donald Trump Says He Won't Quit NATO if Europe Pays Its Way', Politico, 19 March 2024, https://www.politico.eu/article/donald-trump-says-he-wont-quit-nato-if-europe-pays-its-way.

24   See 'Conférence de presse de Charles de Gaulle (Paris, 15 mai 1962)', available from the Luxembourg Centre for Contemporary and Digital History, https://www.cvce.eu/en/obj/press_conference_given_by_charles_de_gaulle_15_may_1962-en-98595c27-9bac-4b12-ab24-770b121b921d.html.

25   See Dag Henriksen and Ann Karin Larssen (eds), *Political Rationale and International Consequences of the War in Libya* (Oxford: Oxford University Press, 2016).

26   In 2023 alone, Meta was fined close to €1.6bn and TikTok €345m under the EU's General Data Protection Regulation.

27   See, for example, Kathrin Hille, Jasmine Cameron-Chileshe and Demetri Sevastopulo, 'Britain "More Helpful" Closer to Home than in Asia, Says US Defence Chief', *Financial Times*, 27 July 2021, https://www.ft.com/content/7fb26630-a96a-4dfd-935c-9a7acb074304.

28   See Nick Childs, 'The AUKUS Anvil: Promise and Peril', *Survival*, vol. 65, no. 5, October–November 2023, pp. 7–24.

29   See Macron, 'Europe Speech'.

Two Cheers for Biden's Ukraine Policy

Peter Harris

United States President Joe Biden pledged to restore US leadership after the tumult of the Trump years. For better or worse, the events of the past three years have provided ample opportunity for him to make good on this promise. The war in Ukraine, in particular, has served as a testing ground for Biden's foreign-policy doctrine – a chance to demonstrate that, when the chips are down, the United States can still implement a far-sighted and inclusive brand of international relations. After more than two years of war, it is worth asking whether Biden's Ukraine policy has been sound, and what lessons can be gleaned to inform future US foreign policy.

The short answer is that Biden deserves two cheers for his approach to the Ukraine crisis. His administration has helped Kyiv batter and bloody the largest army in Europe and assert its sovereign independence in the process – no small feat. Biden has also guarded against the horizontal or vertical escalation of the war that many feared was inevitable. Neither of these policy successes should be taken for granted; not every president could have pulled them off simultaneously. The White House deserves credit for protecting core US interests during one of the most dangerous geopolitical episodes of recent history.

Peter Harris is an associate professor of political science at Colorado State University and author of *Why America Can't Retrench (And How It Might)* (Polity Press, forthcoming in 2025).

Survival | vol. 66 no. 3 | June–July 2024 | pp. 21–34   https://doi.org/10.1080/00396338.2024.2357474

So far, however, Biden's response to the Ukraine crisis has been mostly reactive. More than two years into the war, he has yet to articulate a clear plan for what an achievable post-war settlement might look like – not just between Moscow and Kyiv, but also for the wider European security order. This lack of proactive thinking is a serious – and perilous – flaw in Biden's approach to Ukraine, not least because the United States' citizens deserve to know what sort of future US aid to Kyiv is being used to establish.

Biden the balancer

When Russia began its illegal war of choice against Ukraine in February 2022, it seemed realistic to expect Ukraine President Volodymyr Zelenskyy's government to collapse within a matter of days. Even before Russian tanks rolled into the country and reached the outskirts of Kyiv, Biden was reportedly so pessimistic about Ukraine's chances of repelling the invaders that he offered Zelenskyy an escape plan – a precursor, perhaps, to establishing a government-in-exile in Warsaw, London or Washington.[1]

No such retreat was necessary. Two years on, Zelenskyy is firmly ensconced in his nation's capital. Ukraine has suffered horrendous human, economic and territorial losses, but it has fought back valiantly and indefatigably. At least 42,000 Russian soldiers have been killed in Ukraine, and some analysts estimate that as many as 315,000 are either dead or seriously wounded. Ukrainian forces have destroyed thousands of Russian tanks and hundreds of aircraft, as well as sinking several warships belonging to Russia's vaunted Black Sea Fleet. They have liberated more than half the land occupied by Russia during the early weeks of the war.[2]

Most of the credit for these military successes goes to the Ukrainian people, Ukraine's armed forces and Zelenskyy's adroit leadership. But Biden deserves plaudits, too. From pre-emptively releasing intelligence about Russia's invasion plans to organising punishing economic sanctions on the Russian economy and providing vast amounts of military and economic aid to Kyiv, the Biden administration has played a decisive role in blunting Russia's advances and buoying Zelenskyy's government. It is highly doubtful that Ukraine could have survived two years of terrible war against Russia – a much larger and more powerful adversary, even if beset by poor leadership and low morale – without US backing.

Serving as Ukraine's protector has come at considerable expense. America's ammunition stockpiles have shrunk at an alarming rate as the US defence-industrial base has been hard-pressed to keep pace with Ukrainian demand. In Congress, aid to Ukraine has become a partisan issue. Pro-Trump Republicans held up renewed US military aid for six months, until April of this year. Most US-based observers still agree that assisting Ukraine has been consonant with US interests. This is most obviously true to those who subscribe to the idea that the United States is engaged in an ideological battle with authoritarian regimes in Moscow, Beijing, Pyongyang, Tehran and elsewhere. From this perspective, the war in Ukraine is part of a world-wide effort to defend democratic institutions, US democracy included.[3]

The case for supporting Ukraine should be evident even to those who adopt a narrower definition of US security interests. It is a long-standing orthodoxy that the United States should prevent Europe (and East Asia, its other 'transoceanic flank') from falling under the sway of a hostile power.[4] And while the threat posed by Russia to the security of Europe beyond Ukraine should not be exaggerated, it would be unwise to minimise the danger it poses. There seems to be little doubt that stopping Russia from conquering Ukraine *in toto* has benefitted the United States. An enlarged, battle-hardened Russian Federation with a strengthened hand in Europe surrounded by frightened neighbours would have cut against the United States' broad interest in upholding transatlantic security and stability.

A prudent president

While moving to bolster Ukraine's defences, Biden has avoided support-ing Kyiv in ways that would risk a horizontal or vertical escalation of the war. Early on, this meant ruling out no-fly zones and the deployment of US troops to western Ukraine – ideas that were aired in the US media and enjoyed non-trivial levels of support in US policy circles.[5] As the war pro-gressed, the Biden administration was cautious in supplying offensive weaponry to Ukraine's armed forces. Biden still refuses to order the com-prehensive seizure of Russian-owned financial assets – an act that, if taken, might jeopardise the dollar's central role in the world economy – and has declined to endorse Ukraine's membership in NATO.

Biden's circumspection has invited stern criticism at home and abroad. According to some, Biden's guarded approach to weapons transfers gave Russia time to fortify its positions in southern and eastern Ukraine, badly impairing Kyiv's prospects of liberating all its territory. The most strident hawks argue that Russia's threats of nuclear escalation have been nothing but bluff and bluster all along, accusing Biden of undue timidity. It would have been far better, they insist, for the United States to have adopted a more assertive stance in the face of Russian aggression by drawing and enforcing red lines meant to curb the violence.[6]

For the most part, however, such criticisms are rooted in baseless optimism about worst-case scenarios. It would have been imprudent for Biden to assume from the outset that Russian President Vladimir Putin would never follow through on his threats to escalate the war, whether with tactical nuclear weapons or a conventional attack on NATO territory. Under current defensive arrangements, US forces would be on the front lines if a general European war were to break out – a bleak prospect that ought to alarm any sane leader. Putin's invasion revealed him to be a wanton aggressor, not to mention paranoid, fearful, badly advised and perhaps unwell. Against such an adversary, Biden would have been reckless in the extreme to believe he could control the pace and direction of the war from the Oval Office without having to worry about Moscow's next move. To accuse Biden of lacking courage in such circumstances is to gravely misunderstand what is at stake in Ukraine from the perspective of the United States.

Biden was right not only to reject calls for no-fly zones and direct US military intervention in the conflict, but also to calmly explain to the American people why such prescriptions were folly: because they would risk starting the Third World War.[7] He was prudent to delay the delivery of advanced weapons until his advisers could be more confident that Russia would not respond with escalatory measures. And while it was surely painful, restraining US allies who wanted to go further and faster than the United States was the correct call. These measures have ensured that, terrible as it is, the devastation in Ukraine has not spilled over to other countries and the war has remained a conventional one in which the United States is not an active belligerent.

A vision thing

On balance, Biden's approach to Ukraine can be judged a success, but only a qualified one. While Biden deserves credit for his calibrated orchestration of US support for Ukraine, he has not projected a clear vision of European security in light of the Russia–Ukraine war. This is a serious shortcoming. As a guarantor of 30 European nations' security, America has a major stake in conjuring a workable post-war settlement from the rubble of the war. What matters most to Washington is that the war ends such that the continent can be steered towards a stable security order that firmly diminishes the risk of future conflict rather than erecting a fragile arrangement that might break down at any moment. The former outcome is far from assured. Bringing it about will require US leadership. Key questions at the heart of America's long-term security interests include what sort of settlement the United States expects to see from the Russia–Ukraine war, what concessions (if any) Washington can envisage making as part of an overall agreement, and what concessions it will ask of others, friend and foe alike.

Biden has given little sense of his preferred answers. In fact, he has at times appeared positively unwilling to articulate an American picture of post-war Europe. At the beginning of the war, the president explicitly ruled out the prospect of talks with Russia (or even NATO allies) on a post-war settlement unless Ukraine's leaders were present ('nothing about Ukraine without Ukraine').[8] This was a mistake. Biden can be forgiven for wanting to avoid the suggestion that he was poised to 'sell out' Ukraine and pursue a grubby great-power deal with Putin. At the same time, friendly powers such as Ukraine do not get a veto over US foreign policy, and Biden was wrong to suggest otherwise. It would be practically infeasible for the United States to avoid talking to a regime that governs Eurasia's largest country, controls the world's biggest nuclear arsenal, and has the power to intimidate US allies and partners. Sooner or later, US officials will almost certainly have to negotiate in detail with their Russian counterparts over the future of European security relations. When such talks occur, as they inevitably will, Washington will need to be ruthless in pursuit of US national interests, which will not always overlap with Kyiv's.[9]

Biden also made a rod for his own back by refusing, as a matter of principle, to negotiate the question of NATO membership for Ukraine. At times, he has intimated that barring Ukraine from entering the Alliance would be tantamount to letting Moscow set US foreign policy. This is not the case. It is America's sovereign right to pick and choose the countries to which it extends security obligations; Biden should never have conceded the premise that declining to guarantee the security of Ukraine (or any other nation) would constitute a betrayal. Especially given that Washington is unlikely to support Ukraine's entry into NATO, it makes little sense to rule out negotiations over the future size and shape of the Alliance – an issue of great concern for Moscow. US diplomats will need all the room to manoeuvre they can get if ever they have the opportunity to sit down with their Russian counterparts.

Moreover, Biden's instinctive affirmation and reinforcement of America's security guarantees to NATO, while laudatory on one level, obscure some long-term problems. The reinforcement included deployment of additional US conventional forces to Eastern Europe – around 20,000 troops were sent to Europe in the first few months of the war[10] – as well as the reported return of US nuclear weapons to the United Kingdom. It is easy to intuit the short-term thinking behind such moves: they were intended to reassure NATO allies and deter Russian escalation. But in the long term, it is against US interests to prolong Europe's dependence on the United States for security instead of encouraging the continent to take ownership of its own military defence. The argument here is not that the NATO Alliance is obsolete; it is not. But it could be rebalanced such that Europeans carry more of the load of deterring future Russian aggression. European countries would naturally be disinclined to devote scarce resources toward arms when they have US forces on their soil willing to do the hard work of deterrence for them.

Finally, Biden erred in linking the conflict in Ukraine with America's great-power competition with China. Internationally, the conflation of Russia (a naked aggressor, credibly accused of perpetrating war crimes in Ukraine) with China (not a party to the conflict) was an unnecessary rhetorical framing that contributed to worsening US–China relations at a time when Washington needed Beijing's cooperation in international affairs more than ever. Domestically, it fuelled the narrative that international relations was a starkly Manichaean contest between good and evil, a world view that needlessly complicates the business of diplomacy, leads to crass over-simplifications of what US priorities should be, and constricted Biden's freedom of manoeuvre in Ukraine and elsewhere.[11]

Not only has Biden failed to articulate an affirmative vision for the post-war European order, but his reactive policies have made it more difficult than it otherwise might have been for Washington to play a leadership role in building that order. Some of his mistakes are attributable to short-term exigencies, such as the need to reassure nervous allies and avoid making pessimistic utterances that might have undermined Ukraine's war effort. Whatever the reasons, however, larger strategic questions will soon come to the fore.

The way ahead

How could Biden or a successor improve on his approach to Ukraine? Firstly, it is important to recognise what has gone right. Few put it in these terms, but Biden's approach to Ukraine can accurately be framed as a form of 'offshore balancing' – that is, empowering others (in this case, Ukraine) to do the heavy lifting in containing aggressors in their own regions.[12] In no uncertain terms, Ukraine has proven that even poor, outnumbered and under-resourced nations can defend against much bigger adversaries when they are given the right tools.[13] Its pre-war deterrent, however, was insufficient. While it can't be proven that Putin was deterrable, it's possible that the United States did not equip Ukraine strongly enough prior to the invasion. This was not Biden's mistake alone – it was an error begun under Barack Obama and not adequately addressed by Donald Trump. After the annexation of Crimea in 2014, Washington might have helped Ukraine turn itself into a 'porcupine' that Putin's Russia would never have tried to devour in whole or in part.[14] The United States should have organised substantial deliveries of lethal aid, offered training in advanced weapons systems, partnered with Ukraine to mass produce defensive armaments such as drones and loitering munitions, and deepened intelligence sharing. And it could have been conveyed to Russia that Washington would underwrite Ukraine's national self-defence, should this become necessary.

The primary lesson of the Russia–Ukraine war for US leaders is that threats to militarily defend America's allies and partners are less and less compulsory in a world where smaller nations can repel aggressors by themselves. States living in the shadow of threatening neighbours need arms sales, military cooperation and credible commitments of economic assistance, but they do not necessarily need promises that the United States will come to their direct defence – promises that, in any case, suffer from inherent credibility problems and therefore might have little deterrent value. The key and perhaps counter-intuitive insight here is that vulnerable states themselves are best placed to lodge believable threats against external aggression. The rub is that they usually lack the capabilities to make such threats seem sufficiently severe in the eyes of a larger adversary.

> *US policy should empower European resilience*

Going forward, then, the goal of the United States should be to enable European allies and partners to pose threats to defend themselves that are credible and potent enough to ward off even the most predatory aggressors.[15] This sort of direct deterrence seems better suited to preserving peace in the twenty-first century than extended deterrence, which during the Cold War was primarily conceived to prevent escalation to nuclear conflict at a higher threshold than that of the Russia–Ukraine war, and is less effective in addressing conventional threats especially against non-allies. Yet it is essentially extended deterrence that is presently on offer from the United States.

The overarching goal of US foreign policy in Europe should be to empower the continent – NATO members and non-members alike – to become resilient to external aggression and coercion. This is eminently achievable.[16] If the countries of NATO's eastern flank want additional reassurance, it should be British, French and German military bases that provide them comfort – not US deployments. The way to build a stable regime of direct, general deterrence on the continent is to put in place a phalanx of well-armed, well-trained and survivable conventional militaries capable of defeating Russia on the battlefield. US forces would then be surplus to requirements and could be greatly reduced in number. Europe would be confident in its ability to defend itself and more secure as a result. In terms of its force structure, NATO has been leaning in this direction for the past decade, though it remains significantly dependent on US assets.[17]

What about Ukraine? For starters, Biden should continue to oppose Kyiv's membership of NATO. Moscow would be unlikely to view any US commitment to directly defend Ukraine against future aggression as credible, and admitting Ukraine to the Alliance would risk provoking Russia more than it would deter it. However, Biden could consider offering Ukraine a Taiwan Relations Act-style agreement. This would mean a US commitment to maintain the capability to intervene in a general European war – which is already in America's self-interest – and a pledge to provide arms and economic aid to Ukraine for as long as that country remains vulnerable to Russian predation. There might even be scope for some European NATO members – the Baltics, Poland and the UK, in particular – to establish a separate collective-security agreement with Kyiv, given that these states profess to have a national interest in Ukraine's security per se. Washington should only support such a pact, however, if it could be drafted in such a way that it would not amount to NATO membership through the back door.[18]

As distant as the prospect appears now, at some point the US and its allies will need to return to some sort of diplomacy with Moscow. Western goals will include a full withdrawal from Ukraine, an acknowledgement of Kyiv's sovereign independence, Russia's acquiescence to Ukraine joining the European Union, an international peacekeeping mission along the Russia–Ukraine border, reductions of Russian forces in Belarus and Transnistria, guarantees of Moldovan sovereign independence and a return to arms control. Moscow is unlikely to agree to everything that America wants, of course. But the goal must be to end the war in a way that nudges the superpowers in the direction of more stable, peaceful relations. Accordingly, the cessation of hostilities must be followed apace by good-faith efforts to remove grounds for enmity and belligerence. European-led deterrence will be essential to keeping Russia at bay, but the prospects for lasting peace will remain bleak unless military preparedness is married to hard-headed diplomacy and the eventual removal of obstacles to rapprochement between Russia and the West.

If these recommendations sound like abandonment or appeasement, they should not. America's deployments to Western Europe were never meant to last for 80 years. No country should be expected to occupy other nations – not even its closest allies – for such an extended period of time, especially when the host countries in question are more than capable of providing for their own defence. It is intuitively illogical that the United States – separated from Ukraine by the entire span of the European continent plus the Atlantic Ocean – is shouldering responsibility for rolling back Russian forces in Ukraine while most European governments accept secondary support roles. Europe is rich and powerful enough to back Ukraine today and deter Moscow tomorrow. That they are not leading in either regard is a failure on their part, but it is also an indictment of US grand strategy.

*   *   *

In the late 1940s, journalist and strategist Walter Lippmann recommended that the United States remove its forward-deployed military forces in Western Europe – holdovers from the Allied victory over Nazi Germany – even if the Soviet Union continued to occupy the eastern half of the continent. His reasoning was that, if the Soviets were foolish enough to invade the West after US garrisons had been withdrawn, they would expose themselves as naked imperialist aggressors. With world opinion on their side, the United States and Europe would then have little trouble repelling the Red Army and liberating the whole continent.[19]

If Lippmann's proposal was too risky to entertain in the early Cold War, it is not anymore.[20] Except for Belarus, Moldova and Ukraine, all of Europe is now free from Russian domination. Whereas war devastated much of Europe in the 1940s, today the continent's economies are among the richest in the world – easily large enough to fund conventional militaries to outmatch Russia's. Two Western European governments – Britain and France – have nuclear weapons. There is nothing stopping them from extending a nuclear umbrella over allies and partners to their east.[21] The case that America's presence is necessary to keep the continent safe and secure is losing force. The time will soon come for the United States to initiate a wide-ranging drawdown of its forces in Europe, and to entrust Europeans with the important task of deterring Russian aggression. If a general war in Europe were to break out, the United States could still mobilise to intervene, but stay its hand unless the continental powers proved incapable of providing for their own defence.

Biden may be the wrong leader to implement this sort of long-term vision for Europe. Trump, Biden's most likely immediate successor, certainly is not the right person for the job, lacking as he is in both vision and attention. Eventually, though, America will need to make some big decisions when it comes to European security. It is in nobody's best interests for the transatlantic alliance to persist in a form held over from the Cold War era. The United States is too overstretched abroad, too divided at home and too geographically remote to maintain extended deterrence in perpetuity. Only Europeans can credibly vow to defend themselves for the next 80 years.

Biden's Ukraine policy has been a qualified success. It could be an unbridled triumph if it leads to a recalibration of US security relations in Europe. At present, the European security architecture is in flux and requires US leadership to be put on firmer foundations. This will not be possible unless America retrenches and restores to European capitals something that they have been without for decades: primary authority over their own security and a sustainable vision for a Europe whole and free.

Notes

1   See Carol E. Lee, Courtney Kube and Kristen Welker, 'US Officials Discussed Ukrainian President Leaving Capital if Russia Attacks', NBC News, 21 February 2022, https://www.nbcnews.com/politics/white-house/us-officials-discussed-ukrainian-president-leaving-capital-russian-att-rcna17094.

2   For estimates of Russian losses, see 'More than 42,000 Russian Troops Killed in Ukraine Since Launch of Full-scale Invasion', Radio Free Europe/Radio Liberty, 20 January 2024, https://www.rferl.org/a/ukraine-russian-troops-death-toll/32784518.html; Jonathan Landay, 'U.S. Intelligence Assesses Ukraine War

Has Cost Russia 315,000 Casualties –
Source', Reuters, 12 December 2023,
https://www.reuters.com/world/
us-intelligence-assesses-ukraine-war-
has-cost-russia-315000-casualties-
source-2023-12-12/; Ritu Sharma,
'Russia Lost a Staggering 2400 Tanks,
200 Aircraft, 400,000 Personnel in
Ukraine War: UK Defence Ministry',
EurAsian Times, 20 November 2023,
https://www.eurasiantimes.com/
staggering-2400-tanks-200-aircraft-
400000-personnel/; and Konstantin
Toropin, 'Ukraine Has Liberated 54%
of Territory Seized by Russia, Joint
Chiefs Chairman Says', Military.com,
19 September 2023, https://www.
military.com/daily-news/2023/09/19/
ukraine-has-liberated-54-of-territory-
seized-russia-joint-chiefs-chairman-
says.html.

3   See, for example, Robert Kagan, 'A
Free World, if You Can Keep It',
Foreign Affairs, vol. 102, no. 1, January/
February 2023, pp. 39–53.

4   See Robert S. Ross, 'US Grand
Strategy, the Rise of China, and US
National Security Strategy for East
Asia', *Strategic Studies Quarterly*, vol. 7,
no. 2, Summer 2013, pp. 20–40.

5   Jacob Shamsian, 'Zelensky Says
Biden Personally Ruled Out a "No-
fly Zone" Over Ukraine as Russia
Attacks', *Business Insider*, 1 March
2022, https://www.businessinsider.
com/biden-ruled-out-no-fly-zone-
over-ukraine-zelensky-russia-2022-3;
and Nahal Toosi, 'The Line Biden
Won't Cross on Ukraine', *Politico*, 23
February 2022, https://www.politico.
com/news/2022/02/23/biden-troops-
russia-ukraine-00011049. On US-based
analysts calling for US deploy-

ments to Ukraine and no-fly zones,
see Alexandra Chinchilla and Sam
Rosenberg, 'Why America Should
Send Military Advisers to Ukraine',
Foreign Affairs, 22 September 2023,
https://www.foreignaffairs.com/
united-states/why-america-should-
send-military-advisers-ukraine;
and Caroline Vakil, 'Foreign Policy
Experts Call for "Limited No-fly
Zone" Over Ukraine', *Hill*, 8 March
2022, https://thehill.com/policy/
international/597279-foreign-policy-
experts-call-for-limited-no-fly-zone-
over-ukraine/.

6   See, for example, Mykola Bielieskov,
'Western Fear of Escalation Will
Hand Putin an Historic Victory
in Ukraine', Atlantic Council,
16 April 2024, https://www.
atlanticcouncil.org/blogs/ukrainealert/
western-fear-of-escalation-will-hand-
putin-an-historic-victory-in-ukraine/;
John Raine, 'Time for NATO to
Find a Way Out of the Escalation
Trap in Ukraine', IISS Online
Analysis, 11 March 2022, https://
www.iiss.org/en/online-analysis/
online-analysis/2022/03/
time-for-nato-to-find-a-way-out-of-
the-escalation-trap-in-ukraine/; and
Michael Vickers, 'Biden Must Show
that the U.S. Stands Ready to Support
Ukraine, Militarily if Necessary',
Washington Post, 20 January 2022,
https://www.washingtonpost.com/
opinions/2022/01/20/biden-must-
show-that-us-stands-ready-support-
ukraine-militarily-if-necessary/.

7   See, for instance, Aaron Blake,
'Biden and White House Keep
Talking About World War III',
Washington Post, 17 March 2022,

https://www.washingtonpost.com/politics/2022/03/17/why-biden-white-house-keep-talking-about-world-war-iii/.

8 See Joseph R. Biden, Jr, 'President Biden: What America Will and Will Not Do in Ukraine', *New York Times*, 31 May 2022, https://www.nytimes.com/2022/05/31/opinion/biden-ukraine-strategy.html.

9 See Christopher S. Chivvis, 'America Needs a Realistic Ukraine Debate', *Survival*, vol. 66, no. 1, February–March 2024, pp. 25–40.

10 US Department of Defense, 'FACT SHEET – U.S. Defense Contributions to Europe', 29 June 2022, https://www.defense.gov/News/Releases/Release/Article/3078056/fact-sheet-us-defense-contributions-to-europe.

11 See Lanxin Xiang, 'Biden's Misguided China Policy', *Survival*, vol. 66, no. 3, June–July 2024, pp. 91–104.

12 See Christopher Layne, 'Offshore Balancing Revisited', *Washington Quarterly*, vol. 25, no. 2, Spring 2002, pp. 233–48.

13 See Eugene Gholz, Benjamin Friedman and Enea Gjoza, 'Defensive Defense: A Better Way to Protect US Allies in Asia', *Washington Quarterly*, vol. 42, no. 4, Autumn 2019, pp. 171–89.

14 William S. Murray of the US Naval War College first articulated the 'porcupine' strategy in the China–Taiwan context. See William S. Murray, 'Revisiting Taiwan's Defense Strategy', *Naval War College Review*, vol. 61, no. 3, Summer 2008, pp. 13–38.

15 See T.X. Hammes, 'Defending Europe: How Converging Technology Strengthens Small Powers', *Scandinavian Journal of Military Studies*, vol. 2, no. 1, March 2019, pp. 20–9.

16 See Barry R. Posen, 'Europe Can Defend Itself', *Survival*, vol. 62, no. 6, December 2020–January 2021, pp. 7–34.

17 See, for example, Sven Biscop, 'A New Force Model: NATO's European Army?', Egmont Policy Brief 285, September 2022, https://www.egmontinstitute.be/app/uploads/2022/09/Sven-Biscop_PolicyBrief285_vFinal.pdf.

18 See, for example, Liana Fix, 'The Future Is Now: Security Guarantees for Ukraine', *Survival*, vol. 65, no. 3, June–July 2023, pp. 67–72.

19 See Walter Lippmann, *The Cold War: A Study in U.S. Foreign Policy* (New York: Harper & Bros., 1947).

20 See James Carden, 'Why Walter Lippmann Wanted to Demolish the Ideas Behind Cold War', *Responsible Statecraft*, 13 January 2023, https://responsiblestatecraft.org/2023/01/13/why-we-need-a-walter-lippman-today/.

21 See Benjamin Rhode, 'Europe Without America', *Survival*, vol. 66, no. 2, April–May 2024, pp. 7–18.

NATO's Anniversary Predicament

Sara Bjerg Moller

The NATO Alliance's journey to Washington, where members will celebrate its 75th anniversary this summer, has been beset by several obstacles in recent months. Some of these, such as Russia's faster-than-expected reconstitution of its miliary forces following the disastrous start to its full-scale invasion of Ukraine in February 2022, were beyond NATO's control. Other hazards were self-inflicted. At their finest, NATO allies have provided unprecedented levels of military and humanitarian assistance to Ukraine – close to $200 billion since the war began – and approved ambitious new plans to reform the Alliance's military architecture.[1] At their lowest, the allies have engaged in public rifts over the selection of the next secretary-general and over the status of Ukraine's membership invitation, and finger-pointing over which ally is or isn't contributing various weapons systems to Ukraine.[2] These troubles compounded a mood darkened by the failure of Ukraine's 2023 counter-offensive to make substantial gains, by the US congressional hold-up of Ukrainian aid and by comments from the presumptive nominee of the Republican Party encouraging Russia to 'do whatever the hell they want' to NATO members who are 'delinquent' in meeting the Alliance's Defence Investment Pledge.[3] On at least one point, the allies appear to agree: NATO is at a critical juncture, and the path it selects will shape the Alliance's trajectory for decades to come.

Sara Bjerg Moller is an Associate Teaching Professor in the School of Foreign Service at Georgetown University and a Non-resident Senior Fellow at the Atlantic Council.

Survival | vol. 66 no. 3 | June–July 2024 | pp. 35–42   https://doi.org/10.1080/00396338.2024.2357477

Two years into Russia's brutal and unprovoked war against Ukraine, NATO allies are still wrestling with the medium- and longer-term implications of the conflict for the Alliance. As a result, when its 32 members come together at the Washington Summit in July, they will be confronted with the challenge of attempting to narrow the expanding gap between the Alliance's military strategies, its members' national political objectives and the available resources. At the root of this challenge lies a familiar problem: how to assess the nature of the Russian threat. Most allies acknowledge that Russia is a destabilising actor in the Euro-Atlantic region and poses significant hybrid challenges to individual members, as well as to the Alliance as a whole. These challenges include disinformation campaigns designed to undermine NATO democracies, interference with the Global Positioning System and other airspace violations, and the probing of undersea cables, among other concerning activities.[4] NATO's 2022 Strategic Concept officially classifies the Russian Federation as the 'most significant and direct threat to Allies' security and to the peace and stability in the Euro-Atlantic area'.[5] However, national threat assessments differ regarding Russia's ultimate intentions, particularly whether Moscow could try to mount a direct military challenge against one or more Alliance members. Eastern allies bordering Russian territory, which have long warned their fellow allies about Vladimir Putin's aggressive inclinations, feel vindicated by Moscow's attack on Ukraine and maintain that Moscow could try to test the Alliance's collective-defence mechanism by seeking to reclaim more former Soviet territory in the near future.[6] Earlier this year, Estonia's Foreign Intelligence Service assessed that the Kremlin anticipates a conflict with NATO 'within the next decade'.[7] According to the Estonian military, it's not a matter of whether Russia will invade, 'it's only a question of when'.[8] In May, the newly appointed head of the Polish Military Counterintelligence Service echoed this warning, claiming Moscow is 'certainly already prepared for some mini-operation against one of the Baltic countries'.[9]

In what marks a new development for the Alliance, some northern members now share this outlook. In February 2024, the Danish defence minister warned that Russia could try to test NATO solidarity and its commitment to collective defence 'within a three-to-five-year period'.[10] Just a month earlier, civilian and military officials in Sweden, the Alliance's newest member, publicly warned that 'there could be war in Sweden'.[11] The revised intelligence assessments may have been influenced by increased Russian naval and aerial activity in the region in 2023.[12] Southern members share a different threat assessment, however, with some, such as Spanish Foreign Minister José Manuel Albares, going so far as to state that neither Madrid, nor the European Union, nor NATO was preparing for war.[13] Meanwhile, the US intelligence community, which struggled to convince some European allies of the threat of the Ukraine invasion in winter 2021–22, has assessed that 'Russia almost certainly does not want a direct military conflict with the U.S. and NATO forces'. Instead, it anticipates that Russia will continue engaging in asymmetric activities below what it calculates to be the threshold for provoking a direct military conflict.[14] Even within the northeastern parts of the Alliance, differing viewpoints toward the Russian threat exist. Alexander Stubb, the new Finnish president, has argued that a Russian attack against his country is unlikely.[15]

Mixed messages
Indeed, across the Alliance and within NATO headquarters, officials are grappling with how to appropriately balance national and collective deterrence and defence measures with strategic messaging against Russia. The challenge stems not only from the lack of a shared assessment of vulnerability by allies, but also from a fundamental disagreement over NATO's near-term strategy. The debate transcends national boundaries and manifests in divisions within governments and military establishments alike, as demonstrated by a recent incident in the United Kingdom. Earlier this year, General Patrick Sanders, the chief of the British General Staff, likened the present moment to the pre-1914 situation in Europe and called for a 'citizen army' to prepare for conflict with Russia.[16] His remarks were met with public criticism from both political and military channels. Sanders's controversial remarks were prompted by the knowledge that the British Army, which by next year is expected to number just 72,500, is not large enough to fight Russia in the event of a war. Intended to jump-start a national conversation about the need to place 'our societies on a war footing', his comments

appeared initially to have the opposite effect, leading the prime minister's office to issue a statement categorically ruling out conscription.[17]

The incident exemplifies the delicate balance that European political and military officials must increasingly maintain. Within the Alliance, there are two distinct camps with differing views on how to handle the present challenge. The first comprises those like the British Army chief whose job it is to deliver the armed forces that NATO needs and find themselves unable to do so following decades of cuts to national-defence budgets and ongoing recruitment and retention challenges. Echoing the language of senior NATO officials such as Admiral Rob Bauer, the chair of the NATO Military Committee, who have publicly advocated for a 'warfighting transformation' in Europe, these officials are trying to change commonly held perceptions of NATO as either a peacetime alliance or a cooperative security organisation focused on confronting 'out of area' challenges and threats.[18] The goal of this camp is to prepare allied societies and mobilise the resources needed to implement the ambitious military reforms announced at the Madrid and Vilnius NATO summits.[19]

In the second camp are those who argue that the steady stream of warnings issued over the past year by senior government officials concerning European military deficiencies, and the use of phrases such as 'pre-war generation' and 'pre-war footing', risk sparking panic among the public. After Sweden's top military commander and minister for civil defence warned in January 2024 that Sweden should prepare for war, Swedish opposition leader Magdalena Andersson, under whose government Sweden formally submitted its application to join NATO in May 2022, criticised the government for spreading fear. 'Scaring the population', Andersson wrote, 'will not make Sweden safer'.[20] The head of the British Armed Forces, Admiral Tony Radakin, raised similar objections over the debate unfolding in his own country, stating: 'I worry that the public debate that has played out over recent weeks risks becoming confused and some remarks are alarmist.'[21] Others worry that sounding the alarm about the dire state of Europe's defence capabilities could undermine deterrence by signalling weakness to Moscow. Straddling the two camps are those like President Stubb who, while voicing concern about his fellow European leaders' 'rather belligerent talk' about

Russian plans to test the Alliance's commitment to collective defence, simultaneously argue that, however 'unlikely', Europe 'should prepare for that'.[22] In other words, they advocate for less talk and more preparation.

The difficulty is, of course, that the two are linked; in order to make preparations, officials must first talk. Without making a compelling case to their publics about the persistent threat Russia poses to European security and the necessity for long-term investments in armed forces and defence infrastructure, leaders will find it hard to secure the support of taxpayers for such initiatives. If European officials cannot convince their constituents that Russia is a chronic threat, they will face ongoing difficulties in implementing the necessary defence upgrades needed to deter Russia. Effective deterrence requires capabilities to threaten retaliation, which, at a minimum, necessitates an adequate defence, which costs money.

At present, European governments and publics remain divided over both the nature of the Russian threat and the most effective way to mobilise resources to combat it. After identifying Russia as the number one threat to Germany in 2022, German citizens named it as only the seventh-greatest concern in 2023, below that of rising inequality and mass migration. In Italy, Russia now ranks 12th on the list of risks Italians perceive to their country, behind concerns such as climate change, Islamic terrorism, mass migration, international organised crime and other non-traditional security issues.[23] Even in France, where French President Emmanuel Macron has recently moved to a more hawkish position on Russia and is attempting to mobilise continental support for Europe's autonomous defence, Russia ranks 6th on the threat index, only slightly ahead of Iran.[24]

*   *   *

Europeans will head to the polls this June for EU elections. Americans will follow closely behind in November with presidential and congressional elections. However, the recent behaviour of Republican members of Congress who delayed much-needed aid to Ukraine suggests that, regardless of who ends up in the White House next year, there could be a decline in support for current levels of security assistance to Europe. Further complicating matters,

European allies are now being asked – by none other than NATO Secretary General Jens Stoltenberg himself – to prioritise supporting Ukraine over meeting their own NATO capability targets.[25] Between June and November 2024, NATO leaders will convene in Washington, where they must find a way ahead. Officially, the theme for the 75th anniversary summit will be the 'executability' of the Alliance's new deterrence and defence strategy, which NATO military planners have been diligently developing over the past few years.[26] To achieve this goal, European governments must first tackle the mismatch between strategy, public messaging and national resources that has surfaced since 2022. Navigating the delicate nexus between national and Alliance priorities will not be easy. An unfortunate but likely outcome would be if allies continue with the status quo.

Notes

[1] See Jim Garamone, 'NATO Leader Highlights Programs to Increase Defense, Deterrence', US Department of Defense, 15 February 2024, https://www.defense.gov/News/News-Stories/Article/Article/3678551/nato-leader-highlights-programs-to-increase-defense-deterrence/; and Sara Bjerg Moller, 'NATO at 75: The Perils of Empty Promises', *Survival*, vol. 65, no. 6, December 2023–January 2024, pp. 91–118, https://doi.org/10.1080/00396338.2023.2285606.

[2] See James Angelos and Joshua Posaner, 'Scholz and Macron Feud over Arms for Ukraine', *Politico*, 27 February 2024, https://www.politico.eu/article/olaf-scholz-and-emmanuel-macron-feud-over-ukraine-aid/; and Patrick Wintour, 'Nato Should Not Appoint Mark Rutte Without Broader Discussion, Says Latvia', *Guardian*, 14 March 2024.

[3] See Jill Colvin, 'Trump Says He Told NATO Ally to Spend More on Defense or He Would "Encourage" Russia to "Do Whatever the Hell They Want"', PBS News Hour, 11 February 2024, https://www.pbs.org/newshour/politics/trump-says-he-told-nato-ally-to-spend-more-on-defense-or-he-would-encourage-russia-to-do-whatever-the-hell-they-want. On NATO's Defence Investment Pledge see NATO, 'Funding NATO', 5 April 2024, https://www.nato.int/cps/en/natohq/topics_67655.htm.

[4] See Tommaso Lecca, 'GPS Jamming Is a "Side Effect" of Russian Military Activity, Finnish Transport Agency Says', *Politico*, 3 May 2024, https://www.politico.eu/article/gps-jamming-is-a-side-effect-of-russian-military-activity-finnish-transport-agency-says/; and Miranda Bryant, 'Undersea "Hybrid Warfare" Threatens Security of 1bn, Nato Commander Warns', *Guardian*, 16 April 2024.

5   NATO, 'NATO 2022 Strategic Concept', 29 June 2022, p. 4, https://www.nato.int/nato_static_fl2014/assets/pdf/2022/6/pdf/290622-strategic-concept.pdf.

6   See, for example, Gabrielius Landsbergis (@GLandsbergis), post to X, 30 December 2023, https://twitter.com/GLandsbergis/status/1741204556590018855?s=20.

7   Estonian Foreign Intelligence Service, 'International Security and Estonia 2024', p. 7, https://www.valisluureamet.ee/doc/raport/2024-en.pdf.

8   Lara Jakes and Christina Anderson, 'For Europe and NATO, a Russian Invasion Is No Longer Unthinkable', *New York Times*, 29 January 2024.

9   Quoted in Maciej Miłosz, 'Szef SKW: Służbom potrzeba dystansu od polityki', *Dziennik Gazeta Prawna*, 6 May 2024, https://www.gazetaprawna.pl/wiadomosci/kraj/artykuly/9500938,szef-skw-sluzbom-potrzeba-dystansu-od-polityki-wywiad.html.

10   'Danish Defence Minister Warns Russia Could Attack NATO in 3–5 Years – Media', Reuters, 9 February 2024, https://www.reuters.com/world/europe/danish-defence-minister-warns-russia-could-attack-nato-3-5-years-media-2024-02-09/.

11   Jakes and Anderson, 'For Europe and NATO, a Russian Invasion Is No Longer Unthinkable'.

12   See NATO, 'NATO Intercepted Russian Military Aircraft over 300 Times in 2023', 29 December 2023, https://www.nato.int/cps/en/natohq/news_221598.htm; and Noah Bovenizer, 'Report Highlights Major Increase in Dark Ship Activity in Baltic Sea', *Global Ship Technology*, 12 October 2023, https://www.ship-technology.com/news/major-increase-dark-activity-baltic-sea/.

13   See Maria Tril, 'Spanish Foreign Minister: Neither EU, NATO, nor Spain Prepares for War Despite Russia's Aggression in Ukraine', Euromaidan Press, 26 March 2024, https://euromaidanpress.com/2024/03/26/spanish-foreign-minister-neither-eu-nato-nor-spain-prepares-for-war-despite-russias-aggression-in-ukraine/; and Aurélie Pugnet, 'Enough "Ukraine Only": Spain Wants More Focus on Africa, Asia', Euractiv, 19 September 2023, https://www.euractiv.com/section/defence-and-security/news/enough-ukraine-spain-wants-more-focus-on-africa-asia/.

14   Office of the Director of National Intelligence, 'Annual Threat Assessment of the U.S. Intelligence Community', 5 February 2024, p. 14, https://www.intelligence.senate.gov/sites/default/files/hearings/unclassified_2024_ata_report_0.pdf. On the difficulties experienced by American officials in convincing their European counterparts of the impending invasion, see Shane Harris et al., 'Road to War: U.S. Struggled to Convince Allies, and Zelensky, of Risk of Invasion', *Washington Post*, 16 August 2022.

15   See Maria Kholina, 'Finnish President Considers Russia's Attack Unlikely, While NATO Exercises Is Signal to Moscow', RBC-Ukraine, 8 March 2024, https://newsukraine.rbc.ua/news/finnish-president-considers-russias-attack-1709901533.html. The Finns also appear to be reacting calmly

to the news that Russia intends to deploy a new missile brigade in the Republic of Karelia, which borders Finland. See Thomas Nilsen, 'Finland Relaxed over Moscow's Plans to Deploy Iskander-M Missiles Near Border', *Barents Observer*, 24 April 2024, https://thebarentsobserver. com/en/security/2024/04/ finland-relaxed-over-moscows-plans-deploy-iskander-missiles-near-border.

16 A transcript of his remarks is available at https://www.whatdotheyknow. com/request/general_patrick_ sanders_iavc_spe/response/2576534/ attach/4/20240301%20FOI%20 02502%20Annex%20A%20CGS%20 IAVC%2024%20speech%20FINAL%20 CGS.pdf?cookie_passthrough=1.

17 See Danielle Sheridan, 'Sunak Forced to Rule Out Conscription as Russia War Threat Rises', *Telegraph*, 25 January 2024; and Kieren Kelly, 'Army Chief's Call for Citizen Army "Infuriated" No10 as Top General Called In for "Dressing Down"', LBC, 28 February 2024, https://www. lbc.co.uk/news/army-chief-call-citizen-army-infuriated-downing-street/.

18 See 'NATO Needs "Warfighting Transformation", Top Military Officials Say', Reuters, 17 January 2024, https:// www.reuters.com/world/europe/nato-needs-warfighting-transformation-top-military-official-says-2024-01-17/; and Jack Detsch, 'NATO's Military Has a New Nerve Center', *Foreign Policy*, 28 February 2024.

19 See Moller, 'NATO at 75'.

20 See 'DN Debatt: "Statsministern borde samla folket – inte skrämma och splittra"', *Dagens Nyheter*, 23 January 2024, https://www.dn.se/ debatt/statsministern-borde-samla-folket-inte-skramma-och-splittra/; and Jakes and Anderson, 'For Europe and NATO, a Russian Invasion Is No Longer Unthinkable'.

21 Admiral Tony Radakin, 'Chief of the Defence Chatham House Security and Defence Conference 2024 Keynote Speech', Gov.uk, 27 February 2024, https://www.gov.uk/government/ speeches/chief-of-the-defence-chatham-house-security-and-defence-conference-2024-keynote-speech.

22 Richard Milne and Henry Foy, 'Europe Should Talk Less and Prepare More Against Russian Threat, Says Finnish President', *Financial Times*, 11 April 2024.

23 MSC, 'Munich Security Index 2024', pp. 12–13, https://securityconference.org/ assets/01_Bilder_Inhalte/03_Medien/02_ Publikationen/2024/MSR_2024/ MunichSecurityIndex2024.pdf.

24 *Ibid.*, p. 11; and Hugh Schofield, 'Macron Switches from Dove to Hawk on Russia's Invasion of Ukraine', BBC News, 16 March 2024, https://www.bbc.com/news/ world-europe-68575251.

25 Jens Stoltenberg (@jensstoltenberg), post to X, 17 April 2024, https:// twitter.com/jensstoltenberg/ status/1780596609296027786.

26 See Sean Monaghan, Katherine Kjellström Elgin and Sara Bjerg Moller, 'Understanding NATO's Concept for the Deterrence and Defence of the Euro-Atlantic Area', Center for Strategic and Budgetary Assessments, forthcoming in May 2024.

Civilisational Conflict

Hilton L. Root

While hailing expanded China–Russia cooperation as a 'strategic choice' that was here to stay, Chinese Minister of Foreign Affairs Wang Yi described Moscow as an indispensable partner in 'creating a new paradigm of major power relations that is completely different from the old Cold War era'.[1] Such remarks make it imperative to recognise the constructed self-images of partners and adversaries in the global arena in order to understand what the most profound strategic challenge of our era may be: China's self-fashioning as a 'civilisation-state' to challenge the liberal-international order.[2] It intends not merely to wage a power struggle within the current system, but rather to cast doubt on the system's core values and norms with an eye to fragmenting global standards and elevating alternative governance and development paradigms.

What is a civilisation-state?

A civilisation-state defines its identity and political legitimacy not just through its current geopolitical boundaries or ethnic composition, but more crucially through the long-standing cultural and historical heritage it embodies. Unlike a nation-state – which is customarily based on a shared language, culture or ethnicity within defined borders – a civilisation-state embodies a deep-rooted historical identity and cultural legacy that influences its governance, its diplomacy and its people's perception of themselves.[3]

Hilton L. Root is a professor of public policy at Schar School of Policy and Government at George Mason University and a visiting adjunct professor at the University of International Business and Economics in Beijing.

Survival | vol. 66 no. 3 | June–July 2024 | pp. 43–48   https://doi.org/10.1080/00396338.2024.2357479

China's self-portrayal as a civilisation-state is not unique. Leaders in Hungary, Iran, Russia and Turkiye also endeavour to assert civilisational identities, drawing on narratives of historical greatness to reclaim or reimagine their pasts. They present themselves as guardians of distinct cultural, religious and historical narratives, aspiring to extend their influence beyond national borders. In 1948, historian John King Fairbank presciently remarked that, inspired by China, 'a new cultural nationalism … may in the future outdo the merely political nationalisms in Europe'.[4] Chinese nationalism, unlike the European variety, 'is coterminous with the entire culture, not merely with the state'.[5]

Civilisation-states advocate ideological autonomy, challenging international norms and institutions from their respective vantage points. They criticise the liberal-international order for its Western bias, arguing that it serves the interests of a limited number of nations at the expense of broader inclusivity. Their critiques extend to international bodies, which they perceive as instruments of Western hegemony. A core element of their arguments is non-interference, especially in matters concerning human rights or democratic governance, which China and Russia contend are pretexts for infringements on their sovereignty aimed at destabilising their regimes.

Internal contradictions

Civilisation-states' pursuit of civilisational or cultural imperatives can lead to international conduct that contravenes their avowed principle of respecting state sovereignty. This contradiction arises from the inherent tension between upholding the principle of non-interference in the internal affairs of states – a core aspect of respecting sovereignty – and the inclination to support, intervene or exert influence in matters affecting civilisational identities that can involve ethnic, cultural, religious or historical ties beyond recognised borders.

This is evident in China's approach to regions with which it shares historical or cultural bonds, and in its handling of its own diverse ethnic and cultural regions. Examples include extrajudicial actions, espionage, surveillance and legal jurisdiction over citizens abroad, especially in cases deemed relevant to China's national security or political interests. In particular, the notion that individuals are still under Chinese authority regardless of their citizenship or location conflicts with basic precepts of liberalism.

Russian conduct has similar contradictions, manifest in its interactions with former Soviet states and its conduct in Eastern Europe and Central Asia. While Russia champions respect for state sovereignty in international forums, it has also prioritised coercively advancing Russian cultural and historical influences in Ukraine and aggressively supporting Russian-speaking populations in neighbouring countries.

By leveraging their rich historical and cultural legacies, civilisation-states have assumed a distinctive role in the global order, promoting ideological autonomy that often directly opposes, or outright rejects, liberal-democratic norms. They advocate strong central authority to counterbalance Western liberalism and perceived moral relativism, tainting the liberal order's advocacy of universal rights and laws. Civilisation-states favour ethnic, cultural or religious identities over inclusive definitions of citizenship, contesting the global consensus on human rights and governance.

Economically, these states dispute the equity and sustainability of free-market capitalism, championing models that permit greater state intervention or alternative economic systems, purportedly better suited to their national circumstances and more capable of tackling inequality and developmental hurdles. In another contradiction, this belies the fact that in these societies, state-led economic models reward loyalty and cautious approaches to economic reforms, which can lead to economic decisions in which political stability and the interests of the ruling elites trump optimal allocations of resources and market-driven efficiency.

Civilisation-states' opposition to the Western-led world order is evident. Under President Xi Jinping's leadership, China has vigorously promoted a narrative of national rejuvenation known as the 'Chinese Dream', aiming to restore China's status as a pre-eminent civilisation. Russian President Vladimir Putin and Iranian leader Ayatollah Sayyid Ali Khamenei have similarly invoked their nations' historical and cultural legacies to assert a civilisational stance to justify their domestic and foreign policies. Yet such states do not present a unified front or share a common strategy. While their adherence to visions peculiar to their respective histories links them as opponents of the Western order, it also limits their capacity for strategic unity.

Elusive middle ground

The rise of civilisation-states with ambitions that directly confront the liberal-international order still calls for a strategic reassessment by those dedicated to upholding democracy, human rights and the rule of law. They are compelled to devise comprehensive strategies that not only protect but also promote the order's foundational tenets. Obviously, this entails strengthening the structures of global governance that underpin international law, human rights and democratic norms, as well as bolstering the resilience of liberal democracies through education, cultural diplomacy and the reinforcement of international alliances. Such efforts, however, might not be sufficient to tackle the complex moral dilemmas that civilisation-states pose.

The West must navigate between two approaches, each appropriate in certain circumstances. The first is to be reactive and accept that it cannot change civilisation-states and must learn to cooperate with them despite necessary concessions on human rights. The second is to be proactive and emphasise the commitment to liberal democratic values and to push those interests even when it undermines cooperation with authoritarian states.

When the West chooses, however, to affirm the universality of liberal principles and nurture a global order that honours the dignity and rights of every individual, regardless of ethnic, cultural or religious identity, it must be prepared for countermeasures from civilisation-states. They may draw sympathy and even tacit cooperation from some elements within the liberal order: moral clarity and geopolitics often do not sit well together and inevitably produce difficult trade-offs. And other states, civilisational and otherwise, are likely to join China in rejecting the West's pursuit of a universal moral consensus on humanity's future. This discord underscores the difficulty the West faces in harmonising its normative frameworks with those of other cultures while also declining to recognise the latter's legitimacy and addressing the perceived injustices they have imposed.

The quest for a middle ground, whereby the moral precepts of different societies are accorded equal respect, remains fraught. It affects the West's relations not only with China but also with Russia, the Turkic populations of Asia, and the indigenous populations of Africa.

Finding mutual accommodation

Mutual understanding between China and the West regarding their respective pathways would require narrowing the divergence between their respective modes of causal reasoning. No existing framework reconciles the two. Each side holds an internally consistent viewpoint that is often incomprehensible to the other, resulting in explanations that the opposing side finds biased or flawed and dismisses as propaganda. Accordingly, peaceful coexistence requires that China and the West each understand what is non-negotiable for the other and refrain from insisting that it compromise on it.

Western liberal democracies stress individual freedom, the rule of law, democratic governance and human rights. Significantly curtailing them would amount to relinquishing their identity. China's ruling Communist Party, on the other hand, defines its legitimacy in terms of economic growth, social stability and, increasingly, national rejuvenation and resilience. Its legitimacy is also tied to its governance model: it considers its sovereignty, its territorial integrity and the Communist Party's centrality off limits.

While both sides can broadly agree on the necessity of peace, stability and prosperity for both their own societies and the global community, thus far the West has been unable to convince China's leadership that transitioning towards a more democratic form of governance would leave China's cultural identity or way of life acceptably intact. It would have to demonstrate that democratic values are not inherently at odds with Chinese culture or Confucian heritage – that is, that transparent and accountable democracy offers a framework within which China's traditional values and social norms can continue to thrive.

Assessing whether the values and social norms that are part of Confucian heritage can complement or at least coexist with the principles of constitutional democracy requires a nuanced understanding of both Confucianism and liberal Western democracy. Adherence to the core principles of community, personal austerity, collective effort, filial piety and social harmony has not prevented Japan, South Korea and Taiwan from adopting a version of constitutional democracy. Confucian values could conceivably enrich democratic societies by fostering a deeper sense of community responsibility and ethical leadership. Conversely, democratic principles could introduce mechanisms of accountability and inclusivity to Confucian societies that ensured that respect for authority did not overshadow the need for justice and individual rights. From this perspective, blending traditional Confucian values with democratic principles in a mutually beneficial relationship seems at least plausible.

Notes

[1] Embassy of the People's Republic of China in the United States of America, 'Wang Yi: China and Russia Have Forged a New Paradigm of Major-country Relations that Differs Entirely from the Obsolete Cold War Approach', 7 March 2024, http://us.china-embassy.gov.cn/eng/zgyw/202403/t20240308_11256414.htm/.

[2] The term 'civilization state', as applied to China, was introduced by Lucian Pye. See Lucian W. Pye, 'China: Erratic State, Frustrated Society', *Foreign Affairs*, vol. 69, no. 4, Fall 1990, pp. 56–74. Bruno Maçães, a former Portuguese secretary of state for European affairs, has popularised it. See Bruno Maçães, 'The Attack of The Civilization State', *Noema*, 15 June 2020, https://www.noemamag.com/the-attack-of-the-civilization-state/.

[3] Former empires' dreams of imperial restoration and those of civilisation-states may overlap, but they are not the same. An empire may be composed of several civilisations. The British Empire was not civilisational, although the Russian Empire tried to be.

[4] John King Fairbank, *The United States and China* (Cambridge, MA: Harvard University Press, 1948), p. 89.

[5] *Ibid.*, p. 408.

Russia, the Global South and the Mechanics of the Nuclear Order

Hanna Notte

Russia's full-scale invasion of Ukraine in 2022 marked a watershed for multilateralism. Not only did the war stymie collaboration at the United Nations, it also had a detrimental impact on the multilateral nuclear-negotiating forums and governance bodies, such as the International Atomic Energy Agency (IAEA), the UN First Committee and the Nuclear Non-Proliferation Treaty (NPT). The war paralysed and politicised these forums even as Russia's nuclear sabre-rattling and occupation of Ukrainian nuclear-power plants, and Europe's recommitment to nuclear weapons, demonstrated the ongoing need for nuclear dialogue. More subtly but no less consequentially, the war also caused shifts in states' alignments, priorities and tactics. The implications for the health of the nuclear order may take some time to fully play out, but will likely be profound.

Procedural paralysis

In nuclear forums, the immediate and most visible effect of Russia's invasion of Ukraine was to increase procedural obstacles to their work. At the IAEA in Vienna, heightened acrimony between Russia and Western states affected issues as mundane as meeting agendas, and both sides slowed down routine deliberations through the excessive exercise of the right of reply. The IAEA and the UN First Committee also saw an increased tendency toward voting. At the IAEA, this was apparent at the 2022 General Conference, where Russia and Western states faced off over technical resolutions – usually passed by

Hanna Notte is the director of the Eurasia Nonproliferation Program at the James Martin Center for Nonproliferation Studies (CNS) in Monterey, California, and senior associate (non-resident) with the Europe, Russia, and Eurasia Program at the Center for Strategic and International Studies (CSIS).

Survival | vol. 66 no. 3 | June–July 2024 | pp. 49–57   https://doi.org/10.1080/00396338.2024.2357480

consensus – due to language related to Ukraine and its Zaporizhzhia nuclear-power plant. At the UN First Committee, meanwhile, a growing number of resolutions required voting paragraph by paragraph. This was partially because Russia more frequently tabled texts to compete with Western-backed resolutions, but also because states exploited the rules of procedure, such as the right to introduce amendments on the floor, more liberally.

The NPT review process was disrupted at the 2022 Review Conference, where Russia blocked the adoption of a consensus outcome document, and at the 2023 Preparatory Committee meeting, where, in an unprecedented move, Iran prevented the chair from submitting a 'draft factual summary' of the meeting as a working paper under his own authority, a practice that had become common over the preceding two decades. Russia's and China's tacit support of Iran's breach of traditional diplomatic practice was indicative of the deep acrimony obtaining between them and the West, 18 months into Russia's war.

During the war's second year, some of the immediate procedural repercussions of the invasion subsided. At the IAEA's 2023 General Conference, for instance, a coalition of predominantly Western states supported a new resolution specifically on Ukraine – precisely to avoid the polarisation that had afflicted engagement on the technical resolutions one year earlier. In other forums, however, paralysis and polarisation persisted, only to be further compounded by the Gaza war that began in October 2023.

This state of affairs has caused frustration among the non-nuclear-weapons states, particularly those from the Global South.[1] Especially during the first year of the war, they lamented what they saw as an excessive focus on Ukraine-related issues in nuclear forums. The invasion, which enhanced the salience of nuclear weapons globally, also exacerbated their long-standing dissatisfaction over what they view as insufficient progress toward nuclear disarmament.

Russia's dual strategy

The war's highly visible procedural impact on nuclear forums has tended to mask subtler but no less important efforts by Russia to fragment the existing nuclear order and reduce the West's influence over it. Facing an intense backlash from Western states over its invasion of Ukraine, Russia has been pursuing a dual strategy: it has undermined non-proliferation efforts and chipped away at trust in legacy institutions, while also leveraging these forums in pursuit of greater alignment with non-Western states. Many states in the Global South have looked for opportunities amid the resulting fragmentation, not necessarily out of support for Russia, but because of a growing frustration over their inability to pursue their own priorities in nuclear forums.

Over the past two years, Russia has clearly deprioritised nuclear non-proliferation. Its delegations to NPT meetings in 2022 and 2023 were led by diplomats of relatively low rank, which suggested that Moscow was according less significance to the NPT review process than it did in the past. Having previously cooperated with Western states on the Iran nuclear dossier, Russia emerged as a protector of near-nuclear Iran, stymieing US- and European-led efforts to restore the Iran nuclear deal (JCPOA) in summer 2022 (to be sure, there were other, more significant reasons for the failure of these efforts).[2] Moscow also became more defensive of North Korea and its nuclear activities, recently blocking the renewal of a UN panel of experts that had monitored North Korean sanctions for 14 years.[3]

Russia has accompanied these actions with a campaign that has blamed – in echoes of similar accusations in the past – Western states for the paralysis in multilateral forums. In its recent interventions at the IAEA, Russia has called for the agency to be saved from the 'sad fate' that befell the Organisation for the Prohibition of Chemical Weapons, a disarmament body that has been incapacitated by Russian–Western acrimony for years.[4] Russian diplomats have also sought to undermine trust in the impartiality and professionalism of the IAEA's technical work. According to one diplomat interviewed by the author, Russia has made a habit of asking rhetorical questions about the work of the IAEA Technical Secretariat – as opposed to attacking it directly – which may well have an effect on states that have a limited cadre of specialists and maintain small representations in Vienna.[5]

At the end of the 2023 NPT Preparatory Committee, Russia cast doubt on the impartiality of the Finnish chair, insinuating that he was under 'serious political pressure' that was allegedly preventing him from presenting a more 'balanced' summary of the deliberations.[6] Meanwhile, at the UN First Committee, Russian diplomats have paralysed nuclear diplomacy by introducing amendments and creating other distractions. One non-Western diplomat at the UN mused that the Russians 'must be sleeping with the rules of procedure under their pillow'.[7] Only in multilateral meetings related to nuclear-energy trade has Russia shown any pragmatism.[8]

Russia has also stepped up its engagement with states from the Global South in nuclear forums as part of a broader effort at integrating them into structures of allegiance and partnership that sideline Western states.[9] Instead of strong-arming such countries into supporting its positions or openly criticising those that support votes against Russia, Moscow has focused its attacks on the Western backers of relevant resolutions to underscore the narrative that such resolutions are Western initiatives. Russian diplomats have also stepped up their outreach to non-Western coalitions. They have requested observer status at the G77 – a position Russia had already been granted within the Non-Aligned Movement (NAM) prior to the invasion of Ukraine – and intensified their engagement with regional organisations such as the Agency for the Prohibition of Nuclear Weapons in Latin America and the Caribbean (OPANAL). Russia has also become more aligned with China in multilateral nuclear forums since 2022. Moscow had already sided with Beijing in scrutinising the AUKUS partnership – which Australia, the United Kingdom and the United States had announced in September 2021 – prior to the war. After February 2022, Russia upped its objections to AUKUS and was quick to embrace China's vocal opposition to the initiative.

Targeted groups have been cautious in responding to Russian overtures. Moscow's interest in participating in NAM meetings related to the NPT, for instance, was frustrated when the NAM adopted a new rule restricting attendance to *non*-nuclear-weapons states party to the NPT. Still, one diplomat interviewed for this article noted that while Russia's efforts 'have not yet had a meaningful impact on states' established positions', its use of the NAM platform 'could over time have an impact on states that have less firm positions'.[10]

Discontented Global South

To date, Moscow's efforts appear to have had more success in fragmenting legacy forums than in solidifying alignment with countries of the Global South. However, Russia's ability to fuel fragmentation has been less a product of its own appeal or the skill of its diplomats than of discontent in the Global South with the West's dominance in and approach to multilateral institutions.[11]

Calls by Western states, especially in the first months of the Ukraine invasion, for the rest of the world to fall in line against Moscow caused considerable consternation. Many states – with several notable exceptions[12] – avoided joining the Western chorus, justifying their caution with reference to a general aversion to 'name and shame'. Some privately accused Western states of double standards in calling out some 'bad' actors but not others, citing former US president Donald Trump's 'irresponsible' nuclear rhetoric vis-à-vis North Korea or Israel's bombing of nuclear reactors in Iraq and Syria.[13] A reluctance to criticise Russia on nuclear issues became especially apparent amid a renewed focus on nuclear sharing, caused by Russia's announcement of its intent to deploy non-strategic nuclear weapons to Belarus in March 2023. The United States' own nuclear-sharing arrangements with its allies predate the NPT and were accepted by the Soviet Union when first adopted, though Russia has more recently accused the arrangements of violating the treaty.[14] Russian President Vladimir Putin justified the March 2023 announcement by pointing to American precedent – saying 'there is nothing unusual here … The United States have been doing this for decades'[15] – while at the same time asserting that Russia would not violate its own legal obligations.[16] NATO allies have condemned Russia's move as irresponsible and as 'a fundamental threat to international peace and security'.[17] Meanwhile, at the 2023 NPT Preparatory Committee and 2023 UN First Committee, many non-Western states rejected the idea that there are 'legal' (as practised by NATO) versus 'illegal' (as practised by Russia) forms of nuclear sharing, and most refrained from calling out Moscow's move.

No less important, many states in the Global South have lost faith in legacy nuclear forums – just as Russia would wish – as a result of the war in Ukraine. Frustrated with the paralysis in procedure and concerned that the prospects for achieving nuclear disarmament are becoming ever more remote, these states have shown a growing appetite for 'multi-multilateralism': an à la carte approach to collective action whereby states pivot between different platforms.[18] This appetite was apparent before the Ukraine invasion, but was whetted further by the war's repercussions. At the UN First Committee, ad hoc, open-ended working groups have created space for the aspirations of states that have long been frustrated by the deadlocked machinery of disarmament. Support for the Treaty on the Prohibition of Nuclear Weapons (TPNW), which entered into force in January 2021, also increased after the Ukraine invasion. Several diplomats from the Global South interviewed for this article expressed a growing desire to work in parallel tracks, pursuing progress on disarmament through the TPNW while remaining active in the NPT, though some warned that it was past time the NPT 'got into crisis mode' to avoid losing the support of non-nuclear-weapons states.[19]

*   *   *

Russia's war against Ukraine has ushered in a new era of multilateral nuclear diplomacy. It paralysed processes across existing forums and created opportunities for Russia to further fragment the nuclear order. Of course, as Alexander Bollfrass and Stephen Herzog have argued, the nuclear order has never been perfectly coherent, harmonious, fair or healthy.[20] Russia's invasion did not produce distinctly new problems so much as worsen existing ones, though Russia's occupation of civilian nuclear facilities and nuclear sabre-rattling do represent an unprecedented challenge to nuclear norms. The war also greatly intensified Russia's diplomatic reorientation toward the Global South, with additional implications for the nuclear order.

Western states are not blameless. Set on isolating Russia internationally and forging the broadest possible alliance against it following the invasion, they have alienated many parties in the Global South. It took time for Western states to realise that if they wished for multilateral institutions to continue functioning, they needed to ensure that their disagreements with Russia did not result in procedural paralysis or dominate their agendas with non-Western partners.

Against the backdrop of its war on Ukraine, Russia appears to have lost interest in the health of the nuclear order, except in select areas such as nuclear energy. It is using relevant forums not to foster cooperation, but to discredit the West, chip away at trust in legacy institutions and pursue its own economic interest, all while drawing non-Western states into its orbit. As Russian scholar Dmitri Trenin recently wrote, today's Russia considers the existing, Western-led international order to be beyond repair.[21] Instead, Moscow is looking to construct building blocks for new international regimes, together with the non-Western 'World Majority' – this year it is organising more than 250 engagements as chair of an expanded BRICS, for example.[22] It seems reasonable to expect that Russia will continue to use activities such as these to fragment the existing nuclear order and marshal support for its own positions on nuclear issues.

Acknowledgements

This commentary is based on research the author conducted with support from the Stanton Foundation's Nuclear Security Grant Program.

Notes

1   'Global South' is a highly imperfect term used to refer to a diverse set of countries in Africa, Asia, Latin America and the Middle East. See Comfort Ero, 'The Trouble with "the Global South"', *Foreign Affairs*, 1 April 2024, https://www.foreignaffairs.com/world/trouble-global-south.

2   See Hanna Notte, 'Russia's Invasion of Ukraine: The Iran Nuclear Price Tag', Friedrich Ebert Stiftung, February 2023, https://library.fes.de/pdf-files/international/20083.pdf.

3   See Victor Cha and Ellen Kim, 'Russia's Veto: Dismembering the UN Sanctions Regime on North Korea', Center for Strategic and International Studies, 29 March 2024, https://www.csis.org/analysis/russias-veto-dismembering-un-sanctions-regime-north-korea.

4   See Hanna Notte, 'The United States, Russia, and Syria's Chemical Weapons: A Tale of Cooperation and Its Unravelling', *Nonproliferation Review*, vol. 27, nos 1–3, 2020, pp. 201–24, https://www.tandfonline.com/doi/abs/10.1080/10736700.2020.1766226.

5   Interview with a diplomat of a country in the Global South, conducted on the sidelines of the 2023 NPT Preparatory Committee meeting, Vienna, 8 August 2023.

6   Russian delegate, speaking at the NPT Preparatory Committee meeting, Vienna, 11 August 2023.

7   Interview with a diplomat from a country of the Global South, conducted on the sidelines of the Second Meeting of States Parties to the Treaty on the Prohibition of Nuclear Weapons, New York, 30 November 2023.

8   See Toby Dalton et al., 'Dimming Prospects for U.S.–Russia Nonproliferation Cooperation', Carnegie Endowment for International Peace, 14 March 2024, https://carnegieendowment. org/2024/03/14/dimming-prospects-for-u.s.-russia-nonproliferation-cooperation-pub-91958.

9   See Michael Kimmage and Hanna Notte, 'Containing Global Russia', *War on the Rocks*, 4 March 2024, https://warontherocks.com/2024/03/containing-global-russia/.

10 Interview with a diplomat of a country in the Global South, conducted on the sidelines of the 2023 NPT Preparatory Committee meeting, Vienna, 8 August 2023.

11 See Angela Stent, 'Russia, the West, and the "World Majority"', Russia Matters, Harvard Kennedy School Belfer Center for Science and International Affairs, 25 January 2024, https://www. russiamatters.org/analysis/russia-west-and-world-majority.

12 Such outliers include Ghana, which unlike other states in the Global South specifically referenced the delicate safety and security situation at the Zaporizhzhia nuclear-power plant at the 2022 IAEA General Conference; Guatemala, which criticised the 'illegal, unjustified, and unprovoked invasion of sovereign territory of Ukraine on the part of Russia' at the 2022 UN First Committee; and Ecuador, which condemned Russia's announcement that it would deploy tactical nuclear weapons in Belarus at the UN Security Council on 31 March 2023.

13 Interview with a diplomat of a country in the Global South, conducted on the sidelines of a diplomatic conference near Vienna, 27 May 2023.

14 See Hans Kristensen et al., 'Nuclear Weapons Sharing, 2023', *Bulletin of the Atomic Scientists*, 8 November 2023, https://thebulletin.org/premium/2023-11/nuclear-weapons-sharing-2023/.

15 *Ibid.*

16 Russian officials have argued that the deployment would not violate the NPT since Moscow would not cede control over the nuclear weapons to Minsk. See 'Deploying Russia's Tactical Nuclear Arms in Belarus Does Not Violate NPT – Senior Diplomat', TASS, 1 July 2023, https://tass.com/russia/1641377.

17 'The United States Condemns a Deal Allowing Moscow to Deploy Nuclear Weapons in Belarus', *New York Times*, 25 May 2023, https://www.nytimes. com/2023/05/26/world/europe/russia-belarus-nuclear-weapons.html; and Ambassador Robert Wood, 'Remarks at a UN Security Council Briefing on Threats to International Peace and Security, Additional Response', United States Mission to the United Nations, 31 March 2023, https://usun. usmission.gov/remarks-at-a-un-security-council-briefing-on-threats-to-international-peace-and-security-additional-response/.

18 Stewart Patrick and Emma Klein, 'United Nations, Divided World', Carnegie Endowment for International Peace, 28 September

2023, https://carnegieendowment.
org/2023/09/28/united-nations-
divided-world-pub-90659.

[19] Interview with a diplomat of a country in the Global South, conducted in Vienna, 2 October 2023.

[20] Alexander K. Bollfrass and Stephen Herzog, 'The War in Ukraine and Global Nuclear Order', *Survival*, vol. 64, no. 4, August–September 2022, pp. 7–32, https://www.tandfonline.com/doi/full/10.1080/00396338.2022.2103255.

[21] Dmitry Trenin, 'Dmitry Trenin: Russia Is Undergoing a New, Invisible Revolution', RT, 2 April 2024, https://www.rt.com/russia/595266-ukraine-west-pushed-russia/.

[22] Ekaterina Korostovtseva, 'Yurii Ushakov: BRIKS na dele vyrazhaet interesy mirovogo bol'shinstva' [Yuri Ushakov: BRICS actually expresses the interests of the world majority], TASS, 5 March 2024, https://tass.ru/interviews/20149675.

Noteworthy

Narrower war

'The aerospace unit of the Revolutionary Guards has attacked targets in Israel with dozens of drones and missiles in reaction to the Zionist regime's crimes, including the attack on the consulate section of Iran's embassy in Damascus and martyring our commanders and military advisers in Syria.'

> *Iran's Islamic Revolutionary Guard Corps makes an announcement on Iranian state television on 13 April 2024.[1]*

'By deciding on an unprecedented action, Iran is taking a new step in its destabilizing actions and taking the risk of a military escalation.'

> *French Foreign Minister Stéphane Séjourné comments on Iran's attack.[2]*

'Iran's military action was in response to the Zionist regime's aggression against our diplomatic premises in Damascus. The matter can be deemed concluded. However, should the Israeli regime make another mistake, Iran's response will be considerably more severe. It is a conflict between Iran and the rogue Israeli regime, from which the U.S. MUST STAY AWAY!'

> *Iran's mission to the United Nations releases a statement on 13 April.[3]*

'We have intercepted 99 percent of threats towards Israeli territory. This is a very important strategic achievement.'

> *Israel Defense Forces spokesperson Avichay Adraee hails the success of Israeli countermeasures after Iran's attack.[4]*

'You got a win. Take the win.'

> *A White House official quotes US President Joe Biden in recounting a conversation the president had with Israeli Prime Minister Benjamin Netanyahu on 14 April.[5]*

'The Zionist regime's media supporters, in a desperate effort, tried to make victory out of their defeat, while the downed mini-drones have not caused any damage or casualties.'

> *Hossein Amirabdollahian, Iran's foreign minister, comments on an Israeli drone strike on Iranian targets on 19 April.[6]*

'Feeble!'

> *Itamar Ben-Gvir, Israel's national security minister, comments on the strike in a post to X on 19 April.[7]*

Enough in Gaza

'*The Security Council,*
    Guided by the purposes and principles of the Charter of the United Nations,
    Recalling all of its relevant resolutions on the situation in the Middle East, including the Palestinian question,
    Reiterating its demand that all parties comply with their obligations under international law, including international humanitarian law and international human rights law, and in this regard deploring all attacks against civilians and civilian objects, as well as all violence

and hostilities against civilians, and all acts of terrorism, and recalling that the taking of hostages is prohibited under international law,

Expressing deep concern about the catastrophic humanitarian situation in the Gaza Strip,

Acknowledging the ongoing diplomatic efforts by Egypt, Qatar and the United States, aimed at reaching a cessation of hostilities, releasing the hostages and increasing the provision and distribution of humanitarian aid,

1. *Demands* an immediate ceasefire for the month of Ramadan respected by all parties leading to a lasting sustainable ceasefire, and also *demands* the immediate and unconditional release of all hostages, as well as ensuring humanitarian access to address their medical and other humanitarian needs, and further demands that the parties comply with their obligations under international law in relation to all persons they detain;

2. *Emphasizes* the urgent need to expand the flow of humanitarian assistance to and reinforce the protection of civilians in the entire Gaza Strip and reiterates its demand for the lifting of all barriers to the provision of humanitarian assistance at scale, in line with international humanitarian law as well as resolutions 2712 (2023) and 2720 (2023);

3. *Decides* to remain actively seized of the matter.'

US abstention allows the United Nations Security Council to adopt a resolution on 25 March 2024 calling for a ceasefire in Gaza.[8]

'I made it clear that if they [Israeli forces] go into Rafah … we're not going to supply the weapons and artillery shells.'

US President Joe Biden gives an interview to CNN on 8 May 2024.[9]

Lifeline to Ukraine

'President Biden wants the world to believe that the biggest obstacle facing Ukraine is Republicans and our lack of commitment to the global community. This is wrong.

Ukraine's challenge is not the G.O.P.; it's math. Ukraine needs more soldiers than it can field, even with draconian conscription policies. And it needs more matériel than the United States can provide. This reality must inform any future Ukraine policy, from further congressional aid to the diplomatic course set by the president.

The Biden administration has applied increasing pressure on Republicans to pass a supplemental aid package of more than $60 billion to Ukraine. I voted against this package in the Senate and remain opposed to virtually any proposal for the United States to continue funding this war. Mr. Biden has failed to articulate even basic facts about what Ukraine needs and how this aid will change the reality on the ground.'

US Senator J.D. Vance explains his opposition to a proposed aid package for Ukraine in a New York Times *article published on 12 April 2024.*[10]

'This is a critical time right now. I could make a selfish decision and do something that's different. But I'm doing here what I believe to be the right thing. I think providing lethal aid to Ukraine right now is critically important.'

US House of Representatives Speaker Mike Johnson defends the Ukraine-aid package.[11]

'All of a sudden, he's realizing that the world depends on this. This is not some little political game on the floor.'

US Representative Michael McCaul comments on Johnson's support for the aid package, which at one time the House speaker might have opposed for not containing measures intended to secure the United States' southern border.[12]

'Make no mistake: delay in providing Ukraine the weapons to defend itself has strained the prospects of defeating Russian aggression. Dithering and hesitation have compounded the challenges we face.'

Mitch McConnell, the minority leader of the US Senate, welcomes the passage of the legislation by the US Senate on 23 April.[13]

Trump: just business?

'No politician wants bad press, but the evidence at trial will show that this was not spin or communication strategy; this was a planned, coordinated long-running conspiracy to influence the 2016 election, to help Donald Trump get elected, through illegal expenditures, to silence people who had something bad to say about his behavior, using doctored corporate records and bank forms to conceal those payments along the way. It was election fraud. Pure and simple.'

Matthew Colangelo, a prosecuting attorney in the trial of former US president Donald Trump on charges of falsifying business records, makes an opening statement on 22 April 2024.[14]

'There is nothing wrong with trying to influence an election. It's called democracy. [The prosecution] put something sinister on this idea, as if it was a crime. You'll learn it's not.'

Todd Blanche, a defence attorney for Trump, makes his own opening statement.[15]

Sources

1 'Israel Reports Light Damage After Iran Launches Large Strike', *New York Times*, 13 April 2024, https://www.nytimes.com/live/2024/04/13/world/israel-iran-gaza-war-news.
2 'Iran's Attack on Israel: World Leaders React', Reuters, 14 April 2024, https://www.reuters.com/world/middle-east/reaction-irans-drone-missile-attack-israel-2024-04-13/.
3 Permanent Misson of I.R.Iran to UN, NY (@Iran_UN), post to X, 13 April 2024, https://twitter.com/Iran_UN/status/1779269993043022053.
4 Reged Ahmad et al., 'G7 Releases Statement Condemning Iran Retaliatory Attacks on Israel – As It Happened', *Guardian*, 14 April 2024, https://www.theguardian.com/world/live/2024/apr/13/iran-launches-drone-attack-against-israel.
5 Barak Ravid, 'Scoop: Biden Told Bibi U.S. Won't Support an Israeli Counterattack on Iran', Axios, 14 April 2024, https://www.axios.com/2024/04/14/biden-netanyahu-iran-israel-us-wont-support.
6 Julian Borger and Peter Beaumont, 'World Leaders Urge Calm After Israeli Drone Strike on Iran Ratchets Up Tension', *Guardian*, 19 April 2024, https://www.theguardian.com/world/2024/apr/19/israel-iran-drone-strike-reaction.
7 Itamar Ben-Gvir (@itamarbengvir), post to X, 19 April 2024, https://twitter.com/itamarbengvir/status/1781195747255255220; and Peter Beaumont and Julian Borger, 'Israel Has Mounted Airstrikes on Iran, US Confirms, as Tehran Plays Down Attack',

Guardian, 19 April 2024, https://www.theguardian.com/world/2024/apr/19/israel-iran-airstrikes-ifsahan-tabriz-drones-explosions.
8 United Nations Security Council, 'Resolution 2728 (2024)', 25 March 2024, https://www.un.org/unispal/wp-content/uploads/2024/03/n2408081.pdf.
9 Kevin Liptak, 'Biden Says He Will Stop Sending Bombs and Artillery Shells to Israel if It Launches Major Invasion of Rafah', CNN, 8 May 2024, https://edition.cnn.com/2024/05/08/politics/joe-biden-interview-cnntv/index.html.
10 J.D. Vance, 'J.D. Vance: The Math on Ukraine Doesn't Add Up', *New York Times*, 12 April 2024, https://www.nytimes.com/2024/04/12/opinion/jd-vance-ukraine.html.
11 'How Mike Johnson Got to "Yes" on Aid to Ukraine', *New York Times*, 21 April 2024, https://www.nytimes.com/2024/04/21/us/politics/mike-johnson-house-foreign-aid.html.
12 *Ibid.*
13 'US Senate Passes $95bn Bill Including Aid for Ukraine', *Financial Times*, 23 April 2024, https://www.ft.com/content/2bf55e1b-173b-4b63-b26b-95d9a23f5a58.
14 Supreme Court of the State of New York, *The People of the State of New York vs Donald J. Trump*, p. 877, https://pdfs.nycourts.gov/PeopleVs.DTrump-71543/transcripts/4-22-2024/00060.html.
15 *Ibid.*, p. 896, https://pdfs.nycourts.gov/PeopleVs.DTrump-71543/transcripts/4-22-2024/00079.html.

A War They Both Are Losing: Israel, Hamas and the Plight of Gaza

Daniel Byman

On 7 October 2023, Hamas launched a devastating terrorist attack on Israel, killing almost 1,200 Israelis and seizing around 243 hostages. The scale of the attack was off the charts for a small state – the greatest one-day loss of Jewish life since the Holocaust – and the nature of the killings, which included the deliberate killing of children and old people, as well as mass sexual violence, seared itself into Israel's consciousness.[1] In the months that followed, Israel waged a destructive campaign in Gaza, killing more than 34,000 people, including many children, in an attempt to destroy the terrorist group, putting all Palestinians in Gaza at grave risk of disease and starvation. The campaign continues, albeit at a slower pace than in its initial months.

Both Hamas and Israel may be losing. Each can point to quite real successes against the other, but when the fighting subsides, both are likely to be worse off than they were when the war started.

Hamas can claim to have brought pain to its enemy in a way that the Jewish state has not experienced in its history. Hamas has also restored its previously languishing 'resistance' credentials and, for the time being, increased its popularity among Palestinians at a time when leadership of the Palestinian national movement is in play. It has also at least temporarily

Daniel Byman is a professor at Georgetown University's School of Foreign Service and a Senior Fellow at the Center for Strategic and International Studies. He would like to thank Jon Alterman and Kenneth Pollack for their comments on previous versions of this article. Contact him at dlb32@georgetown.edu.

Survival | vol. 66 no. 3 | June–July 2024 | pp. 61–78   https://doi.org/10.1080/ 00396338.2024.2357484

stalled Israel's regional normalisation. Yet Hamas has paid a tremendous price for these successes, and ordinary Palestinians have paid an even greater one. Hamas's military forces and infrastructure are battered, its leadership under siege and its long-term popularity uncertain.

In addition to hitting Hamas hard, Israel has preserved deterrence vis-à-vis Hizbullah in Lebanon, and dispelled any notions, often bruited, that the Israeli people will not fight hard and suffer casualties. At the same time, Israel has rescued only a few of the hostages Hamas took on 7 October. Its military campaign and slow-rolling of humanitarian aid into Gaza are widely and justly criticised for their indiscriminate impact on ordinary Palestinians. This toll has degraded international opinion of Israel and may be turning a generation of Americans against the Jewish state. Most importantly, Israel has no plan for the day after in Gaza and may find itself mired in a forever war in the strip or compelled to withdraw and allow a battered Hamas to return to power and claim ultimate victory.

Any mid-course assessment must also consider the effects of the Gaza war on the broader region. Hizbullah in Lebanon, the Houthis in Yemen, Iranian-backed militants in Iraq and Syria, and Iran itself have all launched attacks against Israel and the United States. US forces have in turn attacked Iraqi militias and the Houthis, as well as helping defend Israel against Iranian attacks. The United States and Israel have demonstrated their military superiority, and the Israeli partnership with the Gulf Arab states has proven durable and valuable. Iran, however, benefits from a region where the focus is on Israeli aggression and the US embrace of Jerusalem, diverting attention from Tehran's backing of unpopular regimes like Bashar al-Assad's in Syria and its ties to militant groups in the region.

The war is largely at an impasse, with Israel likely to make only marginal military gains in the near term while Hamas clings to survival. The United States enjoys considerable leverage over Israel, and it should use this to push Israel to increase humanitarian aid to Gaza, agree to a ceasefire with Hamas so hostages can be exchanged and begin to install an alternative Palestinian government in Gaza, which in turn will also require changing Israeli policies on the West Bank.

Hamas's gains and losses

It's hard to look at the ruins of Gaza and imagine that Hamas has achieved much, but its leaders probably believe they have made major political advances. Yahya Sinwar and Mohammed Deif – the leader of Hamas in Gaza and the head of Hamas's military forces there, respectively — were the architects of the 7 October attacks and appear to have launched them without informing the external Hamas leadership.[2] Many of Hamas's losses are likely to become more acute over time. But if Israel and external actors handle the aftermath of the war poorly, Hamas may enjoy an eventual triumph.

Hamas is not a mob of fanatics like the Islamic State, but completely discounting its ideology is also a mistake. The group's leaders see Israel as fundamentally illegitimate and believe that the Zionist movement has been at war against the Palestinians since its inception. From that perspective, the sheer quantifiable pain that Hamas has inflicted on Israel – 1,200 Israelis dead and nearly 250 prisoners taken – was itself an achievement in the eyes of Hamas leaders, particularly the more ideological ones like Sinwar and Deif.

Moreover, the 'limited' wars that Israel has conducted since Hamas seized power in Gaza didn't seem so limited from Hamas's point of view. *Operation Cast Lead* in 2008–09 led to more than 1,000 Palestinian deaths in Gaza, *Pillar of Defense* in 2012 more than 100, *Protective Edge* in 2014 more than 2,000, and back-and-forth hostilities in 2021 several hundred. In addition, Israel has raided Gaza with seeming impunity, imposed crippling economic restrictions and otherwise immiserated the Palestinian population there. Now, from Hamas's standpoint, Israel has had a taste of its own medicine. Hamas has also forced Israel to release some 240 Palestinian prisoners, which constitutes a tremendous propaganda victory for the group. (In return, Hamas released 105 captives, mostly Israelis but also 23 Thais and one Filipino who were working near Gaza and got caught up in the raid.)

As noted, Hamas has reasserted itself as a force of resistance. Since winning elections in 2006 and seizing power in Gaza a year later, Hamas has juggled two identities: the government of Gaza and a resistance group dedicated to fighting Israel. Success at either one could win over ordinary Palestinians, making Hamas, not rival secular groups like Fatah or the

Palestinian Authority (PA), the heart of the Palestinian national movement. In recent years, it has appeared that a governance mindset was predominant. Hamas repeatedly negotiated with Israel over fishing rights, work permits and conditions in Gaza. In 2022, Hamas even sat out a round of fighting between Israel and Hamas's frenemy, Palestine Islamic Jihad (PIJ). This seeming passivity led not only supporters of al-Qaeda and the Islamic State but also some activists within Hamas's own military wing to criticise it.

Yet Hamas's ability to win over Palestinians through better government was limited. For years, Israeli economic pressure and international isolation made it hard for Hamas to bring even a modicum of economic health to Gaza. Repeated Israeli attacks destroyed infrastructure and made it clear that the strip's economy was at Israel's mercy. As Hamas cracked down on PIJ and others who wanted to fight Israel in the name of Gaza's economic stability, the group increasingly became a version of its PA rival, perceived as doing Israel's bidding however grudgingly. As governance seemed a dead end, resistance became more alluring. Although its ability to govern Gaza is non-existent today, Hamas has re-established itself as Israel's most hated foe. Hamas leaders probably believe their losses on the governing side are worth the increase in resistance credibility.

Prisoners and their families are an important bloc within Hamas, and gaining the release of prisoners was a major motivation behind the 7 October attacks. In 2006, Israel released more than 1,000 prisoners in exchange for captured soldier Gilad Shalit, and Hamas probably reasoned that it could gain many more such releases with a mass-capture operation.[3] By contrast, the PA – which holds power in the West Bank, has cooperated with Israel on security for many years and has engaged in peace negotiations with Israel – has long sought such releases, only to be repeatedly rebuffed by successive Israeli governments. Hamas's message is vindicated: resistance, not negotiations, produces results.

For now, polls show a significant increase in support for Hamas, especially in the West Bank. A March poll by the highly reputable Palestinian Center for Policy and Survey Research found that 71% of Palestinians in Gaza and the West Bank believe Hamas was correct to launch the 7 October attacks, with almost two-thirds believing Hamas will emerge victorious.

More than 90% of those polled did not believe that Hamas had committed atrocities, making the Israeli response seem even more disproportionate. Few Palestinians blame Hamas for their suffering.[4]

Hamas's popularity comes at the expense of the PA, and at a critical time. Polling also shows that most Palestinians, particularly those in the West Bank, would prefer Hamas's leadership in Gaza to the PA's.[5] The prevailing view is that Hamas has demonstrated that it will act, while the PA has no real theory of success to offer ordinary Palestinians; it suppresses rather than bolsters resistance, and its bet on a peace process to bring about a Palestinian state has appeared increasingly delusional.

The PA itself is in crisis. It has long been plagued by dysfunction, corruption and authoritarianism.[6] As a result, it is deeply unpopular, and Mahmoud Abbas, the 88-year-old chain-smoker who has led it for 20 years, is not going to revive its support. Fearing that it would lose at the polls, it has not held an election since 2006.[7] Israeli settlement

Few Palestinians blame Hamas for their suffering

expansion in the West Bank, settlers' pogroms there and regular raids by the Israeli military have further undermined the PA's credibility, and many Palestinians see it as a handmaiden of the Israeli occupation. Abbas has no clear successor, and it is possible that the more pro-Western Palestinian leadership will splinter when he no longer is able to lead, in which case Hamas could well supplant the PA in the West Bank.

The 7 October attacks and the Israeli response derailed Israel's regional normalisation. To be clear, Israel and Saudi Arabia were not on the verge of normalisation before 7 October. But talks were serious, and the prospect that Saudi Arabia, the most politically and economically important Arab state, would establish relations with Israel was at least plausible, as the plight of the Palestinians could be swept under the rug with a few wiggle words, while political elites in the region focused on the Iranian threat. Today, Arabic-language news outlets present non-stop coverage of the deaths of children in Gaza and the suffering of the people there. Saudi and other Arab leaders cannot forge a full rapprochement with Israel in this environment.

Finally, although it probably was not Hamas's primary aim to disrupt Arab–Israeli normalisation, doing so was a top concern of Iran, which arms, trains and funds Hamas. Tehran rightly fears that Israel–Saudi normalisation is directed against Iran and that it would increase security cooperation between Israel and Iran's Arab rivals, as well as legitimise Israel. Thus, 7 October increased Hamas's strategic value to Iran.

The price of hurting Israel

Hamas's successes came at a steep price for both the group and Palestinians in general. Israel has devastated Hamas's military infrastructure. At the end of April, estimates of the number of Hamas fighters killed ranged from 6,000–8,000 (Hamas figures) to 11,000–13,000 (Israeli figures), with US officials gauging somewhere in between.[8] In any case, the personnel losses constitute a large portion of Hamas's estimated strength of 25,000–30,000 fighters. They are the heart of Hamas's military threat to Israel and key to Hamas's control of Gaza. Hamas has also lost several leaders, including mid-level commanders. Fighters and leaders can be replaced, but it will not be easy: even if Hamas's recruitment remains strong or even grows, capable soldiers and authoritative leaders take time to develop.

While Hizbullah, the Houthis and others have joined the fray, Hamas had hoped for an all-out regional war against Israel. This did not happen, with Hizbullah's forbearance proving a particular disappointment. Although the Lebanese group regularly attacks Israel and an all-out clash remains possible, it has refrained from sending its fighters across Israel's northern border to open a second front or use its massive rocket arsenal to punish and terrorise Israel. Hizbullah is far more capable than Hamas, and its full-scale participation would have been a game changer.[9]

The 7 October fallout also cost ordinary Palestinians dearly. It is hard to know how many Palestinian civilians have died, but the Palestinian Health Authority, generally deemed reliable, reported around 34,000 deaths at the end of April. That figure includes soldiers, but it could well be an undercount according to some international experts. Around 12,000 of the dead are children. On top of the death toll, roughly three-quarters of the population is displaced.[10] The strip is in ruins, and many ordinary

Palestinians have suffered grievous economic as well as personal loss. The destruction of Gaza will increase disease and malnutrition in the longer term. Reconstruction of Gaza is likely to be slow and limited, with people displaced for years to come.

In this light, Hamas's popularity may decline over time. After past attacks, there was initial enthusiasm for striking Israel and then anger at the Israeli response, both of which bolstered Hamas. When Israel imposed further penalties, however, and the cost of Hamas's actions became clear, support for Hamas fell. Already, there are some indications that support for the 7 October attack among Palestinians is declining, particularly in Gaza.[11]

It goes almost without saying that Hamas will find it even harder to engage with Israel in the future. That may not matter to Hamas diehards, but Israel's power dwarfs that of Hamas, and the organisation will inevitably need to engage with Israel at some point. The second intifada, which raged from 2000 to 2005 before slowly petering out, scarred a generation of Israelis, convincing them that Palestinian leaders do not want peace. The memory of 7 October is likely to function similarly, increasing support for Israeli politicians hostile to anything that smacks of Palestinian rights, especially if it involves concessions to Hamas. For now, this may not matter. But Hamas has often followed a political as well as a military strategy. Any hope that Israel might tolerate Hamas playing a quiet role in the Palestine Liberation Organization, having sympathisers participate in governing the West Bank even at a municipal level or otherwise assuming a mainstream political role is greatly diminished.

Israel had grown complacent about the Hamas threat before 7 October, believing the group could not and would not stage such a massive attack on Israel. In the coming years, Israel is likely to take the opposite approach, acting on sketchy intelligence and generally taking a shoot-first-investigate-later approach to Hamas threats. This will result in more Israeli mistakes and deaths of innocent Palestinian, but it will also mean constant pressure on Hamas. Even if Hamas remains popular and legitimate in the eyes of many Palestinians, that pressure may elevate the PA or perhaps some other Palestinian faction seen as more politically acceptable to Israel. At the very least, the rival would have greater Israeli and international support.

Israel's gains and losses

Before 7 October, Israel both negotiated with Hamas and attacked it. The hope was to use a mixture of limited carrots, such as permits for Palestinians in Gaza to work in Israel, to induce good behaviour while employing the threat of force to tamp down Hamas attacks on Israel. This was, by design, an approach without end. Israelis regularly use the term 'mowing the grass' to describe their approach to Palestinian terrorism. They sought simply to manage terrorism, believing that it was enduring and inevitable, and that extinguishing it was unrealistic.[12] Israel, however, would need to regularly strike the Palestinian groups and otherwise disrupt them, or the grass would grow too high again.

Indeed, Israel even sought to boost Hamas politically as a way of weakening the PA and undermining the chances of a two-state solution. By encouraging financial payments to Hamas from Qatar, the Netanyahu government kept Hamas strong. This, in turn, kept Abbas from gaining the upper hand in the Hamas–PA rivalry, and Israel could claim that there was no partner for peace because the Palestinians were divided. 'The Palestinian Authority is a burden', commented far-right Finance Minister Bezalel Smotrich. 'Hamas is an asset.'[13]

This approach appeared to collapse after the massive Hamas attack, which strongly implied that neither inducements nor threats would stop Hamas from killing, capturing and raping on a mass scale. Israel responded to 7 October without any clear goals beyond destroying Hamas and freeing captured Israelis. Yet Israel also cares about restoring deterrence, particularly vis-à-vis Iran, ensuring a modicum of international and especially US support, preserving relations with moderate Sunni states and, in the long run, preventing a repeat of 7 October.

The Israelis claim to have shattered 18 of Hamas's 24 battalions.[14] They have also killed several senior Hamas leaders, among them Marwan Issa, one of the architects of 7 October who was a leading Hamas member in Gaza.[15] Less dramatically, Israeli forces have blown up Hamas tunnels, destroyed strongpoints and ammunition caches, and otherwise eliminated much of Hamas's military infrastructure. Another such attack is unlikely not only because of Hamas's resulting military weakness, but also because

Israel is likely to respond aggressively to even a hint that Hamas is planning a major attack, loath to continue the complacency that allowed 7 October to happen: a year earlier, Israeli intelligence had intercepted the Hamas battle plan and collected specific indicators that it was moving forward, but Israel did not act.[16]

With its harsh military campaign in Gaza, Israel has sent a message to other potential aggressors, notably Hizbullah, about the price of attacking Israel. Hizbullah and Israel have engaged in only a limited back-and-forth since 7 October, and Hizbullah has made clear it does not seek all-out war. Several factors shape Hizbullah's calculus, but the ruin major war would bring to already-fragile Lebanon is likely the primary one.

The Israeli public has also demonstrated a clear will to fight, which is an important element of deterrence. Israel's enemies, including Hizbullah, have long subscribed to a 'spider web' theory whereby Israel looks strong but on close examination is fragile, with casualty sensitivity its greatest weakness. Pre-war internal tensions in Israel added to concerns that the country was too divided to resist its enemies.[17] After 7 October, however, the nation rallied around the military. The massive reserve call-up and the deaths of 600 soldiers on 7 October and in the days immediately thereafter produced grim support, not beseeching protests.[18]

Israel's responses to provocations apparently weigh heavily on Iran and its allies as well. On 1 April, Israel attacked a diplomatic facility in Damascus, killing seven Islamic Revolutionary Guard Corps officers, including two senior ones.[19] On 13 April, Iran responded with a barrage of more than 300 missiles and drones, the first direct attack ever launched against Israel from Iranian soil. The attack fizzled. Israel intercepted most of the drones and missiles with the help of the United States, Jordan and various Gulf states. Israel responded with a small, but precise, strike on an Iranian air-defence system. The exchange demonstrated the strength of Israeli defences and regional Arab states' reluctance to break with Israel even in dark times for the Palestinians. On balance, Iranian personnel outside Iran are vulnerable to Israeli targeting and substantially deterred from directly attacking Israel. Furthermore, Israel has demonstrated to its Sunni Arab partners that it can strike Iran and its proxies with relative impunity and will do so if provoked.

While the Sunni Arab states pay a political price for open cooperation with Jerusalem, Israel now looms as an arguably more valuable military partner.

Hamas still stands

Israel's gains are impressive, but its losses have been daunting. Hamas has declined to release more than 130 of the roughly 240 hostages it took on 7 October, although many of them are probably dead.[20] Israel has been able to extract only three hostages through the use of military force, the others being freed by way of a brief ceasefire and prisoner swap. This record indicates the extraordinary difficulty of hostage rescue – always a stiff challenge – when the hostages are carefully hidden and well guarded. Israel cannot both attack Hamas and swap for hostages, as the terrorist group demands a ceasefire as part of the exchange. The issue is a highly emotional one for Israelis, with no good answer.

Some of Israel's military gains have been limited. Although Israel has killed many Hamas leaders, the two most important, Sinwar and Deif, remained alive as of mid-May. After 7 October, Israel's military spokesman declared Sinwar a 'dead man walking', yet he and Deif have eluded the Israeli military manhunt.[21] More broadly, Israel's military campaign appears largely stalled. It has withdrawn most of its forces from the strip, maintaining a presence in the central area and preventing Palestinians from returning to the north. Further military operations, such as the one against Hamas's remaining stronghold in Rafah, may only yield marginal gains; killing a few thousand more Hamas fighters will not dramatically change the balance of forces. The death of a major figure like Sinwar or Deif would not matter much from a military point of view, though it would yield political benefits for the government of Prime Minister Benjamin Netanyahu. Hamas has a deep bench of leaders and has shown repeatedly that it can weather the loss of senior staff operationally and even thrive politically.

Hamas's long-term position is far stronger than Israel would like. Owing to the high death toll and extreme devastation visited by the Israeli campaign, Gaza will be filled with angry and vengeful young men, ripe for recruitment by Hamas. Even if Hamas is militarily defeated, its theory of resistance – that the only way to create a free Palestine is through violence – remains popular.[22]

The deaths of tens of thousands of Palestinian civilians in Gaza also constitute an immense blot on Israel's international reputation, which was not sterling to begin with. High civilian casualties in Gaza were inevitable, as it is one of the most densely populated places in the world and Hamas fighters intentionally blended in with the population, making it impossible to target Hamas without imperilling civilians. But Israel took this difficult situation and made it worse. Israeli military rules of engagement reportedly allow the killing of up to 20 civilians to take out a single junior Hamas fighter, 100 for a senior leader. By comparison, the United States put the ratio at 30-to-one for Saddam Hussein.[23] A senior Israeli official lamented in April that the Israeli military was shooting first and asking questions later, which is leading to high-profile friendly-fire mistakes, such as the killing of three Israeli hostages shouting in Hebrew and waving a white flag, and the deaths of international aid workers. These errors suggest many Palestinians looking to surrender or simply uninvolved in anti-Israeli action have also been wrongly targeted.[24] Even less justifiably, Israel has blocked or slow-rolled humanitarian aid, with far less getting into the strip than is needed to ensure basic health.[25] Europeans have long seen Israel as a major threat to peace, even more so than Iran, North Korea, Russia and other dictatorships, according to some polls.[26] Since the Gaza war began, demonstrations against Israel have roiled many European cities, and Israeli leaders worry that the International Criminal Court may issue arrest warrants against them because of the Gaza war.[27]

While Israelis might publicly shrug off European criticism, American criticism is another matter. In the United States, approval of Israel's actions fell from over 50% in November to 36% in March. Disapproval was particularly strong among Democrats, with 75% seeing Israel's approach as wrong.[28] Overall favourable views of Israel are falling, and younger Americans are particularly scathing.[29] Mass protests on major-college campuses have raised the profile of the issue in the United States and, occurring in a historically critical election year, have added to pressures on the Biden administration. President Joe Biden, a long-time supporter who embraced Israel after 7 October, has grown more and more critical in his public remarks, and on 8 May decided to at least temporarily halt the supply of munitions that could cause mass casualties to Israel for its assault on Rafah.[30]

Israel's own politics remain fraught. Netanyahu's political position was weak before the war, with many Israelis outraged by allegations of corruption and by his far-right government's attempts to neuter the judiciary and impose other far-right reforms. Some Israelis blame Netanyahu for not taking responsibility for the strategic failure that 7 October reflects. Perhaps most fundamentally, the far right wants to keep the war going, while other Israelis are more willing to accept a ceasefire in exchange for a hostage release.

No day after

Israel's biggest error is especially puzzling to Americans and Europeans with painful memories of the wars in Afghanistan and Iraq: there is no plan for the day after. To keep Hamas down in the long term, Gaza needs a new government, and Israel has dodged this paramount challenge despite repeated calls by the United States to address it.

The logic of American urgency is simple. Groups like Hamas hide among the civilian population and otherwise remain elusive. If military forces leave an area, they re-emerge and reassert control. For example, in a bloody and controversial operation, Israel first captured the Al-Shifa hospital in November. In March, however, several hundred Hamas fighters took control of the area after Israeli forces had left, forcing Israel to go in again.[31] If Hamas is to be destroyed as a political force, something needs to replace it. Otherwise, even with only a few thousand fighters, it can reassert at least limited control over much of the strip.

Territorial control is also vital for the safe delivery of humanitarian aid to Gaza. Israel now imposes many restrictions on anything going into Gaza, but once it passes into the strip, it is often seized by local criminals or desperate people rather than distributed efficiently and fairly. A governing entity could provide law and order, allowing humanitarian workers to do their jobs.[32]

To be sure, political constraints do not make for appealing day-after options. The international community cannot send a peacekeeping force to Gaza without deploying a large number of capable forces with the will and authority to fight Hamas, but volunteers are not forthcoming. While Arab leaders privately scorn Hamas on account of the group's Islamist orientation and Iranian backing, they claim to support the Palestinian people, and their publics are outraged by the Israeli attack and champion Palestinian rights. For them to deploy troops to Gaza to suppress Hamas would complicate their political messaging and put them at odds with their own people.

By default, that leaves the PA, which as noted is deeply flawed. The Biden administration, to its credit, has proposed a revitalised PA that would involve new leadership. In March, Abbas made a gesture in this direction, appointing Mohammad Mustafa, his long-serving economic adviser, as prime minister with an eye to creating a technocratic government.[33] This is a useful step, but Mustafa is hardly a new broom, and in any event such an appointment is only one among many that would need to be made before the PA had the competence to manage a devastated Gaza as well as the West Bank, which it now only tenuously governs.

Political credibility will be even harder to establish. Before 7 October, PA security forces regularly cooperated with Israel against Hamas and other mutual foes, though Israel found them increasingly unwilling and unable to act. At the same time, Abbas seemed to do little in the West Bank to discourage excessively aggressive Israeli military operations undertaken in defence of settlers, who themselves often attacked Palestinian civilians. The situation reached the point where the Biden administration threatened sanctions against several Israeli military units for their 'gross human rights violations' against Palestinian civilians.[34]

The West Bank has been a tinderbox for some time, with both Palestinian and settler violence constant risks. Since 7 October, Israel has grown far more aggressive in the West Bank, and settlers there have run amok. Through the end of April, the Israeli military had arrested more than 8,000 Palestinians in the West Bank, and more than 400 Palestinians had been killed. Although many of those detained were released, the number of Palestinians in Israeli prisons is higher than it was before 7 October, and demonstrations persist.[35] Amnesty International reports that settler violence has 'drastically increased', with murders and property destruction common.[36] The Israeli government has also ramped up land seizures, dispelling any lingering hopes that 7 October would lead to a policy reset.[37] Israel has made it easier for the settler community in the West Bank to arm, and far-right ministers are giving them carte blanche in an already combustible situation, requiring overstretched Israeli troops to be deployed to prevent the situation from exploding.[38]

Perhaps unsurprisingly, only 24% of Palestinians polled in March wanted the PA to rule Gaza, in contrast to 59% who favoured Hamas. Of that 24%, less than half wanted Abbas at the helm, the rest favouring alternative PA leadership.[39]

*   *   *

If there is no credible international or Palestinian actor to govern Gaza, it is likely to become a failed state. There may be pockets of order, but large parts of the strip will be essentially ungoverned. Israel will continue to conduct raids to keep Hamas off balance and prevent it from consolidating control anywhere. The Gaza war's legacy may simply be another indefinite grass-mowing exercise rather than any major change in Israeli policy. Whether deliberate or not, this leaves Israel where Hamas wants it: increasingly isolated internationally, divided internally and embracing policies that marginalise the PA and undermine Israel's regional integration.

Given diminishing Israeli returns and Hamas's unyielding posture, new approaches are necessary. A ceasefire is a logical next step. Israel gains little from the current fighting, and its citizens desperately want surviving hostages and the remains of those who have died returned. This will require painful Israeli concessions in terms of freeing Hamas terrorists and easing military pressure on Hamas, at least in the short term, but there is no viable alternative course.

At the very least, far more humanitarian aid must enter the strip, ideally with some form of escort that prevents massive looting or at such a scale that the black market effectively collapses due to oversupply. This will require streamlining the many hurdles Israel has imposed for aid delivery, as well as increasing overall capacity. Diminishing civilian suffering will ease Americans' criticism of Israel and reduce pressure on Israel's Arab partners.

Most importantly, the planning for the day after needs to begin promptly. The choices are vexing, but no one, including Israel, should welcome an indefinite crisis. To avoid it, someone must govern Gaza. The PA is the best of an array of bad options, and the international community along with Israel should be working to support PA leaders. The success of the PA in Gaza will depend heavily on its performance in the West Bank. Calls for Israel to end settlements, arrest violent settlers and restore a modicum of respect for PA governance there may seem hollow given years of perversely antagonistic policies on the part of multiple Israeli governments, but they must continue. The Biden administration's threats of sanctioning military units, labelling some settler groups as terrorists and conditioning some aid on moderations in Israeli policy in the West Bank are necessary and overdue, and the White House may have to act on them.

Despite appearances to the contrary, the United States has considerable leverage over Israel. Israel not only needs US ammunition and other military assistance for the Gaza war, but it also relies on the United States for intelligence and air-defence assistance to address the ongoing Iranian threat. In addition, Israel is preparing for a possible war with Hizbullah, and its military needs for that conflict will dwarf what was required for Gaza. Israel is sensitive to US concerns, and carefully scrutinises matters such as delays or curtailments in weapons deliveries as potential signs of a larger decrease in support.[40]

Hopes that the Gaza war might restart the peace process or have some other silver lining for now have been flattened, but even this crisis can still be an opportunity. Both the Israeli and the Palestinian leaderships may be in transition, and major changes in either – ideally both – could usher in new approaches focused on ending the blood and tears of the last months. Meanwhile, external actors should seek not only to solve the immediate crisis, but also to set the conditions for longer-term progress, allowing Palestinians and Israelis to wrench some hope from a war they both are losing.

Notes

[1]   See United Nations Office of the Special Representative of the Secretary-General on Sexual Violence in Conflict, press release, 4 March 2024, https://www.un.org/ sexualviolenceinconflict/press-release/ israel-west-bank-mission/.

[2]   See Anchal Vohra, 'Hamas's Political Leaders Aren't in Charge', *Foreign Policy*, 28 November 2023, https://

foreignpolicy.com/2023/11/28/hamas-gaza-qatar-leaders-negotiations-hostages-ceasefire-war-israel/.

3 See Isabel Debre, 'Israeli Hostage Crisis in Hamas-ruled Gaza Becomes a Political Trap for Netanyahu', Associated Press, 8 October 2023, https://apnews.com/article/palestinians-israel-military-prisoners-hostage-hamas-soldiers-e75729364f8c0b453da272365c16d136.

4 Palestinian Center for Policy and Survey Research, Public Opinion Poll no. 91, 20 March 2024, https://www.pcpsr.org/sites/default/files/Poll%20 91%20English%20press%20release%20 20%20March%202024.pdf.

5 Ibid.

6 See, for example, Khaled Elgindy, 'The Palestinian Leadership Crisis', Brookings Institution, 5 January 2016, https://www.brookings.edu/articles/the-palestinian-leadership-crisis/.

7 See Joseph Krauss, 'Abbas Delays Palestinian Elections; Hamas Slams "Coup"', Associated Press, 29 April 2021, https://apnews.com/article/hamas-middle-east-elections-religion-government-and-politics-e88636bc 919f8aab455e01fbbd4b4391.

8 Margherita Stancati, 'In Gaza, Authorities Lose Count of the Dead', Wall Street Journal, 28 April 2024, https://www.wsj.com/world/middle-east/in-gaza-authorities-lose-count-of-the-dead-779ff694.

9 See Seth Jones et al., 'The Coming Conflict with Hezbollah', Center for Strategic and International Studies, 21 March 2024, https://www.csis.org/analysis/coming-conflict-hezbollah.

10 Stancati, 'In Gaza, Authorities Lose Count of the Dead'; and

Alyssa Fowers et al., 'What Would Have Happened to Family and Friends if Gaza Were Home', Washington Post, 5 April 2024, https://www.washingtonpost.com/world/interactive/2024/gaza-numbers-killed-displaced-scale/.

11 Palestinian Center for Policy and Survey Research, Public Opinion Poll no. 91.

12 See Daniel Byman, A High Price: The Triumphs and Failures of Israeli Counterterrorism (Oxford: Oxford University Press, 2011).

13 Quoted in, for example, Mark Mazzetti and Ronen Bergman, '"Buying Quiet": Inside the Israeli Plan that Propped Up Hamas', New York Times, 10 December 2023, https://www.nytimes.com/2023/12/10/world/middleeast/israel-qatar-money-prop-up-hamas.html; and Steven Simon and Jonathan Stevenson, 'The Gaza Horror and US Policy', Survival, vol. 65, no. 6, December 2023–January 2024, p. 40.

14 'Israel Says 18 of 24 Hamas Battalions "Destroyed"', Yahoo News, 16 February 2024, https://news.yahoo.com/israel-says-18-24-hamas-203950351.html.

15 See Dion Nissenbaum and Summer Said, 'Israel Has Killed a Top Hamas Commander in Gaza. It Took Five Months', Wall Street Journal, 20 March 2024, https://www.wsj.com/world/middle-east/israel-has-killed-a-top-hamas-commander-in-gaza-it-took-five-months-76db1be1.

16 See Ronen Bergman and Adam Goldman, 'Israel Knew Hamas's Attack Plan More than a Year Ago', New York Times, 2 December 2023, https://www.nytimes.com/2023/11/30/world/middleeast/israel-hamas-attack-intelligence.html.

17 See 'Nasrallah's Spider Web Theory Is Proving Correct, Haaretz Says', Al Mayadeen English, 26 July 2023, https://english.almayadeen.net/news/politics/nasrallahs-spider-web-theory-is-proving-correct-haaretz-says.

18 See 'Israel Army Says 600 Soldiers Killed Since October 7th', Barron's, 1 April 2024, https://www.barrons.com/news/israeli-army-says-600-soldiers-killed-since-october-7-dcad8bb1.

19 'Iran Says Israel Bombs Its Embassy in Syria, Kills Commanders', Reuters, 1 April 2024, https://www.reuters.com/world/middle-east/israel-bombs-iran-embassy-syria-iranian-commanders-among-dead-2024-04-01/.

20 See 'Israel Appears to Soften Stance in Cease-fire Talks', New York Times, 29 April 2024 (updated 30 April 2024), https://www.nytimes.com/live/2024/04/29/world/israel-gaza-war-hamas.

21 See Neri Zilber, '"Dead Man Walking": How Yahya Sinwar Deceived Israel for Decades', Financial Times, 5 November 2023, https://www.ft.com/content/de78c7a0-f8f0-403e-b0db-eb86d6e76919.

22 This is a tricky issue. As a matter of doctrine, Hamas rejected the two-state solution. But in practice some elements of the group at least seemed willing to accept it. The 7 October attack appears to have negated that possibility.

23 'The Short-sighted Israeli Army', The Economist, 11 April 2024, https://www.economist.com/leaders/2024/04/11/the-short-sighted-israeli-army.

24 See Jacob Magid, 'Senior Israeli Official Laments Culture of "Shoot First, Ask Later" Gaining Ground in IDF', Times of Israel, 3 April 2024, https://www.timesofisrael.com/liveblog_entry/shoot-first-ask-questions-later-senior-israeli-official-laments-culture-creeping-into-idf/.

25 See 'Israel Continues to Block Aid into Northern Gaza; UN Sending Team to Shattered Al-Shifa Hospital', UN News, 1 April 2024, https://news.un.org/en/story/2024/04/1148141.

26 See Peter Beaumont, 'Israel Outraged as EU Poll Names It Threat to Peace', Guardian, 1 November 2003, https://www.theguardian.com/world/2003/nov/02/israel.eu.

27 See Mike Corder, 'What Is the International Court and Why It Has Israeli Officials Worried', Associated Press, 30 April 2024, https://apnews.com/article/israel-hamas-gaza-international-criminal-court-hague-palestinians-1f683a6e2e150d91c415eb1d0a19a44d.

28 Jeffrey M. Jones, 'Majority in US Now Disapprove of Israeli Action in Gaza', Gallup, 27 March 2024, https://news.gallup.com/poll/642695/majority-disapprove-israeli-action-gaza.aspx.

29 Jeffrey M. Jones, 'Americans' Views of Both Israel, Palestinian Authority Down', Gallup, 4 March 2024, https://news.gallup.com/poll/611375/americans-views-israel-palestinian-authority-down.aspx.

30 See Erica L. Green, 'Biden Says the U.S. Will Not Supply Israel with Weapons to Attack Rafah', New York Times, 8 May 2024, https://www.nytimes.com/2024/05/08/us/politics/biden-israel-weapons-rafah.html.

31 See Patrick Kingsley, 'Israeli Army Withdraws from Major Gaza Hospital, Leaving Behind a Wasteland', New York Times, 2 April 2024, https://

www.nytimes.com/2024/04/02/world/
middleeast/gaza-al-shifa-hospital.html.

32 John Davison et al., 'Destruction,
Lawlessness and Red Tape Hobble
Aid as Gazans Go Hungry', Reuters,
26 March 2024, https://www.reuters.
com/world/middle-east/destruction-
lawlessness-red-tape-hobble-aid-
gazans-go-hungry-2024-03-25/.

33 See 'Palestinian Leader Appoints
Longtime Advisor as Prime
Minister in the Face of Calls for
Reform', Associated Press, 15 March
2024, https://apnews.com/article/
palestinians-politics-israel-abbas-
mohammad-mustafa-d7907aa06db3d6
be6f8d59cc29e57897.

34 Anne Flaherty, 'US Holds Off on
Sanctioning Israeli Military Units
Accused of Human Rights Violations
Before Start of War with Hamas', ABC
News, 26 April 2024, https://abcnews.
go.com/Politics/biden-sanction-israeli-
military-units-accused-human-rights/
story?id=109651562.

35 See '"Left to Bleed Out": Israeli Forces
Kill Two Palestinians in West Bank',
Al-Jazeera, 27 April 2024, https://www.
aljazeera.com/news/2024/4/27/israeli-
forces-shoot-dead-two-palestinians-
in-occupied-west-bank; and Omar
Abdel-Baqui, Fatima AbdulKarim and
Anat Peled, 'Another Front for Israel's
Military: Violence Between Settlers

and Palestinians', *Wall Street Journal*,
22 April 2024, https://www.wsj.com/
world/middle-east/another-front-for-
israels-military-violence-between-
settlers-and-palestinians-2a69937b.

36 Amnesty International, 'State-
backed Deadly Rampage by
Israeli Settlers Underscores Urgent
Need to Dismantle Apartheid', 22
April 2024, https://www.amnesty.
org/en/latest/news/2024/04/
state-backed-deadly-rampage-by-
israeli-settlers-underscores-urgent-
need-to-dismantle-apartheid/.

37 See, for example, Laura Bullens,
'Israel's Largest Land Seizure
Since Oslo Accords Deals Fresh
Blow to Palestinian Statehood',
France24, 26 March 2024,
https://www.france24.com/en/
middle-east/20240326-israel-s-largest-
land-seizure-since-oslo-accords-deals-
fresh-blow-to-palestinian-statehood.

38 See Abdel-Baqui, AbdulKarim
and Peled, 'Another Front for
Israel's Military'.

39 Palestinian Center for Policy and Survey
Research, Public Opinion Poll no. 91.

40 See Derek Thompson, 'Interview
with Natan Sachs', *Plain English*,
30 April 2024, https://www.
theringer.com/2024/4/30/24144857/
how-will-the-gaza-war-finally-end-
student-protests-with-natan-sachs.

Iran and Israel: Everything Short of War

John Raine with Ben Barry, Nick Childs, Fabian Hinz and Julia Voo

Iran's attack on Israel on 13–14 April 2024 and Israel's retaliatory strike on Isfahan on 19 April marked a sharp shift in the decades-long conflict between the two states – from indirect to direct military confrontation. It suggested a new phase in which the two states may attack each other's sovereign territory. The complexity of Iran's offensive operations, in particular, was unprecedented. The attacks raised the possibility of 'all-out war' between the two states, which could take the form of direct attacks on sovereign territory and infrastructure, as recently witnessed in the Russia–Ukraine war and the second Nagorno-Karabakh war.[1]

Despite the recent escalation, however, there remain critical constraints on the ability of both Iran and Israel to escalate further to a level of conflict approaching all-out war. They are determined not only by political and geostrategic considerations, but also by the military balance between the two states. While both sides have relatively large defence establishments, they stress different capabilities. Arguably, neither side possesses the military means sufficient to fight a sustained and direct conflict with the other. Excluding Israel's undeclared but universally assumed nuclear capability, neither side has the ability to overwhelm the other militarily. Iran's physical size, its dispersal of assets and its heavily armed asymmetric proxies afford

John Raine is IISS Senior Adviser for Geopolitical Due Diligence. He is the lead author of this article. **Ben Barry** is IISS Senior Fellow for Land Warfare. **Nick Childs** is IISS Senior Fellow for Naval Forces and Maritime Security. **Fabian Hinz** is IISS Research Fellow for Defence and Military Analysis. **Julia Voo** is IISS Senior Fellow for Cyber Power and Future Conflict. This article was adapted from an IISS Online Analysis piece that appeared in May 2024.

Survival | vol. 66 no. 3 | June–July 2024 | pp. 79–90   https://doi.org/10.1080/00396338.2024.2357485

it a resilience that compensates for its shortfall in firepower compared to Israel. Israel, for its part, has sophisticated defences and allies willing to supplement them with critical capabilities.

Structurally unfit for major war

The two states have configured their armed forces primarily to serve broader strategic objectives, and not to fight a major war with each other. Israel's military forces are structured to defend its territory and borders from hostile neighbours, including through forward operations, while Iran's forces are geared to protecting the regime and projecting power into asymmetric conflicts. On balance, however, their force structures have been based on wars of survival rather than conquest.[2] Still, each country has developed military capabilities and plans for possible use against the other.

Iran's armed forces are shaped by the Islamic Republic's history as well as the imperative of survival. The regime's distrust of the conventional army of the shah, coupled with its fervour for the wider Islamic cause, led to the sidelining of regular armed forces in favour of its own Islamic Revolutionary Guard Corps (IRGC) and popular army, the Basij, both charged with defending the state. In addition, the large-scale casualties and costs of its eight-year war with Iraq in the 1980s left the regime determined to avoid conventional war, not least for fear that it would destabilise the country and imperil the revolution. The establishment of the elite Quds Force, charged with exporting the revolution, reflected a new approach to extending Iranian influence and undermining its foreign adversaries. Iran invested heavily in its external asymmetric capability, creating and maintaining a network of regional partners with which it shares strategic aims, ideology (to varying degrees) and, critically, weapons.

Israel has structured its armed forces to defend against state-level aggression from well-armed neighbouring states such as Egypt and Syria, and latterly from asymmetric non-state armed groups. That has left it with a powerful mixture of domain-dominance and intelligence-based capabilities. But despite having powerful strike assets, its armed forces are not designed to fight expeditionary wars beyond its immediate periphery.

While only small and select fractions of the respective forces are likely to be involved in a short conflict, their relative experience overall could conceivably become a factor in a longer one. The two states have differing levels of battle-readiness in terms of personnel and equipment. Iran has a mass-recruitment policy for its domestic security forces, of which only a small percentage has combat experience, although the number is larger within the Quds Force and Hizbullah. This contrasts with the Israel Defense Forces (IDF), whose reservists and professional soldiers have often accumulated experience with multiple weapons systems over several conflicts. But the IDF, despite its considerable record of power projection, has not yet tested its ability to project military power into Iran except through limited aerial and covert means.

Iranian equipment, in particular uninhabited aerial vehicles (UAVs) and missile systems, is in wide use among state actors (Russia, Sudan and Syria) and non-state groups (Hizbullah and the Houthis). Iran's indigenous research-and-development cycle is well honed, as the production and export of its *Shahid*-series UAVs, ballistic missiles and cruise missiles has shown. But while the state's production and research facilities will give some of its weapons systems resilience, they also constitute high-value targets for Israel.

Iran's ability to defend itself against air and missile strikes rests on an ageing air force and on air-defence systems of Russian origin plus older American- and Chinese-origin systems, some updated locally, and domestically produced systems. The effectiveness of Iran's command and control is open to question, especially in light of the disastrous shootdown of a Ukrainian airliner in January 2020 with no firm evidence that capabilities have since improved.

Alliances and partnerships

A further determinant of the military balance is the extent to which each side can leverage its alliances and partnerships. Iran's regional allies are primed for asymmetric conflict with Israel, and can be relied on to defend Iran and to supplement its offensive actions. Iran is likely to seek enhancements from Russia in return for its military support for the war in Ukraine, though it is unlikely Russia would spare the capabilities which would make a major difference to Tehran in the short term.

Israel's allies and partners – the United States in particular but also several European capitals – would be hesitant about supporting, if not openly opposed to, direct Israel military operations against Iran.[3] Fighting in a remote theatre over time would stretch Israel's capabilities and potentially add a new and politically fraught theatre to those of Gaza, the West Bank and southern Lebanon. Israel can be confident in US President Joe Biden's recent statements that the US will defend Israel against further Iranian attacks and the strong showing of Israel's allies and partners in actively defending it against Iranian missiles.[4] But Israel's defence apparatus is not set up diplomatically or militarily for sustained conflict in distant places.

Aircraft and missiles: the key domain

Israel's air force has a demonstrated capability to launch precision strikes at range with aircraft including F-15s, F-16s and F-35s. Iran has only a collection of ageing aircraft to defend its own airspace. However, striking deep into Iran would still represent a logistical challenge requiring significant support. Ballistic missiles, cruise missiles and one-way attack UAVs constitute a key pillar of Iran's deterrence strategy, enabling it to penetrate adversary territory even without a capable air force. Iran has invested heavily in the domestic development of such systems and has acquired a diverse arsenal of missiles with ranges of up to 2,000 kilometres. A US assessment in 2022 estimated that the country possesses up to 3,000 ballistic missiles, even though the percentage of those capable of reaching Israel remains unknown.[5]

Iran's recent strike on Israel, however, exposed the limitations of its missile-centred, asymmetric deterrence strategy. The strike, almost certainly designed to overwhelm Israeli defences, involved more than 100 ballistic missiles and featured some of Iran's most advanced systems. Yet Israeli missile defences – admittedly with the extensive support of US forces and the involvement of several other nations – achieved an extraordinarily high interception rate of the ballistic missiles, shooting down most of Iran's cruise missiles and one-way UAVs before they reached Israel's borders. While Iran might be able to make some quantitative and qualitative improvements to its forces, whether it could significantly scale up future attacks is uncertain. Should confrontation between Israel and Iran escalate into a prolonged exchange of blows, Israeli stockpile numbers would assume critical importance. Although a variety of systems can be used to defend against one-way UAVs and cruise missiles, thwarting medium-range ballistic missiles requires specialised interceptors that are not easily replenished, and the number of *Arrow*-2 and -3 missiles in the Israeli arsenal remains unknown. Israel might be able to count on US ship-based ballistic-missile defences, as it did during the 13–14 April strikes.

Iran has shared substantial rocket, missile and one-way UAV capabilities with allied non-state actors in Gaza, Iraq, Lebanon, Syria and Yemen. But their arsenals' utility against Israel is likely quite limited. The stocks of the Gaza factions have been largely destroyed and depleted in more than six months of war. In Syria, Iran's attempts to build up deterrent capabilities have been degraded by years of pre-emptive Israeli airstrikes. And in Iraq and Yemen, allied groups only have a few weapons that are capable of reaching Israel. The only non-state actor able to make a significant contribution in an all-out war with Israel is Lebanese Hizbullah, whose rocket arsenal is estimated at between 150,000 and 200,000 rockets, including precision-guided missiles.[6] Owing to the close geographical proximity of Lebanon and Israel, overwhelming Israeli missile and air defences may be a more achievable goal for Hizbullah than for Iran itself.

Iran's air-defence challenge is different than Israel's. For one thing, it has a far larger land mass, which yields some advantages in terms of concealment. But its older air-defence missile systems have limited capability and likely also limited operational availability. Its modern long-range systems, such as the S-300PMU2 (RS-SA-20 *Gargoyle*), mainly protect key regime sites including those around Tehran. But the Iranians have developed widely dispersed mobile systems. They are of different designs, which makes it harder for an attacker to mount effective countermeasures, but by the same token stockpiles may be limited. Overall, Israel's limited retaliation for the 13–14 April missile and UAV attack revealed the limits of Iran's air-defence capabilities.

Furthermore, when Israel struck an S-300PMU2 radar installation in Isfahan, it not only destroyed a key piece of defensive equipment but also demonstrated that even Iran's most advanced air-defence system was incapable of countering advanced Israeli stand-off munitions.

Perhaps more significantly, Israel and Iran operate under different criteria of air-defence success. For Iran, surviving to fight another day may be enough, and absorbing some Israeli-inflicted damage and casualties may even work to Tehran's advantage in terms of shoring up domestic support and regional credentials. Any instance of success against an Israeli air campaign, including the downing of even one crewed aircraft, would be an Iranian propaganda coup. Israel, by contrast, faces a national expectation of near complete protection from rocket, missile and UAV attacks, and the government and population have lower tolerances for civilian and military casualties. In cases where such protection cannot be assured, as in northern Israel, domestic calls for military action to degrade adversarial capabilities have increased.

Other domains

Israel has developed a sophisticated if narrowly focused naval force, with missile-armed corvettes and a range of patrol craft that have been effective in defending its sea approaches and contributed to local-area air defence. Increased threats to the country's growing energy interests and assets may prove more challenging. Israel's naval power-projection capacity beyond the eastern Mediterranean and the Red Sea is limited, save for its submarine force, which is assumed to have a land-attack cruise-missile – and by implication nuclear – capability, though Israel would likely remain reluctant to show its hand on this score.

Each country has for some time been engaged in a low-level and partly clandestine shadow war against the other's shipping interests. Tehran has also developed a comprehensive asymmetric capability in the maritime domain, including fast-attack craft, coastal anti-ship missile batteries and one-way UAVs, and has often threatened to close the Strait of Hormuz. Such a move, however, would quickly widen any confrontation and potentially harm Iran's friends and its own economy. More restrained but still disruptive possibilities could include increased seizures of Israeli-connected shipping, additional limited shipping strikes in the Indian Ocean and facilitating further Houthi-led attacks. Direct Israeli response options may be limited but could include targeting Iranian naval assets in the Red Sea, including IRGC ones, or in port via airstrikes.

Israel's superior land capabilities have been designed and deployed to defend its territory, rather than for expeditionary warfare. While Iran has indirectly involved itself in almost every major IDF ground operation of this century by supplying weapons to Hamas and Hizbullah, it has thus far shown no intention of directly confronting the IDF in land operations. The land domain would take on greater strategic significance for Iran if the IDF pivoted from Gaza to southern Lebanon. If this involved land forces at major scale, Tehran would be compelled to consider the extent to which it would intervene to protect Hizbullah's assets. Even were the threat to Hizbullah severe to the point of existential, it seems highly unlikely that Iran would consider advancing its own land forces other than Quds Force personnel. The logistical challenges of moving, maintaining and protecting ageing assets from Israeli air assault would be too stiff, and any potential strategic gain too uncertain, to warrant the risk.

In the covert sphere, both sides have options for escalation that are significantly less risky than open military means. Israel is likely to continue to pursue and intensify its targeted killings of IRGC leaders, possibly linking them to specific capabilities such as UAVs. Furthermore, Israel is considered to have high cyber capability, bolstered by its strong alliance with the United States, and has been willing to use it. Iran, however, has also demonstrated the intent and capability to orchestrate destructive cyber operations via a cadre of non-state pro-Iranian hackers.

Nuclear deterrence

Israel has an absolute advantage in nuclear firepower, but its use is of course subject to serious constraints. The country's nuclear capability has been intended from its inception to preserve – through deterrence and if necessary use – the state's existence. The level of threat Iran poses to Israel's territory and population without significant support, for example, from the Syrian and Lebanese armed forces, would fall below that threshold.

Less straightforward is Tehran's calculation of the benefits of a rush to nuclear weaponisation. It appears for now to be holding to the fatwa of Ayatollah Sayyid Ali Khamenei that the possession and use of nuclear weapons is *haram* (forbidden). But statements from Ahmad Haghtalab, the IRGC commander responsible for protecting Iran's nuclear sites, that Iran may review its nuclear doctrine have compounded existing concerns that Iranian uranium enrichment has substantially exceeded requirements for its civil nuclear programme. Tehran has also been obstructing the work of the International Atomic Energy Agency (IAEA). Despite some apparent agreement on future arrangements, IAEA chief Rafael Grossi's visit to Iran in May 2024 indicated how far apart the two parties are on satisfactory inspections.[7] But if Iran were to mobilise for weaponisation, it is unlikely that it could avoid Israeli and US detection, which would oblige Israel to act. A somewhat novel form of mutual nuclear deterrence would therefore appear to be intact: Iran cannot risk possessing a weapon, and Israel cannot risk using one.

The risk of war
While Iran's and Israel's capabilities are asymmetric, each is able to mount limited strikes against the other's sovereign territory but unable to sustain longer conventional campaigns. Domestic politics, resource implications and logistical challenges constrain both countries from escalating. At the same time, the constraints are unlikely to prevent either side from regarding conventional strikes against sovereign territory and assets as falling within new parameters, and therefore feasible. A major consideration for the Iranian regime will be the need to avoid exposing gaps in its capabilities to Israel, the Iranian population, and its regional allies and partners. Israel, for its part, would need to retain the support of its allies and demonstrate the strategic benefit of striking Iran.

Both sides have incentives for perpetuating a sub-threshold war. Until now, escalation in Israel and Iran's conflict has taken the form of spikes in the tempo of attacks, followed by a period of reset. This may change. If, as seems likely, Israel decides it must significantly reduce Hizbullah's capabilities, this would pose a dilemma for Tehran: it can neither afford to lose Hizbullah nor to respond in a way that invites further Israeli escalation and enlargement. If Iran chooses to escalate without material assistance from another major state actor, its ability to launch an all-out war against Israel will be constrained by its geography and limited military capability.

*   *   *

Fear of escalation in Lebanon has been palpable since Hamas's 7 October 2023 attacks. Immediately thereafter, the US acted to restrain Israel from mounting a pre-emptive strike against Hizbullah based on Israeli intelligence – which turned out to be faulty – indicating imminent Hizbullah action in coordination with Hamas.[8] As the intensity of live-fire operations from both sides has shown over the past six months, the theatre is unstable and volatile. But there remain constraints on the escalation of the current limited conflict between Hizbullah and Israel to the level of war between Israel and Iran.

While the Israeli government is compelled to enable the 80,000 displaced residents of northern Israel to return there and live in safety, and to reassure the wider population that Hizbullah's threat has been contained, this does not require a campaign as extensive as that against Hamas in Gaza. Neutralising Hizbullah as a fighting force would involve finding and destroying its tunnels, caches and operational infrastructure in South Lebanon, Beqaa and Beirut. This would amount to a land war in a neighbouring country, the costs of which would be prohibitive. Israel can protect northern Israel sufficiently by enhancing its targeting of selected Hizbullah capabilities and leaders, and in particular by pushing the group back from its forward positions in the area below the Litani River.

Tehran, for its part, must do enough to ensure Hizbullah's survival but not so much that it provokes the Israelis into potentially catastrophic escalation against the group. While that would not rule out Iranian resupply, it would preclude direct retaliation against Israel – a step Iran was willing to take in April only in response to Israel's direct targeting of

Iranian diplomatic premises and senior IRGC personnel in Syria. Iran sets its level of operational support according to threats and risks to Iran itself, as opposed to its allies and partners. Given the intimate involvement of the IRGC in Hizbullah's command structure and operations, Israel might blur that line either deliberately, in order to weaken Hizbullah's support, or by miscalculation. But the precedent of the 13–14 April Iranian attacks on Israel suggests that Iran would still execute only a limited response designed to forestall escalation.

Military capabilities as well as strategic considerations impose limitations on escalation. Hizbullah's missile and rocket force enables it to strike and deter Israel, but not to defeat it in conventional manoeuvre warfare. The group gained valuable experience in the Summer War of 2006 and again in Syria in 2015, but for it to engage directly with IDF combined forces would place its assets at high risk, especially in light of IDF air supremacy. For the Israelis, a substantial portion of the military and intelligence assets required to launch a land offensive are committed to Gaza and likely to remain there, which compels it to avoid triggering Hizbullah missile attacks and forcing Israel to choose between eradicating Hamas and repelling Hizbullah.

Israel, Iran and Hizbullah alike can pursue limited military goals without running undue strategic or existential risks. Hizbullah Secretary-General Sheikh Hassan Nasrallah has been clear that he does not want Hizbullah to enter the Gaza war.[9] Tehran declared its attack on Israel was the end and not the beginning of a direct conflict. While Israel has made no such limiting comments and vowed to strike targets in Lebanon if necessary, it has not committed to maximalist security objectives in Lebanon. Its priority is to secure Israel, not destroy Hizbullah. These circumstances suggest a degree of strategic equilibrium.[10] Although the situation is hardly stable, it may leave space for a private agreement on discreet channels between the parties clarifying the parameters of conflict and how to avoid the all-out war none of them appears to want.

Acknowledgements

The author is grateful to Douglas Barrie, Henry Boyd and Timothy Wright for their valuable editorial input.

Notes

1   See, for example, Barbara Slavin, 'How to Prevent All-out War Between Iran and Israel', *Haaretz*, 14 April 2024, https://www.haaretz.com/opinion/2024-04-14/ty-article-opinion/.premium/how-to-prevent-all-out-war-between-iran-and-israel/0000018e-dc08-d463-ab9f-dfdcf9760000.

2   See, for example, Esfandyar Batmanghelidj and Mahsa Rouhi, 'Iran's Military Strategy', *Survival*, vol. 61, no. 6, December 2019–January 2020, pp. 183–98; and Raphael S. Cohen, 'Israel's "People's Army" at War', RAND Corporation, 16 January 2024, https://www.rand.org/pubs/commentary/2024/01/israels-peoples-army-at-war.html.

3   See Vali Nasr, 'Why Iran and Israel Stepped Back from the Brink', *Foreign Affairs*, 14 May 2024, https://www.foreignaffairs.com/israel/why-iran-and-israel-stepped-back-brink.

4   See, for instance, Zeke Miller and Michelle L. Price, 'US Works to Prevent an Escalation Across the Mideast as Biden Pushes Israel to Show Restraint', Associated Press, 14 April 2024, https://apnews.com/article/biden-iran-israel-netanyahu-g7-missiles-drone-62cba0eaac095115f8386397b3ded2f4.

5   See, for example, Lawrence Norman, 'Iran Attack Demonstrates Ballistic Missile Capabilities', *Wall Street Journal*, 15 April 2024, https://www.wsj.com/livecoverage/israel-iran-strikes-live-coverage/card/iran-attack-demonstrates-ballistic-missile-capabilities-K5z7NmUpZwXrWsr8PTVK.

6   See, for instance, Eric Tegler, 'Hezbollah's Rocket, Missile and Drone Arsenal Is Huge and Varied', *Forbes*, 15 November 2023, https://www.forbes.com/sites/erictegler/2023/11/15/hezbollahs-rocket-missile-and-drone-arsenal-is-huge-and-varied/?sh=789c89652d21.

7   See Jon Gambrell, 'Iran and the UN Nuclear Agency Are Still Discussing How to Implement a 2023 Deal on Inspections', Associated Press, 7 May 2024, https://apnews.com/article/iran-iaea-nuclear-program-143e3e3c015dbf9c17316ad60ff989da; and Andrew England, 'Iran Open to "Serious Dialogue", Says UN Nuclear Chief', *Financial Times*, 14 May 2024, https://www.ft.com/content/d5e07404-2fed-4f60-ba11-59e6734665c2.

8   See, for example, John Hudson, Yasmeen Abutaleb and Shane Harris, 'Israel's Talk of Expanding War to Lebanon Alarms U.S.', *Washington Post*, 7 January 2024, https://www.washingtonpost.com/national-security/2024/01/07/israel-hezbollah-lebanon-blinken/.

9   See, for instance, Steven Simon and Jonathan Stevenson, 'The Gaza Horror and US Policy', *Survival*, vol. 65, no. 6, December 2023–January 2024, p. 45.

10   See Nasr, 'Why Iran and Israel Stepped Back from the Brink'.

Biden's Misguided China Policy

Lanxin Xiang

The Biden administration has largely continued the confrontational approach towards China initiated by the Trump administration, which includes tariffs, export controls and various sanctions. But President Joe Biden's China policy lacks a coherent and comprehensive strategy. While the administration has articulated its commitment to competing with China and defending US interests, it has been unclear about specific priorities, long-term goals and the means of achieving them. The Biden administration sent mixed signals to China, indicating a willingness to cooperate on certain issues such as climate change and global health while emphasising strategic competition and containment overall. This inconsistency undermines the credibility and effectiveness of US policy.

Biden's China policy rests on two conceptual pillars: great-power relationships as battles between two ideological blocs, one democratic, the other autocratic; and globalisation as a zero-sum game in the struggle for hegemony.[1] Neither concept is original, but the fusion of the two could trigger a conflagration – in particular, by driving the US–China dispute over Taiwan towards military confrontation.

Lanxin Xiang, a contributing editor to *Survival*, is Distinguished Fellow at the Stimson Center, professor emeritus at the Graduate Institute of International and Development Studies in Geneva, and author of *The Quest for Legitimacy in Chinese Politics: A New Interpretation* (Routledge, 2021).

Survival | vol. 66 no. 3 | June–July 2024 | pp. 91–104   https://doi.org/10.1080/00396338.2024.2357482

Democracy versus autocracy

More than just a way to define the nature of great-power relations in the twenty-first century, the democracy-versus-autocracy dichotomy has become the framework for US policymaking. It has restrained policy options by imparting ideological rigidity to great-power politics. US National Security Advisor Jake Sullivan has characterised China as the 'only state with both the intent to reshape the international order and the economic, diplomatic, military, and technological power to do it', and stated that Beijing was 'working to make the world more dependent on China' and 'taking steps to adapt the international system to accommodate its own system and preferences'.[2] US Secretary of State Antony Blinken has implied that there is justification for interference in what China considers internal affairs, saying that its actions 'in Xinjiang, Hong Kong, [and] Taiwan … threaten the rules-based order that maintains global stability' and are 'not merely internal matters'.[3] The upshot of these assertions is that whether the bilateral relationship is competitive, collaborative or confrontational – Blinken's so-called 'Three Cs' – is entirely up to China. The United States need not make any adjustments in its behaviour.

Democracy advocates have often assumed that a democratic political system is not only politically superior but also a precondition for a country's economic take-off, as well as its sustainability. This assumption flies in the face of China's extraordinary economic performance under an authoritarian, one-party system. It is equally specious to premise the United States' adversarial policies on China's abandonment of a democratisation approach it had allegedly once embraced. China's supposed tilt towards Western norms was essentially wishful thinking on the part of the US policy elite based on convergence theory, which posits that, as a society achieves sustained economic growth, it adopts developed societies' political systems.[4] In fact, the reforms Deng Xiaoping initiated more than 40 years ago were never meant to alter the fundamental structure of the Chinese political system. Deng's many public and internal statements all indicated he wanted only perestroika, or economic restructuring, not glasnost, or political openness, to use the Soviet concepts in fashion at the time.

It's an open question why US policy towards China has turned so simplistically adversarial. One reason could be the continued paucity of

Americans' knowledge of Chinese culture and history. Another could be that America's own internal political crisis has been directed outwards.[5]

America's popular turn towards Trumpism over the past several years has clearly pushed China policy in an adversarial direction. Biden administration officials have given grudging credit to the Trump administration for 'updating the diagnosis of the scope and nature of the China challenge' – which, decoded, means launching a trade war with China – while faulting its effort for lacking strategic content. But Donald Trump's approach to China was arguably more effective precisely because he insisted, albeit without specific intent, that great-power politics need not be based on ideology. Even during the Cold War, American officials called the Soviet Union by its official communist name: the 'Union of Soviet Socialist Republics'. Today, Washington has all but supplanted the 'People's Republic of China', the country's official name, with the 'Chinese Communist Party', with the implied aim of delegitimising the regime.

The Biden team's Achilles heel is its blithe ignorance of Chinese history. Western debates over the nature of the Chinese system are not new. The earliest one took place in the mid-seventeenth century. The Chinese Rites Controversy (1645–1742) was a bitter dispute within the Catholic Church over a question raised by the Jesuit missionaries in China as to whether Chinese culture and traditions, such as rituals honouring ancestors, were compatible with Christianity. The Jesuits insisted on the need for accommodation, but most others disagreed. Almost a century passed before a final judgement from the Vatican disavowed the Jesuits' argument.[6]

At that time in Europe, the modern notion of democracy had not yet been established as a comparative tool for disparaging other political systems, so the issue of the legitimacy of Chinese governance did not arise. Since the eighteenth century, Western geopolitical dominance has enabled Western thought to become dominant as well. A new orthodoxy of 'progress' against 'backwardness', 'civilisation' against 'barbarism', and 'the white man's burden' as a supposedly virtuous example of racial supremacism justified colonial expansion into non-Western territories. In the West's vision, its brand of democracy was the pinnacle of political development for all societies. When Francis Fukuyama proclaimed the 'end of history', there was presumptively no room for improvement.

The Biden administration has not moved beyond this imperious mindset even though the recent internal split in the United States over the legitimacy of its democratic system itself has severely undermined it. The administration should finally realise that the democracy-versus-autocracy paradigm has all but collapsed. Yet the Biden administration has endeavoured to rescue it by linking Taiwan directly to Ukraine, increasing global instability.

One China or two?

US–China quibbling over 'One China' versus 'Two China' policies is increasingly moving towards dangerous brinkmanship. The US insists that China has shifted the foundation of the One China policy by military provocations, while China believes that the US is consciously adopting a 'salami-slicing' approach to abandoning the policy and pushing for de facto Taiwanese independence.

The crux of the problem is that the two sides do not agree what constitutes one China. From the founding of the People's Republic of China in 1949 until 1971, the US refused to recognise it as a legitimate state. During that period, for Washington, the Republic of China – that is, Taiwan – under General Chiang Kai-shek represented China. Since the Sino-American rapprochement in the early 1970s, the two sides have consistently talked past each other on the concept of one China. When the United States recognised the People's Republic of China and withdrew its recognition of the Republic of China in 1979, it stated that the government of the former was 'the sole legal Government of China'.[7] This was a major breakthrough.

But does China own Taiwan? In the Shanghai Communiqué of 1972, the United States refused to give in to Chinese demands that it must 'recognise' Chinese sovereignty over Taiwan. Instead, Washington merely 'acknowledged' the Chinese position that Taiwan was part of China.[8] In the third US–China Joint Communiqué in 1982, the United States went a step further, stating that it had no intention of pursuing a policy of 'two Chinas' or 'one China, one Taiwan'.[9] To this day, the US claims that its 'One China position' signifies US recognition of the People's Republic as the sole legal government of China while only acknowledging the Chinese stance that Taiwan is part of China. Hence, the United States maintains formal relations with the People's Republic of China and only unofficial relations with Taiwan. This 'One China' policy has been reaffirmed by each new US administration since it was established.

When geopolitics were simpler and both sides were aligned against the Soviet Union, they were willing to overlook this fundamental clash over Taiwan. Now that the US considers China its main strategic rival, avoiding the dispute is impossible. It is especially dangerous because neither side is willing to recognise the validity of interpretations offered by the other. In China's view, 'One China' should include Taiwan as a matter of sovereign principle. But the US has never really regarded policy as principle. The US objects to Chinese insistence on principle because it will constrain US policy and its flexibility in pursuing its interests. The Biden administration has effectively transformed the United States' One China policy into an unambiguous and less flexible 'one China, one Taiwan policy'. Since this implies the perpetuation of the separation of two Chinese political entities, it is no longer possible for China to believe American protestations that the US does not support Taiwanese independence. Indeed, the policy is in line with the Taiwan independence movement's Plan B, namely, a 'special' country-to-country relationship between Taiwan and the People's Republic, if not necessarily *de jure* status as a sovereign state.[10]

China rightly dismisses this dispensation as a violation of the 'one China principle' and realises that it serves an American geopolitical strategy of containment against China. Under the Biden administration, that strategy and US advocacy for Taiwan's de facto independence are becoming more transparent. As a diplomatic matter, the US cannot officially announce its intention because it officially opposed Taiwanese independence in the third Joint Communiqué in 1982. Thus, it is left to pursue the policy implicitly rather than explicitly.

Strategic ambiguity, which has undergirded mutual deterrence in the Taiwan Strait for five decades, is still useful for the United States. For China, it is over. This discrepancy may cause both sides to make miscalculations. Accordingly, it is high time for China and the US to bring the 'one China, one Taiwan' issue to the table and end the charade of modus vivendi.

Today, however, Beijing's policy elite seems to have lost confidence in dealing with the Biden administration, especially over Taiwan. After Russia's invasion of Ukraine, Biden's purportedly off-script remark about the US commitment to defending Taiwan, which he has repeated several times, began to sound morally convincing in the West.

China's misunderstood rise

In a startling remark that went viral, Blinken recently suggested that the international system was essentially predatory and zero-sum.[11] The view has evolved in the United States that China has launched an economic war against the US in order to take over its global position as the pre-eminent economic superpower. In fact, there is no evidence of that intent.

China, as an advancing global economic power, certainly seeks to enhance its influence and competitiveness in the international economic arena. It has pursued policies aimed at fostering economic growth and development such as the Belt and Road Initiative (BRI), which seeks to enhance infrastructure connectivity and trade between China and other countries so as to expand the former's economic reach and influence globally. Additionally, China has increasingly sought to play a more prominent role in international organisations such as the World Trade Organization and the International Monetary Fund, which does indicate aspirations for greater involvement in shaping the global economic order.

However, China also faces numerous domestic and international challenges and constraints. These include economic imbalances, environmental problems, geopolitical tensions and trade disputes, particularly with the United States. China's leaders often emphasise the goal of achieving a 'peaceful rise' or 'win–win cooperation' in their international engagements, suggesting a desire for constructive economic engagement rather than outright dominance.

The US government tends to dismiss such expressions as deceptive. This is because the Chinese economic miracle is widely misconstrued in the West in general and by the Biden administration in particular. One major factor is simple ignorance. Another is a kind of cultural hubris whereby the Chinese economic miracle must have been either Western-made or the product of some Western mistake or misjudgement about China. In modern economics, genuine dialogue between the West and China has been minimal because the post-Enlightenment West has been so confident of its exclusive possession of economic wisdom.[12] The West still cannot completely accept that the autocratic Chinese system may have advantages over Western democracy.

What the West finds hardest to accept is that China, while stubbornly refusing to become Western, has outperformed the West economically over the past four decades substantially on its own. Thus, the West appears to foreclose the possibility that rapid growth without democracy can sustain the legitimacy of authoritarianism. Yet it also holds the seemingly contradictory view that China, as the world's second-ranking power, for all its supposed inadequacies, will inevitably challenge the incumbent hegemon, and that it constitutes a major threat to Western norms and moral leadership. It was on the basis of this logic that the US weaponised trade policy in the name of national security.

Enlightenment-inspired value judgements have driven most Western analyses of Chinese politics and economy. Chinese tradition, especially Confucianism, has been vilified as a key impediment to the country's economic development. In the Confucian tradition, market mechanisms were valued but moral adjustment was stressed and political legitimacy was not determined by popular elections. Ruling legitimacy depended on a regime's ability to bring well-being and security to its people. The nature of the political system was largely irrelevant, and China became a top economic power anyway. It established a market economic system as early as 300 BCE, in the Warring States period. The system featured private ownership and the free transfer of land, highly specialised and mobile labour, and developed product and factor markets. During the Ming Dynasty (1368–1644), China acquired all the major elements that proved essential for the British Industrial Revolution in the eighteenth century. Yet the revolution occurred in Britain and the Chinese economy lagged behind Europe's.[13]

The German sociologist Max Weber, who first studied the phenomenon, suggested that China lacked the cultural roots required for modern industrialism and capitalism, while others posited a large disequilibrium between supply and demand. Both assessments were factually unfounded.[14] The core reason China skipped the Industrial Revolution was that the traditionally insular Chinese view of the state cut against the main driver of the revolution: conquering outside territories to fuel mass production. Adam Smith adapted the laissez-faire principle – originally a Chinese insight – to his free-trade philosophy, which was self-consciously aligned with proselytising Christian morality. Global free trade advanced the spread of religious doctrine and was often seen as being prompted by a divine call, or an 'invisible hand'. Historically, hegemony through trade originated in Europe. The Chinese did not consider it essential to sustaining ruling legitimacy. Western thinkers have thus posited a missed historical opportunity for China that never really existed.

China's descent from the economic top tier, precipitated by the British Opium Wars, had been considered irreversible until recently. Eurocentric historians had deliberately ignored the dominant role China played in the world economy between 1100 and 1800 CE. As late as 2006, historian David Landes, the leading advocate for the supremacy of Western economic principles, was still debunking the 'Asian economic miracle' as insignificant.[15] Organisation for Economic Co-operation and Development historian Angus Maddison disavowed such cultural arrogance, tracking the history of Chinese economic growth since 960 CE. His study demonstrated that China's recent rise was in fact a return to economic superstardom, which the Middle Kingdom had enjoyed for many centuries.[16]

For Western strategists, the real question should be, what does economic development mean for a resurgent China? The term 'economy' (jingji, 经济) in the Chinese language does not describe pure economic or commercial activities. It simply means 'managing everyday life of the society and providing sufficient resources for the state' (jingshi jiguo, 经世济国). In this conception, state and economy can never be separated into two mechanical spheres; the body politic and the body economic are organically connected. Furthermore, maintaining a fine balance between internal demand and supply is considered the best model for the state to manage the economy. Although China created the first international trading network – the so-called Silk Road – 2,000 years ago, active trade with foreign countries was never believed capable of playing a decisive role for the health of the domestic economy. The need for sustained GDP growth is a recently imported concept and an alien vision.

There is no doubt that, during the reform and opening process, China benefitted enormously by drawing on Western competitive methods based on concepts such as comparative advantage and leverage financing. From the very beginning of this period, however, Deng's design for China's reform called for maintaining the power of the state over the economy. In 1980, during her first interview with foreign media, Italian journalist Oriana Fallaci inquired as follows: 'The four modernizations will bring foreign capital into China, and this will inevitably give rise to private investment. Won't this lead to a miniaturized capitalism?' Deng replied:

> In the final analysis, the general principle for our economic development is still that formulated by Chairman Mao, that is, to rely mainly on our own efforts with external assistance [being] subsidiary. No matter to what degree we open up to the outside world and admit foreign capital, its relative magnitude will be small and it can't affect our system of socialist public ownership of the means of production. Absorbing foreign capital and technology and even allowing foreigners to construct plants in China can only play a complementary role to our effort to develop the productive forces in a socialist society.[17]

Is this resolutely authoritarian, socialist state ready to deal with the trade war launched by the United States? The Biden administration tends to forget three factors that may bolster Beijing's resistance. Firstly, China under a communist regime has had extensive experience in dealing with economic isolation and even a comprehensive blockade by the West, from 1950 to 1972. Secondly, the country's deeply entrenched self-reliance principle has rekindled its patriotism and resolve.[18]

Thirdly, in the high-tech sector, the US CHIPS Act and other tough measures – what Sullivan has called 'small gardens, high fences' – cannot stop or slow for long Chinese development in cyber, artificial intelligence and space technologies. Historically, technology diffusion has been unstoppable, and China enjoys organisational advantages in financing and coordinating national resources for high-tech research and application. China has been mobilising internal and external resources to offset the effect of a trade war and potential decoupling efforts by the US or Europe. European Commission President Ursula von der Leyen devised the more measured concept of 'de-risking' to guide Europe's dealing with China. But China itself has been de-risking for some time, especially by enhancing economic ties with friendly nations within the BRICS group and other countries in the Global South. From this vantage, Xi Jinping was prescient in launching the BRI ten years ago. Barring a wholesale Western economic blockade against China, the US alone cannot choke the Chinese economy even with the 60% tariffs suggested by Trump.[19] More broadly, it is hard to believe that the self-proclaimed 'Tariff Man' can make America great again by implementing another version of the Smoot–Hawley Tariff Act that failed the United States so disastrously in the 1930s.

The danger of great-power politics

In the face of common threats to humankind, such as climate change and viral pandemics, relations between the major powers are supposed to improve rather than get worse. There was a common trope during the Cold War that if hostile aliens invaded planet Earth, the US and the Soviet Union would put aside their grudges and work together to resist the invaders.[20] The world has already experienced three strategic shocks in this century: transnational jihadist terrorism, the international financial crisis and the COVID-19 pandemic. However, the major powers have declined to join hands and have instead intensified the rivalries, confrontations and security dilemmas among them, all emerging weaker.

The United States' strategic shift after 9/11 led to the costly failures of the wars in Afghanistan and Iraq, which damaged America's reputation and credibility. Then, the global financial meltdown exacerbated America's internal discord, producing extreme populism and Trump's election as president. Until the 6 January 2021 insurrection at the US Capitol, most had believed that the American system would always retain the resilience to right itself. That event has dimmed the US as the beacon of democracy and the rule of law. Now, as the defeated president who precipitated it seeks to be elected again and stands a reasonable chance of succeeding, the durability of American democracy itself is in question. In addition, criticism of the West's double standards has broadened. While America and Europe condemn Russia for war crimes in Ukraine, they do not direct comparable opprobrium towards Israel for its conduct in Gaza. This inconsistency casts grave doubt on the integrity and viability of a rules-based international order. The US, described by the late Madeleine Albright in 1998 as 'the indispensable nation', hardly seems to merit that description now.

China's weaknesses are also being exposed. The Chinese assessment that 'the East is rising and the West is falling' (*dongsheng xijiang*, 东升西降) is a colossal strategic miscalculation. It not only exaggerates China's influence in the West, but also underestimates the United States' strong reactions to such a claim, notwithstanding its ongoing domestic political crisis. More broadly, the phrase 'decline of the West' underplays America's economic, military and technological strength. The proposition that 'the West is falling' is more about serious fractures in Western, especially American, societies, and the main reason for that is not the rise of China. The notion that 'the East is rising' does not take into account the fragility of the Chinese economic system. Tough administrative and technical measures in the early days of the pandemic did indeed work, but they were not sustainable. China's lifting of controls did not bring about the expected rebound in consumer spending, which was offset by other factors. Unemployment is rising sharply due to weaknesses in real estate and manufacturing. The costs of the property-sector collapse have been absorbed largely by writing off debts. Given a declining and ageing population, latitude for using public spending to prop up the economy is severely limited.

Regarding Russia, moreover, its failure to conquer Ukraine demonstrates its fundamental weaknesses. Russia's military technology has proven obsolete, and its organisational and command capabilities have steeply declined. While it still possesses the world's largest nuclear arsenal, its undiversified economic model, heavily reliant on oil and natural gas, is not sustainable in the long run.

*   *   *

The most recent strategic shock – the COVID-19 pandemic – has not benefitted any one of the major powers, and none of them now appears strong enough to secure a decisive, lasting advantage. This reality renders the two exclusionary pillars of US national-security policy – democracy versus dictatorship and zero-sum logic – inappropriate. The core lesson of the pandemic is that the international community, including the United States, should give top priority to strengthening cooperation. In this light, America's tentative return to realpolitik in great-power relations – hinted at by Sullivan's omission of the democracy-versus-autocracy paradigm in his remarks in January at the Council on Foreign Relations following his meeting with Chinese Foreign Minister Wang Yi in Bangkok[21] – should be welcome. Given current domestic political conditions in the United States, however, it might not last.[22]

In any event, nobody should expect the summit between Xi and Biden in San Francisco in November 2023, or other recent diplomatic interactions between China and the United States, to yield a framework for bilateral stability. Chinese leaders only grudgingly play along with this conceit of reconciliation, believing that Biden seeks mainly a tactical pause to enhance his chances for a second term. Xi's goal is strategic stability, especially over Taiwan, a goal that has failed to gain traction in Washington. For Beijing to take engagement with the Biden administration seriously, Biden's team would have to dispense with its inconsistent positions and condescending attitude. Otherwise, Chinese officials may conclude that a new Trump administration, however erratic Trump's behaviour may be, would offer China a better chance to reset the relationship, if only because they understand his crudely transactional methods.

Notes

1   See White House, 'National Security Strategy', October 2022, Part I, https://www.whitehouse.gov/wp-content/uploads/2022/10/Biden-Harris-Administrations-National-Security-Strategy-10.2022.pdf. See also Antony J. Blinken, 'The Administration's Approach to the People's Republic of China', speech at George Washington University, 26 May 2022, https://www.state.gov/the-administrations-approach-to-the-peoples-republic-of-china/.

2   See White House, 'Remarks and Q&A by National Security Advisor Jake

Sullivan on the Future of U.S.–China Relations', 30 January 2024, https://www.whitehouse.gov/briefing-room/speeches-remarks/2024/01/30/remarks-and-qa-by-national-security-advisor-jake-sullivan-on-the-future-of-u-s-china-relations/.

3   'How It Happened: Transcript of the US–China Opening Remarks in Alaska', Nikkei Asia, 19 March 2021, https://asia.nikkei.com/Politics/International-relations/US-China-tensions/How-it-happened-Transcript-of-the-US-China-opening-remarks-in-Alaska.

4   See, for example, Francis Fukuyama, *The End of History and the Last Man* (New York: Free Press, 1992); W.W. Rostow, *The Stages of Economic Growth: A Non-Communist Manifesto,* 3rd ed. (Cambridge: Cambridge University Press, 1991); and David Shambaugh, *China's Future* (New York: Polity, 2016). Shambaugh argues that only a transition from 'hard authoritarianism' to 'soft authoritarianism' and 'semi-democracy' is likely to enable China to achieve continued economic development.

5   For a detailed analysis, see Lanxin Xiang, *The Quest for Legitimacy in Chinese Politics: A New Interpretation* (Abingdon: Routledge, 2021).

6   *Ibid.*

7   US Department of State, Office of the Historian, 'Address by President Carter to the Nation', 15 December 1978, https://history.state.gov/historical documents/frus1977-80v01/d104.

8   With respect to China's attempt to change the Chinese text from the original 'acknowledge' to 'recognize', Warren Christopher, then deputy secretary of state, testified at a US Senate

hearing: 'We regard the English text as being the binding text. We regard the word "acknowledge" as being the word that is determinative for the US.' Shirley A. Kan, 'China/Taiwan: Evolution of the "One China" Policy – Key Statements from Washington, Beijing, and Taipei', Congressional Research Service, 10 October 2014, p. 39, note 90, https://sgp.fas.org/crs/row/RL30341.pdf.

9   US Department of State, Office of the Historian, 'The August 17, 1982 U.S.–China Communiqué on Arms Sales to Taiwan', https://history.state.gov/milestones/1981-1988/china-communique.

10   See 'Interview of Taiwan President Lee Teng-hui with *Deutsche Welle* Radio', 9 July 1999, available at https://www.taiwandc.org/nws-9926.htm.

11   See, for instance, Zhao Ziwen, 'Amid US–China Rivalry, Washington Takes Aim at Allies Who Avoid Choosing Sides, Observers Say', *South China Morning Post,* 24 February 2024, https://www.scmp.com/news/china/diplomacy/article/3253046/amid-us-china-rivalry-washington-takes-aim-allies-who-avoid-choosing-sides-observers-say.

12   For an example of this viewpoint, see David S. Landes, *The Unbound Prometheus: Technological Change and Industrial Development in Western Europe from 1750 to the Present,* 2nd ed. (Cambridge: Cambridge University Press, 2003).

13   The English historian Joseph Needham (1900–95) popularised the question of why this was the case even though China had been more advanced than other countries in

what became known as the 'Needham Puzzle'. For a detailed analysis, see Justin Yifu Lin, 'The Needham Puzzle: Why the Industrial Revolution Did Not Originate in China', *Economic Development and Cultural Change*, vol. 43, no. 2, January 1995, pp. 269–92.

[14] See Mark Elvin, 'The High-level Equilibrium Trap: The Causes of the Decline of Invention in the Traditional Chinese Textile Industries', in W.E. Willmott (ed.), *Economic Organization in Chinese Society* (Stanford, CA: Stanford University Press, 1972).

[15] David S. Landes, 'Why Europe and the West, Why Not China?', *Journal of Economic Perspectives*, vol. 20, no. 2, Spring 2006, pp. 3–22. See also David S. Landes, *The Wealth and Poverty of Nations: Why Some Are So Rich and Some So Poor* (New York: W. W. Norton & Co., 1998).

[16] See Angus Maddison, *Chinese Economic Performance in the Long Run, 960–2030 AD*, 2nd ed. (Paris: OECD Center for Development Studies, 2007). See also Nigel Inkster, *The Great Decoupling: China, America and the Struggle for Technological Supremacy* (London: C. Hurst & Co., 2021).

[17] 'Answers to the Italian Journalist Oriana Fallaci', 21 and 23 August 1980, available at https://dengxiaopingworks.wordpress.com/2013/02/25/answers-to-the-italian-journalist-oriana-fallaci/.

[18] Chinese-American scientists and engineers, whose predecessors played a decisive role in developing China's first atomic bomb in 1964, are leaving the US for China en masse, partly as a result of purges and investigations in US universities and labs. See, for example, Ryan Quinn, 'Chinese Scientists Increasingly Leaving U.S.', *Inside Higher Ed*, 5 July 2023, https://www.insidehighered.com/news/faculty-issues/research/2023/07/05/study-chinese-scientists-increasingly-leaving-us.

[19] See, for example, Rebecca Picciotto, 'Trump Floats "More than" 60% Tariffs on Chinese Imports', CNBC, 4 February 2024, https://www.cnbc.com/2024/02/04/trump-floats-more-than-60percent-tariffs-on-chinese-imports.html.

[20] See, for instance, Danny Lewis, 'Reagan and Gorbachev Agreed to Pause the Cold War in Case of an Alien Invasion', *Smithsonian Magazine*, 25 November 2015, https://www.smithsonianmag.com/smart-news/reagan-and-gorbachev-agreed-pause-cold-war-case-alien-invasion-180957402/.

[21] See White House, 'Remarks and Q&A by National Security Advisor Jake Sullivan on the Future of U.S.–China Relations'.

[22] See Lanxin Xiang, 'Biden's China Policy Tweak Is Welcome, but It's Still Based on a Fantasy', *South China Morning Post*, 18 February 2024, https://www.scmp.com/comment/opinion/world/article/3252218/bidens-china-policy-tweak-welcome-its-still-based-fantasy.

Forever Bound? Japan's Road to Self-defence and the US Alliance

Lotje Boswinkel

In December 2022, the government of Japanese Prime Minister Kishida Fumio announced a major transformation of Japan's security and defence policy, including an unprecedented budget increase, the acquisition of deep-strike capabilities and sweeping command-and-control reform.[1] A key driver of the revision was the recognition that Japan's defence posture is no longer adequate given the rapidly deteriorating security situation in the Asia-Pacific, and more particularly China's military build-up. Traditionally, Japan's Self-Defense Forces have been able to conduct localised operations to repel attacks within or at Japan's territorial borders, while relying on the United States to come to its support for more complex operations. However, faced with China's highly advanced reconnaissance-strike complex – which threatens to deny Japanese and US forces' freedom of manoeuvre in and around Japan – decision-makers in Tokyo have concluded that the Self-Defense Forces should be able to 'disrupt and defeat invasions against its nation much earlier and at a further distance' within the next ten years.[2]

Concretely, this would entail a shift towards a forward-leaning denial strategy whereby Japan would seek the ability to disrupt an adversary's command, control, communications, computers, intelligence, surveillance and reconnaissance (C4ISR) infrastructure; defeat its missiles and other

Lotje Boswinkel is a PhD candidate and researcher at the Centre for Security, Diplomacy and Strategy (CSDS) at the Brussels School of Governance, Vrije Universiteit Brussels.

Survival | vol. 66 no. 3 | June–July 2024 | pp. 105–128   https://doi.org/10.1080/00396338.2024.2357483

weapons systems; and destroy its precision weapons-launching systems.[3] To achieve this, Japan needs to invest not only in capable air and missile defences, counter-strike missiles, and adequate air and land platforms, but also in appropriate strategic enablers and a broader defence-industrial and technological base that can underpin its operational and war-fighting readiness. As many such roles and capabilities fall outside Japan's traditional strengths, a key question arises: can Tokyo deliver on its ambition to 'disrupt and defeat an invasion by [its] own initiative' within the ten-year time frame it has set for itself?[4]

A preliminary analysis of Japan's ten-year defence plan yields a mixed picture. Traditionally, the Self-Defense Forces have had a tactical and sectorial focus, with little ability to conduct joint or combined operations, and few capabilities to strike targets over longer distances or to operate in complex precision-strike contexts.[5] However, Japan is making headway in overcoming these shortcomings through significant investments in its C4ISR infrastructure, the establishment of a joint operations command, and efforts to improve readiness, mobility and training. Tokyo is also committed to bolstering its space, cyber and electronic-warfare assets, strike and missile-defence capabilities, and uncrewed systems.[6] While these efforts are certainly impressive, the question remains whether Japan's defence reforms will be sufficient considering the pace and extent of China's military modernisation, and the broader deterioration of Japan's security environment.

Moreover, as Japanese forces grapple with the challenge of operating increasingly sophisticated weaponry in a more contested environment, new dependencies on the United States are emerging. A noteworthy example is Japan's reliance on the US kill-chain architecture for the deployment of its newly acquired stand-off capability. While Japan's integration into a US targeting infrastructure promises important benefits in terms of military effectiveness, it also comes with questions and challenges. One has to do with whether Tokyo is comfortable with fully integrating into this architecture, including target selection. Another relates to ongoing US concerns about Japanese information security. Last but not least, a framework of dependence provides no alternatives to abandonment concerns. In any case, such reliance on the United States will complicate Japan's effort to achieve full-fledged operational and war-fighting readiness, and to assume 'primary responsibility' in deterring and defending against threats to its homeland.[7] Indeed, as the Asia-Pacific security landscape grows more contested, an increasingly capable Japan is also becoming increasingly bound to its US ally.

A new security landscape

Japan's 2022 reform follows a decade of growing alarm among Japanese leaders over China's rising defence budget, build-up of theatre air and missile capabilities, naval activities around the Senkaku/Diaoyu islands, and belligerent rhetoric towards Taiwan. Perhaps most importantly, China has pursued an anti-access/area-denial (A2/AD) strategy whereby it seeks to prevent the deployment of opposing forces into an operational theatre and reduce their freedom of manoeuvre once present.[8] To achieve this, it has developed a centralised, land-based reconnaissance-strike complex composed of long-range sensors, command-and-control networks and precision weapons. Beijing has expanded and improved its missile arsenal, air-defence systems and fighter-bomber fleet; built a robust submarine and surface force; and invested in domain-denial capabilities including electromagnetic-pulse attacks, anti-satellite capabilities, cyber-attack functions and seabed warfare.[9] These capabilities would hold at risk Japanese and US bases and troops located in the Japanese archipelago should China seek to deny their utility in a regional contingency, seize the contested Senkaku/Diaoyu islands or secure access to choke points in the East China Sea. Japan's southwestern islands such as Yonaguni, Ishigaki and Miyako could be at particular risk of amphibious attack.[10]

Japan's threat environment is further complicated by North Korea's development and deployment of an increasingly advanced, accurate and mobile missile arsenal capable of conducting pre-emptive first-strike, retaliatory second-strike and battlefield counter-force attacks.[11] Indeed, Japan's defence revision followed a year in which Japan was unsettled by Pyongyang's test of a *Hwasong*-17 intercontinental ballistic missile capable of reaching the United States and an intermediate-range ballistic-missile launch over Japanese territories. North Korea has developed the ability to strike targets across Japan from multiple directions and numerous locations, and to use nuclear blackmail to prevent the United States from using its forces in Japan.

Finally, Japanese threat perceptions have worsened as a result of Russia's invasion of Ukraine in February 2022. Concerned by the precedent it may set for other revisionist powers, Prime Minister Kishida famously warned that 'Ukraine today may be East Asia tomorrow'.[12] While Kishida may have had China principally in mind when he made this remark, leaders in Tokyo have also grown increasingly worried about Russian activities and intentions in the Asia-Pacific region. The Japanese Ministry of Defense has repeatedly warned of an increase in Russian military exercises and deployments in the Pacific and Arctic oceans, as well as Russia's increased military cooperation with China. In recent years, the Chinese and Russian militaries have conducted regular joint flights and naval exercises in and over the Sea of Japan and the East China Sea.[13] Meanwhile, military cooperation between Russia and North Korea has also been growing since the beginning of the war in Ukraine, further alarming Tokyo.[14]

The changing strategic landscape has implications for the division of labour within the US–Japan alliance. Both China and North Korea are investing in capabilities aimed at keeping US forces out of their near theatres and holding the US homeland at risk. In doing so, they seek to undermine US effectiveness to operate in and around Japan, and potentially Washington's willingness to assist Japanese defence efforts. Perhaps more importantly, the fact that Chinese and North Korean strategic ambitions appear to concentrate on Taiwan and the South China Sea (China) and the Korean Peninsula (North Korea) is likely to disperse US strategic attention across the region, away from Japan. Japanese leaders also have growing concerns about America's waning military superiority, distraction by domestic unrest, and rising public and congressional scepticism towards overseas engagements.[15] As a result of these challenges, alliance cooperation between US and Japanese forces may be shifting from a functional division of labour towards a geographical one. While traditionally, the US was to provide operational and strategic cover to Japan's more tactically focused operations, today the US would focus on Taiwan and the broader region while the Self-Defense Forces would defend Japanese territories, particularly in Japan's southwest.

With the 2022 strategic update, leaders in Tokyo have acknowledged that Japan's ability to assume such responsibility for its own defence would require a far more significant strategic overhaul than that already set in motion by the government of Abe Shinzo (2012–20).[16] To make 'the opponent realize that the goal of invasion of Japan is not achievable by military means, and that the damage the opponent will incur makes the invasion not worth the cost', Japan has begun to shift towards a forward-focused denial strategy. This includes an advanced integrated air- and missile-defence system, stand-off capability, and cross-domain (such as cyber and electromagnetic) and uncrewed assets to disrupt an opponent's C4ISR infrastructure.[17] To ensure operational and war-fighting readiness, Japan is ramping up investments in its command-and-control and intelligence functions, mobility and resilience.[18] Simultaneously, Japan is seeking to reinforce its defence-industrial and technological base, deeming this a 'virtually integral part of a defence capability'.[19] In bolstering its capabilities, strategic enablers and defence-industrial capacity, Tokyo thus seeks to fulfil an expanded role within the US–Japan alliance.

Tokyo seeks an expanded role within the alliance

In order to assess Japan's ability to assume primary responsibility for its own security over the next ten years, it is useful to think about three distinct but interrelated layers: 1) the direct operational implementation of the country's forward-focused denial strategy through investments in capable air and missile defences, counter-strike missiles, and adequate air and land platforms and units; 2) the enabling of these operations through a robust C4ISR infrastructure, jointness, cross-domain capabilities and force mobility; and 3) the broader industrial and technological infrastructure that underpins the first two layers and allows high-intensity combat in a major war to be sustained. As this analysis will show, Japan's ability to assume 'primary responsibility' varies significantly across the three layers. The effort to reinforce the Self-Defense Forces' air-defence capability is a case in point: while Japan is stepping up to the extent that it may be in a position to protect its aerial domains, it continues to rely on US enabling capabilities, as well as American weapons platforms such as F-35s and Joint Strike Missiles.

Layer 1: platforms, capabilities, posture

Japan's ability to deter and defend at greater distances is contingent upon a first layer of platforms, capabilities and posture reforms aimed at defeating and destroying adversary missile and weapons systems, including their launchers. Starting with the Abe administration, Japan has moved to expand its already impressive submarine fleet;[20] convert its *Izumo*-class helicopter destroyers into light-aircraft carriers; procure F-35B vertical-landing fighters;[21] and extend its F-35A fleet.[22] The Self-Defense Forces have stationed anti-air and anti-ship missiles at strategic points along the Ryukyu (Nansei-shotō) island chain and created an amphibious troop unit to defend Japan's vulnerable far-off islands that mark important choke points or contested areas.[23] Through these efforts, Japan is reinforcing its air- and sea-defence capability. With the 2022 strategic revision, Tokyo is adding long-range missiles to the Self-Defense Forces' deterrence and defence capability based on the logic that a 'left-of-launch' or 'shoot-the-archer' strategy could prove more effective in offsetting China's quantitative missile advantage. For this purpose, Japan is purchasing US ship-launched *Tomahawk* cruise missiles, extending its Type 12 missiles for surface, sea and air launches, and developing hypersonic ballistic missiles.[24]

Today, the Japanese Maritime Self-Defense Force consists of a large destroyer fleet, highly advanced submarine and anti-submarine-warfare capabilities, and an extensive mine-sweeping capacity. The size of its P-3, P-1, OP-3C and EP-3 patrol-aircraft fleet, combined with numerous intelligence, surveillance and reconnaissance (ISR) assets on surface, sub-surface and ground-based platforms, leaves Japan well equipped to defend sea lines of communication, conduct choke-point control and perform ISR missions around Japan. In addition to purchasing *Tomahawk* cruise missiles and extending its indigenous Type 12 missiles, the Maritime Self-Defense Force is growing its *Aegis*-equipped destroyer fleet from eight to ten.[25] Two new *Aegis*-system-equipped vessels – expected to become operational in fiscal years 2026 and 2027 – will cover and protect Japan's entire archipelago against

North Korean short- to intermediate-range ballistic missiles.[26] The Maritime Self-Defense Force's existing *Aegis* destroyers will henceforth be more readily available to respond to potential contingencies in the East China Sea.

Even if relatively small, Japan's Air Self-Defense Force has a highly skilled pilot crew and a robust fleet with some of the world's most advanced air platforms. Over the last decade, it has ramped up the procurement of F-35A aircraft, which are known for their effectiveness in non-permissive environments and executing network-centric operations – as well as for their inter-operability with US forces.[27] It has furthermore added E-2D Airborne Early Warning and Control aircraft, C-2 transporters, uncrewed RQ-4B *Global Hawk*s with ISR capabilities, and the KC-46A refueller and transport aircraft. Of course, changes like these cannot be accomplished overnight: full delivery of F-35s and E-2D aircraft will take another decade, during which time the Air Self-Defense Force will continue to rely on its retiring E-2C Airborne Early Warning and Control aircraft and older F-15 fleet. In recent years, Japan equipped its F-35s with Joint Strike Missiles and its F-15Js with Joint Air-to-Surface Stand-off Missile-extended Range cruise missiles. In addition to upgrading and reinforcing Japan's ISR, air-defence and command capabilities, these procurements add significant firepower to the Air Self-Defense Force.[28]

The Self-Defense Forces' third service, the Ground Self-Defense Force, has gradually shifted towards greater mobility and a dispersed posture, not least through the formation of brigade-sized units capable of rapid deployment to Japan's numerous smaller islands. The country has invested in anti-air and anti-ship capabilities, developed an ambitious amphibious troop unit, and deployed missile units to the islands of Miyako, Amami Oshima and Yonaguni, all of which mark important choke points in the East China Sea.[29] To address the Ground Self-Defense Force's continued reliance on large combat divisions suited for defence against large-scale territorial invasions of Japan's main islands, the 2022 Defense Buildup Program seeks to further reorganise its divisions and brigades into deployable mobile units.[30] In doing so, the Ground Self-Defense Force's focus is progressively moving away from a more static posture in the north towards a more mobile force geared towards defending Japan's southwest.

While these changes are impressive, some bottlenecks remain. Today, roughly 70% of Japan's ammunition continues to be stored on Hokkaido, Japan's northernmost main island located more than 2,000 kilometres away from Japan's islands in the East China Sea. Building new depots in Japan's southwest, and securing existing ones, will take time.[31] And while new types of missiles such as *Tomahawks* are being procured ahead of schedule, one RAND study questions whether ongoing efforts (and spending) are sufficiently intense or timely.[32] Budgetary constraints cast doubt on the decision to focus on expensive stand-off missiles capable of striking targets deep inside China. In the case of a conflict over Japan's southwestern islands, the country's policymakers may back away from approving this type of attack against a nuclear-armed adversary. Instead, for the in-theatre defence of smaller islands, shorter-range missiles could be preferable, both politically and strategically.[33] Whether Japan is able to achieve sufficient mass here alongside its costly deep-strike investments is questionable. More generally, the acquisition of new platforms and capabilities across this first layer could face budgetary challenges. Even if Japan appears set to achieve the spending metrics of at least its first five-year plan, inflation and a weak yen are undermining Japan's purchasing power at a time when its forces are buying more and more foreign equipment.

Meanwhile, Japan's lack of strategic depth makes passive defence measures such as the hardening of bases and dispersion of key assets indispensable to enhancing force survivability and resilience.[34] Yet efforts to improve facilities are only slowly gathering pace. In 2023, 80% of the Self-Defense Forces' 23,254 facilities did not meet the Ministry of Defense's standards for resilience against enemy attack.[35] To address this issue, ¥4 trillion (almost $26 billion) has been allocated to improve resiliency in 2023–27 – an increase of 300% compared to the previous five-year period.[36] Yet the ministry's 2023 budget allocations were mostly limited to relatively cheap and ineffective measures such as conducting revetments or building additional parking.[37] It is unclear how many bases will ultimately be hardened. This, in combination with an overall lack of dispersion, leaves Japanese capabilities and supplies vulnerable. To illustrate, an attack on the Naha air base in Okinawa hosting Japan's P-3C and UH-60J squadrons could deal a severe blow to Japan's anti-submarine-warfare capability.[38] The preparation of civilian bases and ports for military use is one step towards increasing the resiliency of the Self-Defense Forces' maritime and air infrastructure, but efforts may prove insufficient in a mature precision-strike context.[39]

Despite such ongoing challenges, Japan's investments in strike and defence capabilities across the three services are promising. By 2032, Japanese forces will have an aerial fleet made up of F-35, patrol and Airborne Early Warning and Control aircraft, extensive and capable undersea and surface vessels, and an increasingly mobile ground force. All three services will see their firing power significantly enhanced.

Layer 2: strategic enablers

Japan's effective use of its newly (or soon-to-be) introduced platforms, capabilities and postures depends on a layer of joint and enabling capabilities that allow a military to operate effectively in contested environments. To achieve this, Japan is investing in its C4ISR infrastructure, jointness, cross-domain capabilities and force mobility. Despite notable advances in this area, Japan's historical underinvestment will not be easily overcome, and the complexity of Japan's threat environment will continue to demand more elaborate and sophisticated enabling infrastructure.

C4ISR, jointness and cross-domain capabilities

To improve its ISR capabilities, Japan has made organisational changes and investments to improve internal processes for collection, assessment and distribution of intelligence.[40] Efforts commenced in the late 1990s with Tokyo's decision to build spy satellites, yet reform only truly gathered pace with the passage of the Designated State Secrets Law and the establishment of the National Security Council in 2013. These two developments helped overcome coordination and communication inefficiencies between Japan's various intelligence units and security-policy functions.[41] Soon after, Tokyo passed the Cybersecurity Basic Law, created the Cybersecurity Headquarters, and adopted a Basic Space Plan, paving the way for Japan's military use of space in an unprecedented strategic overhaul.[42] In 2018, the National Defense Program Guidelines announced the pursuit of a space structure for ground- and space-based situational monitoring and capabilities to disrupt adversaries' C4ISR structures.[43] This marked the first time that Japan had decided to deploy offensive space capabilities. The planned launch of 50 low-orbit space satellites to monitor military targets reflects this significant policy shift, even if several challenges remain unaddressed.[44]

Still, Japan's intelligence, surveillance and reconnaissance capabilities need to be sufficiently resilient to survive and operate in a contested A2/AD context. Whereas most of Japan's ISR platforms would perform important roles in peacetime intelligence collection and support combat operations against non-state actors, they are less suitable for non-permissive environments. For instance, most of Japan's airborne sensing platforms, including its RQ-4 *Global Hawks*, are easily tracked via radar, leaving them vulnerable to hacking, spoofing, jamming and interception. Meanwhile, the Self-Defense Forces lack advanced/special-mission ISR platforms, including ground moving-target indication radars; overhead, persistent, infrared capabilities; and measurement- and signature-intelligence systems. And while Japanese forces have extensive intelligence-collection platforms, their processing, exploitation and dissemination capacity falls short.[45]

Japan is therefore under pressure to step up its electronic-warfare capabilities. China's layered defence system of long-range missiles, aircraft, ships and submarines depends on sensors and communications operating in the electromagnetic spectrum. The success of any defensive operation within such an environment is contingent on a significant electronic-warfare capability that can protect the defender's assets and disrupt those of the adversary.[46] To catch up with its neighbour's investments, Japan has been upgrading its own electronic-warfare capabilities. The decision to expand the Self-Defense Forces' F-35A/B fleet has been one such step, the ongoing outfitting of the country's F-15 aircraft with an advanced electronic-warfare system another.[47] Japan is also developing a new stand-off electronic-warfare aircraft to be based on its C-2 airlifters and procuring RC-2 spy planes designed for gathering electronic intelligence.[48]

Through these investments in C4ISR assets and cross-domain capabilities, Japan is making initial steps towards bolstering its operational and war-fighting readiness. Yet, somewhat paradoxically, the introduction of highly sophisticated capabilities such as F-35s and stand-off missiles further increases the Self-Defense Forces' dependence on US enablers. As *Tomahawks* require US intelligence, surveillance, reconnaissance, targeting and battle-damage-assessment assets, for the foreseeable future Japan will have neither the operational nor the political autonomy to use this capability.[49] Even for the country's future indigenously developed counterstrike missiles, it is likely that the Self-Defense Forces will continue to rely on US enablers given the extensive and extremely costly ISR, targeting and damage-assessment requirements.[50] In addition, Japan's limited Suppression of Enemy Air-Defence capabilities has led some to describe the possibility of the country independently striking targets deep inside China as 'simply not realistic'.[51] The same could apply to North Korea's mobile missile launchers. Similarly, the effective deployment of Japan's F-35 fleet will depend on US Suppression of Enemy Air-Defence capabilities. Such dependencies are unlikely to be overcome in the next decade and will constrain Japan's operational readiness.

Japan's ability to defend its territories is further contingent on consolidation and jointness across the Self-Defense Forces' three military services, and between civilian and military authorities.[52] When facing an advanced-reconnaissance strike complex, the ability to conduct multi-domain operations is key. Meanwhile, various of Japan's new defence roles and capabilities, including its amphibious unit and stand-off capability, require ever closer cooperation between the Maritime, Ground and Air Self-Defense Forces. While reforms have been significant in some areas, including the National Security Council, in others they have fallen short. Until now, the Self-Defense Forces have relied on the overstretched Joint Staff Office for strategic-level coordination between the three services, with Joint Task Forces being used for temporary missions. Truly joint, cross-service assets such as the *Global Hawks* surveillance drones have remained scarce.

That being said, in a move that represents a breakthrough from both an operational and an organisational perspective, the three services are now being unified under a joint service commander.[53] By the end of March 2025, a joint operations command will be established to boost the Self-Defense Forces' operational capacity and ability to conduct multi-domain operations

– including in space, cyber and the electromagnetic spectrum.[54] It will play an indispensable role in the operationalisation of Japan's counterstrike capabilities, for which missile systems are expected to be deployed across the three services. What is more, the joint operations command will enhance operational coordination and bilateral planning with the United States, as its new commander can serve as a direct counterpart to the commander of the United States' Indo-Pacific Command (INDOPACOM).

Closer operational integration between the two allies will be indispensable as Japan takes on greater responsibilities and the alliance shifts to a more operational relationship.[55] As mentioned, the deployment of Japan's counterstrike capabilities requires the US and Japan to closely coordinate strike operations in real time given Japan's reliance on the US kill-chain architecture. Against this backdrop, Prime Minister Kishida and US President Joe Biden announced in April 2024 their intention to 'bilaterally upgrade [their] respective command and control frameworks to enable seamless integration of operations and capabilities and allow for greater interoperability and planning between US and Japanese forces'.[56]

As impressive as these reforms might be, questions remain about the scale and pace of their implementation. Concretely, it remains to be seen whether the new joint operations command will be able to efficiently streamline multi-domain planning; whether and when outstanding inter-operability issues between the Self-Defense Forces' three services may be solved; or when newly developed joint doctrines may take effect. Inter-service mistrust – which casts a shadow upon Japan's amphibious capabilities – is a challenge that may not be easily overcome.[57] Indeed, as Japan seeks to create a truly joint and integrated force, a change of mindset may prove more challenging than material investments.

Finally, long-standing recruitment problems additionally call into question Japanese defence-reinforcement efforts across this second layer.[58] To illustrate, the Self-Defense Forces seek to jump from operating three *Global Hawks* to a full-fledged force within ten years, but such an expansion will require skills that are hard to recruit. The planned quadrupling of Japan's cyber-defence force faces similar problems as there is fierce competition for the necessary skills from the private sector.[59]

Force mobility

As the locus of Japan's defence shifts to the country's southwest, long-standing shortages in its logistical-support capabilities are growing increasingly problematic. Consisting of 416 inhabited and 6,432 uninhabited islands, the Japanese archipelago covers 378,000 km² of territory and stretches across a claimed exclusive economic zone measuring 4,470,000 km².[60] In the event of hostilities in the East China Sea, the Self-Defense Forces would need to move defence materiel and troops over significant distances: Japan's Ryukyu island chain includes 55 islands and islets, and stretches around 1,200 km from the southern tip of Kyushu to the westernmost island of Yonaguni. Mobility is thus critical, but the forces' lift and refuelling capabilities are insufficient both in numbers and in effectiveness when operating in non-permissive, precision-strike environments.

Despite various acquisitions, Japan continues to lack strategic-airlift capabilities capable of carrying heavy payloads over great distances. In recent years, Tokyo has invested in tactical airlift by expanding the country's fleet of C-130Hs (capable of carrying maximum payloads of approximately 19,000 kilograms over 1,900 km) with the indigenously designed C-2 aircraft (capable of carrying payloads weighing nearly 30,000 kg over 4,800 km).[61] Combined, the Air Self-Defense Force now operates 27 fixed-wing (C-130H and C-2) aircraft dedicated to airlift (excluding the C-1s that are being phased out).[62] With 14 C-2s in its current inventory and plans to add six more over the next five years, Japan can be said to have mid-range capabilities: the C-2 was developed with peacekeeping missions in mind and cannot transport oversized cargo such as tanks (neither can Japan's C-130s). Meanwhile, the C-2's extensive landing and take-off requirements mean the aircraft is ill-equipped to serve smaller islands. In contingencies, this aircraft would therefore serve mainly to transport forces and lighter payloads from Japan's principal islands to Okinawa. For transport of oversized cargo, Japan would depend on the United States.

For transport to the rest of the Ryukyu islands, Japan is reliant on its UH-60JA and CH-47J/JA medium- and heavy-lift helicopters.[63] Only the latter can transport large equipment and personnel simultaneously, making the CH-47J/JA *Chinook* the most suitable aircraft to move large volumes of supplies through unimproved landing zones located beyond the reach of larger, fixed-wing aircraft (such as C-130Hs). However, CH-47s cannot carry useful payloads beyond 150 nautical miles (approximately 280 km) from landing surfaces that can accommodate C-130s and C-2s without intermediate refuelling.[64] And while the Self-Defense Forces together operate more than 100 such aircraft, in a contingency this capacity would be strained due to damage-related maintenance needs and the forces' role in evacuating civilians from war zones.[65] Aware of these shortcomings, Japan is forming two squadrons of V-22 *Osprey* tilt-wing aircraft to augment its tactical-aircraft fleet. Compared to CH-47s, these aircraft fly over longer distances and at greater speed, and are thus intended to rapidly move troops, equipment and supplies from expeditionary ships or airfields into combat zones, providing the country with an amphibious operational-manoeuvre capability.[66] Still, in considering the Self-Defense Forces' combined fixed- and rotary/tilt-wing aircraft fleet, Japan's airlift capability is likely to fall short when needed to operate over long distances with sparse airfield infrastructure.

Japan's sealift capabilities pose even greater challenges. The Maritime Self-Defense Force operates three ageing *Osumi*-class tank-landing ships capable of heavy transport.[67] With only three such platforms, damage to one would severely impair Japan's sealift capability. The Maritime Self-Defense Force's other sealift platforms cannot make up for this: its six Land Craft Air Cushion vessels are not designed for longer distances and mainly serve to load and unload the tank-landing ships, while the Self-Defense Forces' two Landing Craft Utility ships have very limited payload capacity.[68] Under its current defence plans, Japan will procure eight lighter sealift capabilities, including logistic-support vessels, Landing Craft Utility ships and manoeuvrable boats, but has no plans to expand or replace the tank-landing-ship fleet. Instead, the Self-Defense Forces intend to rely on private-finance initiatives for larger transport needs, but legal hurdles could well hinder the use of civilian vessels for military purposes.

Japan's geography similarly poses problems to its forces' mid-operation-refuelling capabilities. Any engagement of Chinese ships and aircraft far from Okinawa would require an extensive refueller fleet. In 2023, Japan possessed just four KC-767 and two KC-46A fighter refuellers (in addition to two KC-130Hs for helicopter refuelling).[69] For extended land operations by the V-22

Osprey fleet, the Self-Defense Forces have no dedicated refuelling capabilities. While Japan plans to procure an additional 13 aerial-refuelling aircraft (including four KC-46As by 2025), this effort may prove insufficient given Japan's geography.[70] The Maritime Self-Defense Force has similar quantity issues with its replenishment ships: it operates five oilers – both classes of which are relatively old – with no plans to increase this number. This means that sustained operations further away from the nearest Maritime Self-Defense Force port in Sasebo (on Kyushu) could face difficulties unless fuel tanks are prepositioned in the Ryukyu islands (such as Okinawa) or if commercial ports are used. The introduction of two large tankers will help with the transport of fuel from the mainland to Okinawa, but will not enable Maritime Self-Defense Force destroyers and minesweepers to sustain longer out-of-port operations. Japan's ability to conduct air- and sealift would thus depend on advanced warning that allows for the prepositioning of capabilities, supplies, munitions and fuel.[71]

Layer 3: defence-industrial and technological infrastructure

The third and final layer concerns Japan's ability to sustain a defence-industrial and technological base fit for high-end and potentially protracted conflict. As the war in Ukraine has highlighted, defence-industrial capacity plays a key role in attritional wars between advanced militaries.[72] In recent years, China's defence-industrial base has increasingly shifted to a wartime footing, producing ever larger quantities of land, maritime, air, space and other capabilities.[73] Japan's operational and war-fighting readiness will thus be contingent on access to high-end capabilities and ammunition supplies. While these can be either purchased abroad or indigenously produced, a state depends, at least in part, on a strong domestic base given that imports, even from allies, are inherently uncertain. Vulnerabilities would arise if the exporter's defence-industrial base were stretched thin or if supplies were disrupted in case of a contingency. In recent years, however, Japan's defence-industrial and technological base has grown less capable of delivering key capabilities to the Self-Defense Forces.

In the last decade, Japan has increasingly turned to foreign suppliers for its military acquisitions. Between 2014 and 2023, the share of domestic procurement in Japan's defence budget fell from 89.3% to 76.5%. Especially for the contract value of major equipment such as aircraft, imports are fast outpacing domestic procurement. Given Japanese investment in US-made F-35s, KC-46s, E-2Ds and V-22 *Ospreys*, between 2016 and 2022 as much as 90% of major aircraft contracts were with foreign partners, especially the United States. One key reason for the increase in US Foreign Military Sales to Japan is a decline in joint development between the two countries. While Japanese defence industries have always relied heavily on joint development and technology transfers, the rising sophistication and development costs of today's capabilities have eroded US willingness to release defence-equipment licences.[74] To illustrate, Mitsubishi Heavy Industries produced F-15s under licence in the past, but is only allowed final assembly and inspection of F-35s today.

Another reason for the decline in Japan's indigenous defence production has been the country's strategic reorientation.[75] The Self-Defense Forces' new focus on forward denial is affecting the types of capabilities Japan is buying: where previous procurement efforts focused on land equipment such as tanks and armoured vehicles, today the emphasis has shifted towards maritime and aerial capabilities, missiles and missile-defence systems, and cross-domain assets. Japan's recent defence-budget increase has thus been absorbed almost entirely by the procurement of aircraft and missiles, while investments in land equipment have gone down. Growth prospects for companies focusing on land equipment are dwindling, leading Japanese companies to withdraw from the defence business altogether. Those that remain are finding it harder to achieve economies of scale, which is encouraging the Ministry of Defense to select foreign products instead.[76] Japan's history of export restrictions does not help: despite significant reforms in 2014, many companies are still unable to effectively tap into foreign markets due to a lack of competitiveness or an export strategy.

Japan's decline in indigenous production should be considered in light of its broader effort to move away from traditionally protectionist military-industrial practices and towards closer defence-industrial integration with the US and other partners. By the mid-1990s, Japan was already emphasising the importance of defence-equipment and technology cooperation with the United States through the 1995 National Defense

Program outline, and was working to jointly develop the SM-3 Block IIA missile interceptor with its American ally.[77] In the first half of the 2010s, Japanese leaders introduced several important reforms aimed at furthering arms trade and cooperation. In 2011 and 2014, Japan reformed its export policy to enable joint development and production. It then established the Acquisition, Technology and Logistics Agency to coordinate acquisition policies and timelines, and thereby to promote international defence-industrial collaboration. Finally, Japan adopted its state-secrets law to promote information exchanges on sensitive technologies.[78] While these changes were implemented to strengthen Japan's domestic defence-production and technological base, they have yet to bear much fruit. Attempts to export Japanese P-1 patrol aircraft to Britain or submarines to Australia have failed. Even so, Japan has concluded various strategic partnerships with other countries to explore options for joint research and development or equipment collaboration, including France, India, the Philippines and the United Kingdom. Of these projects, the joint development of a fighter jet with Britain and Italy via the Global Combat Air Programme has been particularly noteworthy.

Thus, while Japan has sought to strengthen its defence-industrial and technological base by abandoning protectionist policies and practices, its reliance on foreign supplies and especially US Foreign Military Sales has only deepened over the last decade. As capability requirements grow more sophisticated and focused on aircraft and missiles, US supplies will make up an ever-larger share of the Self-Defense Forces' procurement budget.

*　　　*　　　*

No matter how impressive Japan's reforms, the complex nature of the strategic environment could ultimately stand in the way of the country's ambition to assume primary responsibility for deterring and defending against threats at a greater distance. China's highly advanced reconnaissance-strike complex (including its cross-domain denial capabilities) – as well as, to a lesser extent, North Korea's missile build-up – mean that Japan must make significant investments in sophisticated capabilities in the aerial and maritime domains while ensuring their effective use through an advanced C4ISR structure and greater jointness.

Japan has come a long way in overcoming its traditional reliance on the United States in the first layer, even if challenges such as force resilience remain. When it comes to the second layer of enabling capabilities, the record is more mixed. The growing sophistication of Japan's platforms and weapons systems requires an ever more advanced C4ISR infrastructure. Developing an independent kill chain to effectively deploy deep-strike capabilities that can engage mobile targets at great distances is not an easy task, requiring a scale of funding not currently allocated and stretching well beyond the outlined decade. Meanwhile, the nature of the threat places a premium on mobility, and Japan's lift and refuelling capabilities could well fall short. In the third layer, Japan is growing only more dependent on the US defence-industrial and technological base, to the detriment of its own.

Japan appears to be making important strides in terms of operational and war-fighting readiness. Yet somewhat paradoxically, as Japan adopts a more proactive approach to security policy and embraces new missions, it might be pulled closer to the United States. The Self-Defense Forces may well wish to assume primary responsibility for their own theatre; however, their ability to deter and defend against threats to Japan's territory will ultimately be contingent on the degree of cooperation and integration with US forces in the region.

Acknowledgements

The author would like to thank Luis Simón, Antonio Calcara, Michito Tsuruoka, Hirohito Ogi, Satoru Mori, Kohei Nakamura, Tongfi Kim, Daniel Fiott and Eva Pejsova for their input and comments on earlier versions of this paper. Sole responsibility for the article's content lies with the author.

Notes

[1] These reforms are outlined in National Security Council of Japan, 'National Defense Strategy', 16 December 2022; National Security Council of Japan, 'National Security Strategy of Japan', 16 December 2022; and Japan Ministry of Defense, 'Defense Buildup Program', 16 December 2022.

2 National Security Council of Japan, 'National Security Strategy of Japan', p. 20.

3 For a discussion of what the author calls Japan's 'forward denial' posture, see Hirohito Ogi, 'Evolving Japan–US Command and Control Cooperation for Forward Denial', United States Studies Centre, 20 November 2023.

4 Japan Ministry of Defense, 'Defense of Japan 2023', White Paper, 2023, p. 229, https://www.mod.go.jp/en/publ/w_paper/wp2023/DOJ2023_EN_Full.pdf.

5 See Christopher W. Hughes, *Japan's Re-emergence as a 'Normal' Military Power*, Adelphi 368–9 (Oxford: Oxford University Press for the IISS, 2004).

6 See Ken Jimbo, 'Deterrence by Denial: Japan's New Strategic Outlook', Stimson Center, 22 February 2023.

7 Japan Ministry of Defense, 'Defense of Japan 2023', p. 229.

8 See, for example, Thomas G. Mahnken, 'China's Anti-access Strategy in Historical and Theoretical Perspective', *Journal of Strategic Studies*, vol. 34, no. 3, June 2011, pp. 299–323; and Andrew S. Erickson, Ashley J. Tellis and Travis Tanner, 'China's Modernization of Its Naval and Air Power Capabilities', in Ashley J. Tellis and Travis Tanner (eds), *Strategic Asia 2012–13: China's Military Challenge* (Seattle, WA: National Bureau of Asian Research, 2012), pp. 60–125.

9 Thomas G. Mahnken et al., 'Tightening the Chain: Implementing a Strategy of Maritime Pressure in the Western Pacific', Center for Strategic and Budgetary Assessments, 23 May 2019, https://csbaonline.org/research/publications/implementing-a-strategy-of-maritime-pressure-in-the-western-pacific/publication/1; and Toshi Yoshihara, 'Going Anti-access at Sea: How Japan Can Turn the Tables on China', Center for a New American Security, 12 September 2014.

10 See Yoji Koda, 'The U.S.–Japan Alliance: Responding to China's A2/AD Threat', Center for a New American Security, 13 June 2016.

11 See Bruce Klingner, 'Japanese Strike Capabilities: Security Advantages for U.S. Alliance, Challenges to Overcome', Heritage Foundation, 16 August 2021.

12 Prime Minister's Office of Japan, 'Keynote Address by Prime Minister Kishida Fumio at the IISS Shangri-La Dialogue', 10 June 2022, https://japan.kantei.go.jp/101_kishida/statement/202206/_00002.html.

13 See Japan Ministry of Defense, 'Development of Russian Armed Forces in the Vicinity of Japan', March 2024, https://www.mod.go.jp/en/d_act/sec_env/pdf/ru_d-act.pdf.

14 See 'US, South Korea, Japan Raise Concerns over Russia–North Korea Military Cooperation', Reuters, 23 September 2023, https://www.reuters.com/world/us-south-korea-japan-raise-concerns-over-russia-north-korea-military-cooperation-2023-09-23/.

15 Michael Unbehauen and Christian Decker, 'Japan Cancels Aegis Ashore: Reasons, Consequences, and International Implications', *Air Force Journal of Indo-Pacific Affairs*, vol. 3, no. 4, 2020, pp. 97–127.

16 On Japan's defence reforms under Abe, see, for instance, Adam P. Liff, 'Japan's Defense Reforms Under Abe:

Assessing Institutional and Policy Change', in Takeo Hoshi and Phillip Y. Lipscy (eds), *The Political Economy of the Abe Government and Abenomics Reforms*, 1st ed. (Cambridge: Cambridge University Press, 2021), pp. 479–510.

17 Japan's security documents refer to 'cross-domain operation capabilities' when highlighting investments in cyber, space and the electromagnetic spectrum. See National Security Council of Japan, 'National Defense Strategy', pp. 25–6.

18 Japan Ministry of Defense, 'Defense Buildup Program', p. 4; and National Security Council of Japan, 'National Defense Strategy', p. 12.

19 National Security Council of Japan, 'National Defense Strategy', p. 33.

20 See Bradley Perrett, 'How Japan Could Quickly Build Up Its Submarine Force', *Strategist*, 18 April 2023, https://www.aspistrategist.org.au/how-japan-could-quickly-build-up-its-submarine-force/.

21 See 'Japan Starts Conversion of Second Izumo Helicopter Carrier', *Janes*, 1 April 2022, https://www.janes.com/defence-news/news-detail/japan-starts-conversion-of-second-izumo-helicopter-carrier.

22 See Xavier Vavasseur, 'Japan Officially Selects F-35B Fighter as STOVL Aircraft', Naval News, 17 August 2019, https://www.navalnews.com/naval-news/2019/08/japan-officially-selects-f-35b-fighter-as-stovl-aircraft/.

23 On developments in the Ryukyu islands, see Asia Maritime Transparency Initiative, 'Playing Chicken in the East China Sea', 28 April 2017, https://amti.csis.org/playing-chicken-east-china-sea/; and Tim Kelly and Nobuhiro Kubo, 'Exclusive: Japan's Far-flung Island Defense Plan Seeks to Turn Tables on China', Reuters, 18 December 2015, https://www.reuters.com/article/idUSKBN0U1071/. On the amphibious troop unit, see Ankit Panda, 'Japan Activates Amphibious Rapid Deployment Brigade', *Diplomat*, 9 April 2018, https://thediplomat.com/2018/04/japan-activates-amphibious-rapid-deployment-brigade/.

24 See 'Japan Signs $2.8 Billion Deals for Long-range Missile Development', *Defense News*, 11 April 2023, https://www.defensenews.com/global/asia-pacific/2023/04/11/japan-signs-28-billion-deals-for-long-range-missile-development/.

25 See Luke Caggiano, 'Japan to Purchase U.S. Tomahawk Missiles', Arms Control Association, March 2023, https://www.armscontrol.org/act/2023-03/news/japan-purchase-us-tomahawk-missiles; and Yoshihiro Inaba, 'Here Is Our First Look at Japan's Type 12 SSM (Upgraded)', Naval News, 17 August 2022, https://www.navalnews.com/naval-news/2022/08/here-is-our-first-look-at-japans-type-12-ssm-upgraded/.

26 See 'Japan's New ASEV Ships Will Boast an Impressive 128 VLS Cells', Naval News, 3 June 2023, https://www.navalnews.com/naval-news/2023/06/japans-new-asev-ships-will-boast-an-impressive-128-vls-cells/.

27 See 'Japan: Toward the Establishment of a Dynamic Defense Force', ch. 7 in National Institute for Defence Studies,

'East Asian Strategic Review 2012', https://www.nids.mod.go.jp/english/publication/east-asian/pdf/2012/east-asian_e2012_07.pdf; and Paul Kallender-Umezu, 'Japan's Fighter Procurement Crunch', Defense News, 6 June 2015, https://www.defensenews.com/air/2015/06/06/japan-s-fighter-procurement-crunch/.

28 See Christopher W. Hughes, *Japan as a Global Military Power: New Capabilities, Alliance Integration, Bilateralism-plus*, 1st ed. (Cambridge: Cambridge University Press, 2022), p. 32.

29 See 'Japan to Deploy Missile Unit on Island near Taiwan', *Japan Times*, 27 December 2022, https://www.japantimes.co.jp/news/2022/12/27/national/yonaguni-japan-missile-deployment/; and 'GSDF Amphibious Unit Now Seen as "Partner" of U.S. Marines', *Japan Times*, 21 July 2023, https://www.japantimes.co.jp/news/2023/07/21/national/gsdf-amphibious-unit-marines-partner/.

30 Japan Ministry of Defense, 'Defense Buildup Program'. See also Samuel P. Porter, 'A Solution for Japan's Military Mismatch', *Foreign Policy*, 15 March 2023.

31 See 'Japan Nears Plan for Ammo Storage Network Closer to Taiwan', Nikkei Asia, 7 January 2023, https://asia.nikkei.com/Politics/International-relations/Taiwan-tensions/Japan-nears-plan-for-ammo-storage-network-closer-to-Taiwan.

32 David A. Ochmanek et al., 'Inflection Point: How to Reverse the Erosion of U.S. and Allied Military Power and Influence', RAND Corporation, 25 July 2023. See also 'Japan to Procure U.S. Tomahawk Missiles Earlier than Planned', *Asahi Shimbun*, 5 October 2023, https://www.asahi.com/ajw/articles/15021823.

33 See Eric Heginbotham, Samuel Leiter and Richard J. Samuels, 'Pushing on an Open Door: Japan's Evolutionary Security Posture', *Washington Quarterly*, vol. 46, no. 2, 3 April 2023, pp. 47–67.

34 See Stacie L. Pettyjohn, Andrew Metrick and Becca Wasser, 'The Kadena Conundrum: Developing a Resilient Indo-Pacific Posture', *War on the Rocks*, 1 December 2022, https://warontherocks.com/2022/12/the-kadena-conundrum-developing-a-resilient-indo-pacific-posture/.

35 In fact, 40% do not even meet earthquake-resistance standards. Jacob Stokes, Lisa Curtis and Joshua Fitt, 'Strengthening the Shield: Japan's Defense Transformation and the U.S.–Japan Alliance', Center for a New American Security, 2023.

36 Japan Ministry of Defense and Self-Defense Forces, 'Fundamental Reinforcement of Japan's Defense Capabilities: Why Now?', March 2023, https://www.mod.go.jp/en/images/guidline_pamph_english.pdf.

37 See Heginbotham, Leiter and Samuels, 'Pushing on an Open Door'.

38 See Yoshihara, 'Going Anti-access at Sea'.

39 See 'Japan Names 33 Airports, Ports to Be Upgraded for Defense Use', Nikkei Asia, 28 September 2023, https://asia.nikkei.com/Politics/Defense/Japan-names-33-airports-ports-to-be-upgraded-for-defense-use.

40 See Richard J. Samuels, *Special Duty: A History of the Japanese Intelligence Community* (Ithaca, NY: Cornell University Press, 2019).

41 See Mayumi Fukushima and Richard J. Samuels, 'Japan's National Security Council: Filling the Whole of Government?', *International Affairs*, vol. 94, no. 4, July 2018, pp. 773–90, https://doi.org/10.1093/ia/iiy032.

42 See 'Japan's Space Program Comes of Age', nippon.com, 14 August 2015, https://www.nippon.com/en/features/h00116/japan's-space-program-comes-of-age.html.

43 See Japan Ministry of Defense, 'National Defense Program Guidelines', 2018; and Nanae Baldauff, 'Space and Strategy: Japan's National Security in Space and Europe', Centre for Security, Diplomacy and Strategy, 13 December 2023.

44 See Naoki Matsuyama, 'Japan Eyes Network of 50 Satellites to Track Enemy Missiles', *Asahi Shimbun*, 15 November 2022, https://www.asahi.com/ajw/articles/14759571; and Russell Thomas, 'Japan's Budding Space Program Grounded by Persistent Setbacks', *Japan Times*, 20 March 2023, https://www.japantimes.co.jp/news/2023/03/20/national/science-health/japan-space-exploration/.

45 See Jeffrey W. Hornung, 'Japan's Potential Contributions in an East China Sea Contingency', RAND Corporation, 2020.

46 See Aki Nakai, 'Japan Gears Up for Electronic Warfare', *Diplomat*, 5 September 2018, https://thediplomat.com/2018/09/japan-gears-up-for-electronic-warfare/.

47 See Inder Singh Bisht, 'Boeing to Upgrade Japan's F-15s with Advanced Electronic Warfare Suite', *Defense Post*, 18 September 2023, https:// www.thedefensepost.com/2023/09/18/japanese-f15-electronic-warfare/.

48 See Akhil Kadidal, 'Japan to Use C-2 Airlifter for Stand-off EW Aircraft', *Janes*, 2 May 2022, https://www.janes.com/defence-news/news-detail/japan-to-use-c-2-airlifter-for-stand-off-ew-aircraft; and Daisuke Sato, 'Japan Military Accepts First RC-2 Modern Spy Plane', Defence Blog, 2 October 2020, https://defence-blog.com/japan-military-accepts-first-rc-2-modern-spy-plane/.

49 Christopher B. Johnstone and Zack Cooper, 'Getting U.S.–Japanese Command and Control Right', *War on the Rocks*, 28 June 2023, https://warontherocks.com/2023/06/getting-u-s-japanese-command-and-control-right/.

50 See Kisho Yoshida, 'Acquiring Counterstrike Capabilities Is No Simple Matter for Japan', *Japan Times*, 14 December 2023, https://www.japantimes.co.jp/commentary/2023/12/14/japan/japan-counterstrike-capability/.

51 Eric Heginbotham and Richard J. Samuels, 'Active Denial: Redesigning Japan's Response to China's Military Challenge', *International Security*, vol. 42, no. 4, 1 May 2018, pp. 128–69.

52 Traditionally, Japan's three services have enjoyed greater inter-operability with their US counterparts than with each other. See Michael J. Green, *Line of Advantage: Japan's Grand Strategy in the Era of Abe Shinzō* (New York: Columbia University Press, 2022).

53 See Robert Ward and Yuka Koshino, 'Japan Steps Up: Security and Defence Policy Under Kishida', in IISS, *Asia-Pacific Regional Security Assessment 2023* (Abingdon: Routledge for the IISS, 2023), pp. 116–36.

54 See 'Japan Enacts Laws to Set Up Joint Command for Self-Defense Forces', Nikkei Asia, 10 May 2024, https://asia.nikkei.com/Politics/Defense/Japan-enacts-laws-to-set-up-joint-command-for-Self-Defense-Forces.

55 See Christopher Johnstone, 'When Actions Match Words: Japan's National Security Strategy at One Year', Washington Quarterly, vol. 47, no. 1, 15 April 2024, pp. 167–83.

56 White House, 'FACT SHEET: Japan Official Visit with State Dinner to the United States', 10 April 2024, https://www.whitehouse.gov/briefing-room/statements-releases/2024/04/10/fact-sheet-japan-official-visit-with-state-dinner-to-the-united-states/.

57 See Benjamin Schreer, 'Arming Without Aiming? Challenges for Japan's Amphibious Capability', in Texas National Security Review, 'Policy Roundtable: The Future of Japanese Security and Defense', 1 October 2020, https://tnsr.org/roundtable/policy-roundtable-the-future-of-japanese-security-and-defense/.

58 See 'Shortage of SDF Personnel Hurts Push to Bolster Japan's Defenses', Asahi Shimbun, 24 August 2023, https://www.asahi.com/ajw/articles/14988285; and Junnosuke Kobara, 'Japan's Latest Security Threat: Its Declining Birthrate', Nikkei Asia, 2023, https://asia.nikkei.com/Politics/Japan-s-latest-security-threat-its-declining-birthrate.

59 See 'The Glitch in Japan's Plans to Bolster US Defence', Reuters, 26 April 2024, https://www.reuters.com/world/glitch-japans-plans-bolster-us-defence-2024-04-26/.

60 Manabu Ueda, 'Japan Has 6,432 Desert Islands, Hot Spots for Tourists, Brokers', Asahi Shimbun, 19 May 2020, https://www.asahi.com/ajw/articles/13385842.

61 Jeffrey W. Hornung and Mike M. Mochizuki, 'Japan: Still an Exceptional U.S. Ally', Washington Quarterly, vol. 39, no. 1, 2 January 2016, pp. 95–116.

62 IISS, The Military Balance 2023 (Abingdon: Routledge for the IISS, 2023), p. 261.

63 The UH-60JA, CH-47J/JA and V-22 are Japan's only smaller aircraft capable of transporting at least a dozen personnel over longer distances. Only the latter two can do heavy lifting of both large equipment and personnel. The Ground Self-Defense Force operates 40 UH-60JA Black Hawk and 53 CH-47J/JA Chinook helicopters (with an additional three CH-47 aircraft in the pipeline), and is in the process of forming two squadrons with a combined total of 17 V-22 Osprey aircraft. The Air Self-Defense Force operates 15 CH-47JA aircraft. IISS, The Military Balance 2023, pp. 259, 261.

64 See John Stillion, David T. Orletsky and Anthony D. Rosello, Intratheater Airlift Functional Needs Analysis (FNA) (Santa Monica, CA: RAND, 2011).

65 See Ochmanek et al., 'Inflection Point'.

66 See Hornung, 'Japan's Potential Contributions in an East China Sea Contingency'.

67 The reason for this is historical: during the Cold War, Japan was focused on the Soviet threat in the north and most of its materiel was already prepositioned on the northern island Hokkaido.

68 See Hornung, 'Japan's Potential Contributions in an East China Sea Contingency'.

69 IISS, The Military Balance 2023, p. 261.

70 See Japan Ministry of Defense, 'Defense Buildup Program'; and Akhil Kadidal, 'Japan to Acquire Two Additional KC-46 Tankers', *Janes*, 1 December 2022, https://www.janes.com/defence-news/news-detail/japan-to-acquire-two-additional-kc-46-tankers.

71 See Ochmanek et al., 'Inflection Point'.

72 See Cathal J. Nolan, *The Allure of Battle: A History of How Wars Have Been Won and Lost* (Oxford: Oxford University Press, 2017); and Iskander Rehman, *Planning for Protraction: A Historically Informed Approach to Great-power War and Sino-US Competition* (Abingdon: Routledge, 2023).

73 See Seth G. Jones and Alexander Palmer, 'Rebuilding the Arsenal of Democracy: The U.S. and Chinese Defense Industrial Bases in an Era of Great Power Competition', Center for Strategic and International Studies, March 2024.

74 See Sadamasa Oue, Hirohito Ogi and Rintaro Inoue, 'Comparative Study of Defense Industries', Institute of Geoeconomics, 2023.

75 On Japan's indigenous defence industry, see, for example, Michael J. Green, *Arming Japan: Defense Production, Alliance Politics, and the Postwar Search for Autonomy* (New York: Columbia University Press, 1995).

76 See Oue, Ogi and Inoue, 'Comparative Study of Defense Industries'.

77 See Bjørn Elias Mikalsen Grønning, 'Operational and Industrial Military Integration: Extending the Frontiers of the Japan–US Alliance', *International Affairs*, vol. 94, no. 4, 1 July 2018, pp. 755–72.

78 *Ibid.*

Preventing Nuclear War

Edward Ifft

Nuclear war, alongside climate change and a devastating pandemic, is the greatest threat to the planet. The world is beginning to see the consequences of climate change and has recently had a glimpse of what a pandemic without effective vaccines might look like. Though there has been nuclear use, there has never been a nuclear war. Preventing it generated a great deal of effort during the Cold War, but the prospect of nuclear Armageddon receded once the Cold War ended and the world seemed on the path to cooperation and peace. The world has avoided a nuclear war for nearly 80 years. However, this is not a time for complacency. Russia's war in Ukraine, accompanied by reckless rhetoric from the Kremlin, has brought the threat posed by the thousands of extant nuclear weapons back to the forefront of international security. The Congressional Commission on the Strategic Posture of the United States recently concluded that the United States was not prepared to face and deter two adversaries that were nuclear peers, and that the risk of nuclear use had grown.[1] The movie *Oppenheimer* has also returned nuclear weapons to prominence in the public mind.[2]

Without specifically mentioning nuclear weapons, Russian President Vladimir Putin made a series of ominous threats that plainly alluded to such weapons right from the beginning of the 2022 Russian invasion of Ukraine.

Edward Ifft, now a Distinguished Visiting Fellow at the Hoover Institution at Stanford University, helped negotiate and implement many of the key nuclear-arms-control agreements of the past 50 years, primarily as a senior US State Department official. This paper is based on a talk he gave at an international conference in Vienna in June 2023.

Survival | vol. 66 no. 3 | June–July 2024 | pp. 129–144   https://doi.org/10.1080/00396338.2024.2357486

These have been analysed in detail elsewhere.[3] Putin's statement on 24 February 2022 – the day of the invasion – is illustrative: 'Russia remains one of the most powerful nuclear states. Moreover, it has a certain advantage in several cutting-edge weapons. In this context, there should be no doubt for anyone that any potential aggressor will face defeat and ominous consequences should it directly attack our country.' He continued with another menacing warning:

> I would now like to say something very important for those who may be tempted to interfere in these developments from the outside. No matter who tries to stand in our way or all the more so create threats for our country and our people, they must know that Russia will respond immediately, and the consequences will be such as you have never seen in your entire history. No matter how the events unfold, we are ready. All the necessary decisions in this regard have been taken. I hope that my words will be heard.[4]

Sergei Karaganov, honorary chairman of Russia's Council on Foreign and Defense Policy, sharpened the issue by suggesting that the limited use of nuclear weapons in the Russia–Ukraine war could be 'a difficult but necessary decision'.[5] Such influential figures as Russian historian Dmitri Trenin and former Russian president Dmitry Medvedev supported this position.[6] After several world leaders strongly condemned these apparent nuclear threats, the Russian Foreign Ministry and Putin himself denied that Russia was contemplating the use of nuclear weapons and noted that even considering it would lower the threshold for their use. The US and NATO wisely remained calm throughout this period. Nevertheless, UN Secretary-General António Guterres warned that 'humanity is just one misunderstanding, one miscalculation away from nuclear annihilation'.[7]

It is worth recalling that nuclear threats are not really new. As US president, Donald Trump threatened North Korean leader Kim Jong-un with 'fire and fury like the world has never seen'.[8] Since the world witnessed Hiroshima and Nagasaki in 1945, one wonders what catastrophic scenario Trump had in mind. When James Baker was US secretary of state, he threatened his Iraqi counterpart, Tariq Aziz, with nuclear reprisal if Iraq took certain non-nuclear actions against US forces – perhaps a successful deterrent, although Iraq might not have had the capability or intention to carry out the attacks Baker feared. In any case, the G20, at its meeting in India in September 2023, issued a statement that 'the use or threat of use of nuclear weapons is inadmissible'.[9] This would appear to rule out even official American statements, sometimes made in military crises, to the effect that all options are on the table.

Policy and doctrine

Official Russian military doctrine declares that the Russian Federation reserves the right to use nuclear weapons in response to use of nuclear weapons or other weapons of mass destruction against it or its allies, or in response to aggression using conventional weapons that threatens 'the very existence of the state'.[10] The latter phrase is almost certainly drawn from the 1996 advisory opinion of the International Court of Justice on the circumstances which could justify the use of nuclear weapons.[11] In the context of the war in Ukraine, it would be reasonable to say that there is nothing that Ukraine could do that would threaten the existence of the Russian Federation. However, the Russian view on this might be that the seizure of territory that Russia believes belongs to it would meet the criterion.

For purposes of comparison, the relevant US policy is that 'the United States would only consider the use of nuclear weapons in extreme circumstances to defend the vital interests of the United States or its allies and partners'.[12] In the past, US officials have characterised such 'extreme circumstances' as the use of nuclear weapons or possibly a broad-scale attack using biological weapons or other weapons of mass destruction. The stated policies of the two primary nuclear powers are thus perhaps more similar than might be expected, although decisions made in the heat of battle might involve significantly divergent interpretations.

At the 2020 Review Conference of the Nuclear Non-Proliferation Treaty (NPT) – which was actually held in 2022 – Putin and US President Joe Biden reaffirmed the Reagan–Gorbachev pledge that 'nuclear war cannot be won and must never be fought'.[13] The five countries recognised as nuclear-weapons states under the treaty, which are also the five permanent members of the United Nations Security Council, collectively followed with a similar endorsement. But the formulation seems purposefully to reference 'nuclear war' rather than nuclear use. It is in no way a no-first-use (NFU) commitment. The United States has consistently declined to make such a commitment, most recently in its 2022 Nuclear Posture Review. Russia made the commitment for some years but withdrew it. China, on the other hand, has steadfastly held to an NFU policy and urges other nuclear-weapons states to adopt one as well.

Both Ronald Reagan and Mikhail Gorbachev were pursuing the goal of total elimination of nuclear weapons and wished to avoid any use of them. But they almost certainly had in mind a general nuclear exchange, as opposed to the limited use of nuclear weapons. It seems clear that a nuclear-weapons state could 'win' a war against a non-nuclear-weapons state through the use of its nuclear weapons. Thus, the Reagan–Gorbachev proclamation, though useful and important, does not seem especially relevant to the war in Ukraine, assuming it retains its current limited character.

One other aspect of great-power nuclear policies seems worth noting. The international community has worked hard to maintain the 'nuclear taboo' against any use of nuclear weapons. Since the negotiation of the Comprehensive Nuclear-Test-Ban Treaty in 1996, this taboo has extended even to the testing of nuclear weapons. An assumption has long been that any use of nuclear weapons would rapidly escalate to a full catastrophic nuclear exchange and the end of civilisation as we know it. War games frequently collapse with the first use of nuclear weapons, since further steps seem too horrible to contemplate or are simply unknowable. Yet the Russian threats that have recently emerged make the actual use of nuclear weapons quite imaginable. In this light, it might be prudent to consider how leaders of major powers should react to that prospect.

The three Cs

The structures and mindsets that need to be in place for preventing a nuclear war are similar to those needed to deal with the crisis that would result from the limited use of nuclear weapons. Decades of experience show, of course, that it is easier to prevent nuclear war than to prevent war in general. In the opinion of most experts, by far the most likely way a nuclear war would begin is with a conventional war that was going badly for one side. How nations would deal with a nuclear crisis is probably more dependent on who the leaders are at the time than on what their bureaucracies are thinking or their stated policies are. Accordingly, there are three key areas to consider.

Firstly, intergovernmental contacts, especially between senior officials, are crucial and can lead to greater understanding and trust at the personal level. Regular summit meetings with both allies and adversaries should be expected and pursued even when relations are poor and dramatic results cannot be achieved. Diplomatic channels, military-to-military channels and those involving academic institutions, scientific organisations and think tanks are all useful. They can facilitate the exchange of plans, warnings, reassurances and explanations. The uniquely American idea that refusing to talk to one's adversaries somehow contributes to settling problems with them seems self-defeating. The fact that the United States has shut down the exchange of data between US and Russian scientists on climate change in the Arctic because of the war in Ukraine is difficult to understand.

Arms-control inspections, particularly those under the New START Treaty, have provided a particularly valuable opportunity to establish contacts. A case could be made that these have been the most effective liaison between the United States and Russia in the security area (though they have been suspended, initially because of COVID-19 and more recently due to the war in Ukraine). At first glance, their success seems improbable since the primary task of inspectors is to search for violations by the other side. However, the engagements have been frequent and conducted professionally and respectfully by both sides. Detailed documents, approved at the highest levels, guide how inspectors carry out their work, advancing and enriching the process. The documents themselves were negotiated meticulously by delegations compelled to address deep disagreements in both substance and style, but who interacted on a first-name basis almost daily for long periods. Such arms-control activities serve as a model for how mutual trust and understanding can be achieved.

Secondly, communications can always be improved. There have long been 'hotlines' between Washington and Moscow, and this system should be extended to all five nuclear-weapons states recognised by the NPT. The National and Nuclear Risk Reduction Center (NNRRC) in the US State Department and its opposite number in the Russian Ministry of Defence have continued to function in spite of the war in Ukraine, as have their counterparts in many other countries. The NNRRC serves a number of arms-control agreements – principally the New START Treaty but also the Chemical Weapons Convention, the International Atomic Energy Agency Additional Protocol and the Vienna Document 2011 – along with the Cyber Security Confidence Building Measures regime and the Incidents at Sea and Prevention of Dangerous Military Activities agreements.

The Russia–Ukraine war has disrupted crucial communications

Such channels are generally reserved for emergencies and provide prompt, secure and reliable information between states in multiple languages. They can also convey 'goodwill' messages, as they did after the 9/11 attacks. The NNRRC handles approximately 4,000 messages per year. It has transmitted and received more than 25,000 messages under the New START Treaty alone since its entry into force in 2011. While Russia and the United States have pledged to continue to observe the central limits in the treaty, they are no longer implementing the daily, detailed exchanges of data required by the treaty and essential to its verification.[14] In June 2023, the US proposed talks 'without preconditions' on New START and a possible follow-on agreement or agreements. Russia has rejected this, citing the situation in Ukraine.[15]

US military leaders say that they would like better contacts with their counterparts in both Russia and China. The fact that they apparently could not reach anyone in Beijing during the January–February 2023 balloon episode is most disturbing. Biden and Chinese President Xi Jinping, however, agreed at their November 2023 meeting to re-establish military-to-military contacts. The Russia–Ukraine war has been allowed to disrupt crucial communications in other areas. First the United States and then Russia blocked high-level discussions to address the expiration of the New START Treaty in 2026. This is the last remaining legal regime that constrains the number and deployment of US and Russian nuclear weapons; finding a framework to replace it would very likely be a difficult and time-consuming process.

There have certainly been bilateral communications between Russia and the US about the Ukraine crisis, but perhaps not in the depth that the seriousness of the conflict requires. Before the invasion, French President Emmanuel Macron had several personal interactions with Putin, as did others including Xi. Since the 2022 invasion began, the United States has sent several high-level officials to Moscow, but lower-level contacts have been blocked. Few if any robust Track Two channels – that is, those between non-official but influential players sometimes with official access – appear to be in use. With the right participants, these can be very useful when diplomatic and military-to-military channels are unable to function. A number of other key countries, including China, Saudi Arabia and Turkiye, have met recently with Putin. Communications with Kyiv and within NATO have been excellent. While the current US policy of not having international discussions on anything to do with Ukraine without a Ukrainian representative in the room is understandable, it may limit opportunities to make progress in ending the crisis. In a crisis, informed communications may be more desirable and important than actions. It is possible that other channels that are not known publicly are, or soon will be, in use.

Crisis management is the third obvious area of focus. The 1962 Cuban Missile Crisis is probably the event most thoroughly studied from this point of view, and the analysis is not finished yet.[16] New documents recently released from the Russian archives reveal shocking misunderstandings and mistakes. NATO's 1983 *Able Archer* exercise and various false alarms on early-warning networks were additional scary incidents that provide important lessons in crisis management.[17] In several cases, sheer luck was a key ingredient in the avoidance of a nuclear disaster. Security-policy leaders from 50 countries have recently declared that the reduction of strategic risks and the avoidance of war between nuclear-weapons states are the 'foremost responsibilities' of the five nuclear-weapons states recognised by the NPT.[18] Henry Kissinger made similar admonitions in an eight-hour interview with

The Economist shortly before his death in 2023. He noted that governments lack any settled principle on which they could establish order and 'much margin of political concession', such that 'any disturbance of the equilibrium can lead to catastrophic consequences'.[19]

The United States and Russia agreed years ago to establish a data-exchange centre in Moscow that would be jointly manned 24/7 to exchange early-warning information on missile and space launches, but never followed through with it. When conditions improve, the sides could finally operationalise this crisis-management tool. A similar facility in Beijing could be useful.

Is limited use of nuclear weapons credible?

For decades, leaders and experts have focused on deterrence theory and the prevention of any use of nuclear weapons. Countries have built up nuclear stockpiles and delivery systems, large and small, with a view to making them reliable and survivable. Military staffs have established plans, whether credible or not, for a nuclear response to nuclear first use to fortify deterrence. Even so, the arms-control community has generally resisted thinking about any use whatsoever of nuclear weapons, which is part of a general reluctance to consider what would and should happen if nuclear use on a small scale were to occur. Some believe that the results would be too terrible to contemplate, rapidly escalating to full-scale nuclear war, while others do not wish to seem to legitimise such a scenario. These head-in-the-sand attitudes seem roughly analogous to refusing to prepare for the next pandemic because that would somehow make such a pandemic more likely. The circumstances and rhetoric surrounding the war in Ukraine are warnings that such an approach is not prudent. After years of thinking about how to prevent any use of nuclear weapons, it may be time to consider seriously how to respond to the use of a small number of tactical nuclear weapons in a local conflict.

The Ukraine situation has illuminated that scenario most brightly, but others have brought it into sharper relief as well. Tactical nuclear weapons could conceivably be used if North Korea attacked South Korea with a massive conventional bombardment and ground invasion. If South Korean forces could not stop such an assault with conventional means before South Korea, including Seoul, were devastated, the United States might decide to stop the offensive with a few tactical nukes. A Russian invasion of a Baltic state might prompt a similar calculation on Washington's part. Scenarios such as these, which bring into play US extended deterrence, are a principal reason that the United States has been unwilling to adopt an NFU policy.

Some Russian planners are said to be considering the use of a few tactical nuclear weapons to stop a Ukrainian attempt to invade Crimea, which Russia occupied and illegally annexed in 2014–15.[20] It would be dangerous to underestimate the importance of Crimea in the Russian psyche, given its history, the manner in which it was transferred from Russia to Ukraine in 1954, its current Russian population and the Russian naval facilities located there. Russian war games also appear to posit a Western invasion centring on Saint Petersburg, only a few hours' drive from the NATO border. If Moscow were willing to contemplate using battlefield nuclear weapons to avoid defeat in Ukraine, it would probably do so in the event of a strategic incursion on unambiguously Russian soil. A Chinese limited nuclear attack on US naval assets attempting to thwart a Chinese invasion of Taiwan is quite imaginable. One could also foresee scenarios involving India and Pakistan's selective use of small nuclear weapons. More generally, ongoing efforts to develop smaller-yield nuclear weapons that are consequently more useable appear to lower the nuclear threshold, making limited use for specific, limited ends more plausible.

It is worth noting that all of these scenarios could be justified as defensive, last-resort employments of nuclear weapons. And of course, countries invariably seek to justify their nuclear-weapons programmes as defensive or solely for deterrence. Putin's veiled threat to use them was directed only at NATO countries that might be tempted to 'interfere' in the war. When the Chechen warlord Ramzan Kadyrov urged the use of nuclear weapons against Ukraine, the Kremlin quickly rebuked him.[21] At the same time, there is obviously an important distinction between an attack on an adversary's cities using high-yield nuclear weapons, which would clearly be offensive even if justified as retaliatory, and the use of nuclear weapons to repel an invasion of its established or claimed territory. The morality of any use of nuclear weapons is highly debatable, of course, but surely the two types of scenarios sketched here would fall at different places on the morality spectrum, the latter being discomfitingly more justifiable. The United States and NATO clearly recognised this distinction when they buried atomic demolition munitions (ADMs) on West German territory to repel a potential Warsaw Pact invasion during the Cold War.

Thinking the unthinkable

In the event that the three Cs prove insufficient to prevent some limited use of nuclear weapons, what should be the response? There would be many variables in play. What is the attacker's explanation for its actions and what does it propose should happen next? What sort of retaliation or punishment against it would contribute to the resolution of the conflict? On whose territory did the attack take place? Was the nuclear use essentially a demonstration or a genuine operational measure with serious battlefield consequences? Was the attack a true game-changer? Is an agreed pause to allow time for negotiation feasible, and are the sides in fact willing to negotiate? Is a credible mediator available?

Presumably, the attacker would hope that the strike would lead to a resolution on favourable terms with no further use of nuclear weapons. It would no doubt attempt to justify its actions and might threaten further nuclear attacks unless its terms were met. The rest of the world would voice shock and outrage, perhaps demanding a crushing nuclear response. Diplomatic relations would be broken off immediately. The UN Security Council would be called into emergency session, as would NATO.

The wisest response would set punishment and reparations aside in the immediate aftermath and concentrate on preventing further escalation, especially using nuclear weapons. A military response would be appropriate if reasonably calculated to prevent further attacks. For the United States, this probably would work vis-à-vis, say, North Korea, but would be highly escalatory vis-à-vis Russia or China. Reliable and secure communications would be absolutely crucial, and should be made through established channels, drawing on the experience gained from past interactions among leaders. The familiarity between the leaders shown in the 1964 movie *Dr. Strangelove* was actually quite salutary, though the level of intelligence portrayed on each side left much to be desired. The communications in the Cuban Missile Crisis proved effective in the end, but they were slow, perhaps overly formal and sometimes confused.

Although some 13,000 nuclear weapons are still with us, efforts to prevent nuclear war have been successful since the nuclear age began in 1945 – a result that might not have been predicted 70 years ago. What is needed, as a key part of that ongoing effort, is some serious attention to how to deal with a situation in which nuclear use has already occurred. This could include more realistic simulations in which all the players do not simply go home at the first use of nuclear weapons.

Red lines

Red lines also have a role to play. In relations between states, red lines should be a device for avoiding nuclear war and other catastrophes. They can do this primarily by averting misunderstandings about when some action or an event occasioned by State A will cause State B to react in some way that is highly undesirable to State A. For this to happen because State A did not realise how strongly State B felt about the issue would be unfortunate for all parties. Of course, State B could be bluffing, in which case the credibility of similar warnings in the future would be greatly weakened. On the other hand, State A may understand perfectly well what will happen if it crosses State B's red line and decide to go ahead anyway because it feels the issue is so important.

Given these complications, red lines should be selectively imposed and carefully considered, generally communicated privately and taken very seriously. In rare cases, a state might wish to make a red line public in the hope that this will somehow strengthen the desired prohibition. This could work but, perhaps more likely, it could also be viewed as a challenge or dare by the other side. It might also constrain freedom of action for the side that established the red line, to its regret.

Unfortunately, the concept of red lines has infiltrated the public imagination at the risk of becoming almost meaningless. Misbehaving children publicly cross parents' boundaries with no consequences, and leaders casually establish red lines with no expectation of having to enforce them. Speculation as to exactly where certain red lines lie has become a distracting parlour game. The fact remains that there is a long list of historical cases in which terrible death and destruction has occurred, or dire results only narrowly avoided, because world leaders failed to establish a red line or neglected to communicate it clearly, or another leader failed to understand that it existed or where it was. Consider, for example, Saddam Hussein's 1990 invasion of Kuwait, the Cuban Missile Crisis and Putin's invasion of Ukraine.

Not every official declaration that another country should not do something, or that doing so would have consequences, should automatically be considered a red line. Demarches are not always intended to be outright demands or ultimatums. If they were, international relations would become a dangerously unnavigable maze of red lines on a daily basis.

Poorly communicated red lines can have perverse and unintended effects. In particular, the receiving side may believe that it has a green light to take hostile actions right up to the articulated red line with no consequences. The danger this poses is obvious. A famous example is the shelling of islands by China in 1954 after US secretary of state Dean Acheson and under secretary Christian Herter indicated that they were outside the United States' security perimeter in the Western Pacific.

A more recent example of a misguided red line is the Obama administration's public warning to the Syrian government in 2012 that the movement or use of chemical weapons would have dire consequences.[22] Not only did Obama's red line fail to deter Syria from using chemical weapons, but the United States decided not to punish Syria for crossing it, damaging US credibility. The diplomatic alternative that the Obama administration pursued – Syria was forced to join the Chemical Weapons Convention, and 1,300 tons of weapons and precursor chemicals were destroyed and 27 production facilities demolished in an impressive international effort – was a far better result than firing a few cruise missiles into Syria would have produced. Nevertheless, the United States' lack of a military response has been construed as a policy failure.

There is an alarming trend in the casual use of the term 'red line', illustrated by the proliferation of stories with titles such as 'Biden Shows

Growing Appetite to Cross Putin's Red Lines'.[23] The media seem to view the imposition of red lines as an exercise in playground dare and counter-dare, or a test of manhood. If the overuse and trivialisation of red lines continues, governments may soon be tempted to put everything they wish not to happen into a large bundle surrounded by red lines. A valuable diplomatic tool for avoiding dangerous misunderstandings in the conduct of international relations – including those that could lead to nuclear use – would then be lost.

Notes

[1] See Congressional Commission on the Strategic Posture of the United States, 'America's Strategic Posture: The Final Report of the Congressional Commission on the Strategic Posture of the United States', October 2023, https://www.ida.org/-/media/feature/publications/a/am/americas-strategic-posture/strategic-posture-commission-report.ashx.

[2] See, for example, Jonathan Stevenson, 'Oppenheimer: The Man, the Movie and Nuclear Dread', *Survival*, vol. 65, no. 5, October–November 2023, pp. 153–60.

[3] See, for example, Aleksey Arbatov, 'The Ukrainian Crisis and Strategic Stability', Russian International Affairs Council, 18 July 2022, https://russiancouncil.ru/en/analytics-and-comments/analytics/the-ukrainian-crisis-and-strategic-stability/; and Lawrence Freedman, 'The Russo-Ukrainian War and the Durability of Deterrence', *Survival*, vol. 65, no. 6, December 2023–January 2024, pp. 7–36. See also William Alberque, 'Russia Is Unlikely to Use Nuclear Weapons in Ukraine', IISS Online Analysis, 10 October 2022, https://www.iiss.org/blogs/analysis/2022/10/russia-is-unlikely-to-use-nuclear-weapons-in-ukraine.

[4] President of Russia, 'Address by the President of the Russian Federation', 24 February 2022, http://en.kremlin.ru/events/president/news/67843.

[5] Sergei A. Karaganov, 'A Difficult but Necessary Decision', Russia in Global Affairs, 13 June 2023, https://eng.globalaffairs.ru/articles/a-difficult-but-necessary-decision/.

[6] See Andrey Baklitskiy, 'What We Learned from Recent Calls for a Russian Nuclear Attack', Carnegie Endowment for International Peace, 20 July 2023, https://carnegieendowment.org/politika/90232.

[7] Quoted in, for instance, Edith M. Lederer, 'UN Chief Warns World Is One Step from "Nuclear Annihilation"', Associated Press, 1 August 2022, https://apnews.com/article/russia-ukraine-covid-health-antonio-guterres-2871563e530f9a676d7884b3e2d871c3.

[8] Quoted in, for example, Peter Baker and Choe Sang-Hun, 'Trump Threatens "Fire and Fury" Against North Korea if It Endangers U.S.', *New York Times*, 8 August 2017, https://

www.nytimes.com/2017/08/08/world/asia/north-korea-un-sanctions-nuclear-missile-united-nations.html.

9   Quoted in, for example, Shannon Bugos, 'G-20 Majority Condemns Russian Nuclear Threats', *Arms Control Today*, December 2022, https://www.armscontrol.org/act/2022-12/news/g-20-majority-condemns-russian-nuclear-threats.

10 See, for example, Amy F. Woolf, 'Russia's Nuclear Weapons: Doctrine, Forces, and Modernization', Congressional Research Service, updated 21 April 2022, p. 8, https://sgp.fas.org/crs/nuke/R45861.pdf.

11 See International Court of Justice, 'Advisory Opinion on the Legality of the Threat or Use of Nuclear Weapons', General List No. 95, 8 July 1996, https://law.justia.com/cases/foreign/international/1996-icj-rep-66.html.

12 US Department of Defense, '2022 Nuclear Posture Review', October 2022, p. 9, https://apps.dtic.mil/sti/trecms/pdf/AD1183539.pdf.

13 See 'Joint Soviet–United States Statement on the Summit Meeting in Geneva', 21 November 1985, available from the Ronald Reagan Presidential Library and Museum, https://www.reaganlibrary.gov/archives/speech/joint-soviet-united-states-statement-summit-meeting-geneva.

14 See Edward M. Ifft with James Goodby, 'Beyond New START', Hoover Institution, Stanford University, 27 January 2023, https://www.hoover.org/research/beyond-new-start; and Edward M. Ifft, 'Beyond New START: Addendum', Hoover Institution, Stanford University, 24 February 2023, https://www.hoover.org/research/

beyond-new-start-addendum. See also Mike Albertson and Nikolai Sokov, 'Beyond New START: Two Forecasts for Future Russian–US Arms Control', Research Paper, International Institute for Strategic Studies, April 2023, https://www.iiss.org/globalassets/media-library---content--migration/files/research-papers/2023/04/beyond-new-start-two-forecasts-for-future-russian-us-arms-control.pdf; and Pranay Vaddi and James M. Acton, 'A ReSTART for U.S.–Russian Nuclear Arms Control: Enhancing Security Through Cooperation', Carnegie Endowment for International Peace, 2 October 2020, https://carnegieendowment.org/2020/10/02/restart-for-u.s.-russian-nuclear-arms-control-enhancing-security-through-cooperation-pub-82705. For a Russian view, see Arbatov, 'The Ukrainian Crisis and Strategic Stability'.

15 See Libby Flatoff and Daryl G. Kimball, 'Russia Rejects New Nuclear Arms Talks', *Arms Control Today*, March 2024, https://www.armscontrol.org/act/2024-03/news/russia-rejects-new-nuclear-arms-talks.

16 See Sergey Radchenko and Vladislav Zubok, 'Blundering on the Brink: The Secret History and Unlearned Lessons of the Cuban Missile Crisis', *Foreign Affairs*, vol. 102, no. 3, May/June 2023, pp. 44–63.

17 See, for example, Gordon Barrass, '*Able Archer 83*: What Were the Soviets Thinking?', *Survival*, vol. 58, no. 6, December 2016–January 2017, pp. 7–30.

18 See European Leadership Network and Asia-Pacific Leadership Network, 'Group Statement: Protecting Nuclear Arms Control Is a Global Imperative',

17 May 2023, https://www.
europeanleadershipnetwork.org/
group-statement/protecting-nuclear-
arms-control-is-a-global-imperative/.

19 'Henry Kissinger Explains How
to Avoid World War Three', *The
Economist*, 17 May 2023, https://www.
economist.com/briefing/2023/05/17/
henry-kissinger-explains-how-to-
avoid-world-war-three.

20 Author's private communication with
a Russian colleague.

21 See Sam Farbman, 'Telegram,
"Milbloggers" and the Russian State',

Survival, vol. 65, no. 3, June–July 2023,
pp. 107–28.

22 See 'Reassessing Obama's Biggest
Mistake', *The Economist*, 22 August
2023, https://www.economist.com/
international/2023/08/22/reassessing-
barack-obamas-red-line-in-syria.

23 John Hudson and Dan Lamothe,
'Biden Shows Growing Appetite
to Cross Putin's Red Lines',
Washington Post, 1 June 2023,
https://www.washingtonpost.
com/national-security/2023/06/01/
ukraine-f-16s-biden-russia-escalation/.

The Gulf States' Pragmatism in Afghanistan

Hasan T. Alhasan and Asna Wajid

The Gulf Arab states were among the first countries to bear the consequences of the United States' August 2021 departure from Afghanistan. As
the Taliban bulldozed its way back to power, US commercial and military
aircraft ferried tens of thousands of fleeing Afghans to airports, military
bases and temporary housing facilities in the Gulf, where many remain
in limbo. Although Saudi Arabia and the United Arab Emirates (UAE)
had been the only countries other than Pakistan to recognise the Taliban-
controlled Islamic Emirate of Afghanistan in the late 1990s, the two Gulf
states have long since switched from supporting to combatting Islamist
groups worldwide. The Taliban's return to power nourished fears in the
Gulf that Afghanistan could become a rear base for al-Qaeda in the Arabian
Peninsula (AQAP), as the group's Gulf franchise is known, which could
then regain the ability to carry out attacks against the Gulf states. Given
the relationship that Iran and the Taliban had nurtured on the basis of
their shared animosity towards the United States, the Taliban's return also
prompted concerns that Iran's Central Asian influence would expand. And
as the Taliban banned female education and limited individual freedoms,
the Gulf states sought to protect their reputations by joining the West in
curtailing ties with the group.

Hasan T. Alhasan is IISS Senior Fellow for Middle East Policy. Asna Wajid is a research assistant at the IISS.

Survival | vol. 66 no. 3 | June–July 2024 | pp. 145–158   https://doi.org/10.1080/00396338.2024.2357487

As Western attention shifted elsewhere and the enduring nature of Taliban rule became clear, however, the Gulf states – notably Qatar, the UAE and to a lesser extent Saudi Arabia – have overtly engaged senior Taliban leaders to advance their own security and economic interests. These states see a geo-economic opportunity to expand their presence in Asia's energy and emerging connectivity architecture. They are shedding their inhibitions about rebuilding more visible relations with the Taliban in the hope of gaining a long-term advantage in Afghanistan despite international sanctions and the reputational risks associated with the group.

A rocky relationship

After the 9/11 attacks and US-led invasion of Afghanistan, the Gulf states sought to dissociate themselves from the Taliban, which was widely seen as al-Qaeda's accomplice. The Taliban also found common cause with Iran in seeking to expel NATO forces from Afghanistan. Saudi Arabia tried but failed to drive a wedge between the Taliban and al-Qaeda, a sworn enemy of the pro-Western Saudi kingdom.[1] Although Riyadh had initially complied with Afghanistan's president Hamid Karzai's requests in 2008 and 2010 to facilitate peace talks with the Taliban, it discontinued those efforts as the group remained closely aligned with its adversaries.[2] But the Taliban, notably the Haqqani network, continued to seek private donations in Kuwait, Qatar, Saudi Arabia and the UAE.[3]

Meanwhile, the UAE and Qatar competed for the opportunity to broker peace talks between the United States and the Taliban. With the creation of the Taliban office in Doha in 2013, Qatar gained a major advantage. Although the UAE's relationship with the Taliban suffered a setback when a bomb attack attributed to the group claimed the lives of five Emirati diplomats in January 2017 in Kandahar, it nevertheless hosted at least one round of peace talks in December 2018. However, the Taliban's preference for Qatar, seen by the group as a more neutral facilitator, meant that Doha would remain the principal venue of US–Taliban talks until the signing of the peace agreement in 2020.[4]

When the Taliban regained control of the country in August 2021 and imposed a strict regime of social control including restrictions on the movement and education of women, the Gulf states distanced themselves from the group to signal their disapproval. They resorted to humanitarian aid as a low-risk tool for asserting influence in Afghanistan without being seen as endorsing the Taliban, sending hundreds of tonnes of humanitarian aid to help alleviate food shortages and difficult winter conditions.[5] Financial commitments soon followed.[6]

The Gulf states are now displaying greater willingness to deal with the Taliban even as the group and its leaders remain under international sanctions. Qatari Prime Minister and Foreign Minister Sheikh Mohammed bin Abdulrahman Al Thani became the first foreign official to meet, in May 2023, with Taliban Supreme Leader Mullah Hibatullah Akhundzada in Kandahar. The UAE has since approved the Taliban's control of Afghanistan's embassy in Abu Dhabi; in October 2023, the group appointed Badruddin Haqqani, a key member of the powerful Haqqani clan, as its envoy to the UAE.[7] Taliban Defence Minister Mullah Mohammad Yaqoob, the son of the group's founder Mullah Mohammad Omar, has become a frequent official guest of Gulf leaders. In December 2022, UAE President Sheikh Mohamed bin Zayed Al Nahyan received him in Abu Dhabi.

Even the Saudis, who had been loath to associate with the Taliban and denied Taliban leaders diplomatic visas for the annual hajj pilgrimage in 2022, have changed their tune. In 2023, Saudi Crown Prince Muhammad bin Salman received Mullah Yaqoob as a guest of the state. Mullah Yaqoob attended Qatar's 2024 Doha International Maritime Defence Exhibition and Conference accompanied by the Taliban's Acting Chief of Defence Staff Qari Fasihuddin Fitrat.[8] Given that Afghanistan is a landlocked country with no coastguard or navy, the Taliban's appearance at Qatar's flagship maritime-security event was likely intended to underscore Doha's general comfort in dealing with the group.

Security interests

The Gulf states' security interests in Afghanistan include countering terrorism, Iranian influence and drug trafficking. The Taliban could be expected to take a hard line on drugs for religious reasons and has done so.[9] But its return to power threatened to exacerbate threats posed by Iran and al-Qaeda.

The Gulf states' growing ties with the Taliban are partly intended to manage these security challenges and sway the group in a favourable direction.[10]

The Taliban has built a close relationship with Iran, the Gulf Arab states' main regional rival, over the two decades since the 2001 US-led invasion, establishing an office in the Iranian city of Mashhad to coordinate efforts with the Islamic Revolutionary Guard Corps against NATO forces. The Gulf Arab states, especially Saudi Arabia, are concerned that Iran will seek to exploit its relationship with the Taliban to widen its influence within Afghanistan beyond its traditional stronghold of Herat and in the greater Middle East.[11] Iran's record supports this concern. At the height of the Syrian civil war, Iran recruited tens of thousands of Afghan Shia Hazaras – most of whom were living as refugees in Iran – into the Fatemiyoun Brigades to fight alongside Syrian President Bashar al-Assad's forces, whom Saudi Arabia and Qatar were seeking to overthrow.[12]

So far, the Taliban's threats to Gulf states' interests have been contained. The three-million-strong Afghan-refugee population in Iran has produced grievances and occasional border clashes. Although the Taliban and Iran have made efforts to resolve their differences over sharing the waters of the Helmand River, Afghanistan is not falling under Iran's influence. Furthermore, the Gulf states' own improved relations with Iran, which have held in spite of the Gaza war, may be helping to dissuade Iran from antagonising them in Afghanistan.[13]

The Taliban's continued association with al-Qaeda is perhaps a more salient source of anxiety for the Gulf states. In the early to mid-2000s, al-Qaeda absorbed hundreds of Saudi militants returning from Afghanistan following the downfall of the Taliban regime, some of whom later coalesced into AQAP.[14] Following a series of bomb attacks in Riyadh, the Saudi government cracked down on the franchise and forced it to regroup in neighbouring Yemen. It is considerably weaker than it was a decade ago and is at times co-opted by various warring factions in Yemen. Recently, its militant and media activity have shown signs of a resurgence, however.[15] Meanwhile, al-Qaeda continues to operate under Taliban protection in Afghanistan and has in fact established new training camps and weapons depots.[16] The United States' killing of al-Qaeda leader Ayman al-Zawahiri in a drone strike in August 2022 in Kabul shed light on the organisation's ongoing relationship with the Taliban, belying the Taliban's denials that it was harbouring leaders of the terrorist group.[17] While the Taliban has repeatedly extended assurances that it would not allow Afghanistan to be used as a launching pad for transnational terrorist attacks, Zawahiri's successor, Saif al-Adel, believed to be living in Iran, is seeking to exercise tighter control over al-Qaeda in Afghanistan and AQAP.[18]

The Gulf states' geo-economic ambitions

Beyond security, the Gulf states have commercial interests in Afghanistan and increasingly view it as a potential node in Asia's broader energy and transportation connectivity networks.

The UAE enjoys the most significant commercial relationship with Afghanistan proper, partly by virtue of the large Afghan diaspora in the Emirates, estimated at around 150,000 people, and Dubai's attractiveness as a business hub. The UAE is one of Afghanistan's top trading partners.[19] Established in 2005, the Afghan Business Council in Dubai is the only such entity in the Arab world and, in 2010, Dubai hosted the first Afghanistan International Investment Conference to help Kabul attract foreign investors into Afghanistan's economy.[20]

Today, the UAE dominates at least two key sectors in Afghanistan: telecommunications and aviation. The UAE's Etisalat is the largest telecom operator by share of market value in Afghanistan, where it has operated since 2007. Etisalat was the first operator to roll out a 3G network in Afghanistan in 2012 and, in 2021, was involved in standing up the infrastructure required to upgrade Afghanistan's mobile broadband network to 5G.[21] In the aviation sector, the UAE's state-linked GAAC Holding won a contract for managing security and ground operations at Kabul International Airport in September 2022, beating a rival bid by Qatar and Turkiye.[22] In October 2023, Dubai's low-cost carrier Flydubai became the first international airline to resume flights to Kabul since the Taliban's takeover, followed shortly by the Sharjah-headquartered Air Arabia.[23]

State-owned energy investors in the Gulf including Saudi Arabia's ACWA Power and the UAE's Masdar are eyeing Kazakhstan's, Tajikistan's and

Uzbekistan's renewable-energy sectors. Qatar and the UAE have pledged to invest in Uzbekistan's gas infrastructure. In January 2024, the UAE and Turkmenistan reached an agreement whereby the Abu Dhabi National Oil Company would help develop the third phase of Turkmenistan's large Galkynysh Gas Field, which could end up carrying 33 billion cubic metres of natural gas per year to Afghanistan and Pakistan if a long-delayed pipeline project is revived.[24] Farther east, Saudi Arabia pledged a $10bn investment in a refinery in Pakistan's Gwadar Port, which constitutes Afghanistan's main international-trading connection.[25]

The closing statement of a 2024 Gulf Cooperation Council (GCC)–Central Asian ministerial meeting identified several railway projects as potential areas of cooperation.[26] The Trans-Afghan Railway, which seeks to connect Afghanistan, Pakistan and Uzbekistan at an estimated cost of $5bn, has attracted both Emirati and Qatari interest. The three Asian states signed a memorandum of understanding in July 2023 and have held high-level meetings with officials from the UAE and Qatar to discuss the feasibility of the project.[27] Central Asian states including Kazakhstan and Kyrgyzstan are also reportedly looking to attract investments from Qatar in planned transportation corridors including the Trans-Caspian International Transport Route, which would link China to Europe, and the China–Kyrgyzstan–Uzbekistan railroad.

Expanded investment in Central and South Asian connectivity networks places the Gulf states, especially the UAE and Qatar, in an advantageous position as future development partners for Afghanistan. Given the potential for insecurity in Afghanistan to spill over into their neighbourhood, the Gulf states now have a commercial interest in ensuring stability, amplifying their need to engage directly with the Taliban to protect it.

Risks and rewards of pragmatism

The UAE's and Qatar's pragmatic approach towards the Taliban is deeply opportunistic. The two Gulf states see distinct advantages in engaging the group from a position of strength, especially as Western capitals have been hesitant about engaging with the Taliban. The UAE's and Qatar's overtures fit with the Taliban's efforts to attract foreign investments, develop

Afghanistan's economy and build a case for wider de facto recognition.[28] The Taliban administration is courting a wide array of investors including Iran, Pakistan and Russia; awarded a Chinese state-owned enterprise a contract to extract oil and gas from the Amu Darya basin; and signed $6.5bn-worth of contracts in the mining sector with investors from China, Iran, Turkiye and the United Kingdom.[29]

Nevertheless, the UAE's and Qatar's public engagement with the Taliban beyond the circumscribed arenas of conflict resolution or humanitarian aid carries reputational, legal and security risks. The United Nations Security Council's sanctions regime against the Taliban, in place since 1999, imposes asset freezes, travel bans and restrictions on support for the group and its members.[30] There is no clear prospect of de-listing the Taliban.[31] Moreover, the Taliban continues to resist international pressure for reinstating female education or protecting other individual freedoms.

Another source of risk – especially since Gulf Arab states are undertaking long-term, capital-intensive commitments that are difficult to exit – is that Afghanistan continues to lack legal infrastructure for regulating and protecting foreign investments and resolving commercial disputes. And despite the drop in insurgent activity since the Taliban's takeover, terrorist organisations, notably the Islamic State – Khorasan Province (ISKP), have the potential to surge and destabilise the country.[32] The UAE and Qatar do not appear to have a clear strategy for leveraging their economic heft or relations with the Taliban to mitigate such threats.

Saudi Arabia's cautious approach to the Taliban carries risks of its own. Riyadh has resisted Qatari proposals for direct engagement by the GCC bloc, preferring instead to work through its ally Pakistan and the Organisation of Islamic Cooperation (OIC).[33] Riyadh's risk aversion has yet to yield clear returns. For instance, Saudi-backed efforts at the OIC to persuade the Taliban to relax its restrictions on female education on religious grounds have fallen flat.[34] It is possible that the Taliban perceives Saudi Arabia as too closely wedded to Pakistan. Pakistan's relations with Taliban-ruled Afghanistan hit a low as Islamabad embarked in October 2023 on a campaign to deport hundreds of thousands of undocumented Afghans.[35] Cross-border ISKP attacks launched from Afghanistan and the growing involvement of Afghan nationals in Tehrik-e Taliban Pakistan (TTP) attacks in Pakistan have also inflamed relations between Islamabad and Kabul, prompting border incursions by Pakistani troops.[36]

While Saudi Arabia, along with the UAE and Qatar, was an observer in the Moscow Format Consultations on Afghanistan, it remains locked out of other regional forums, including the India-led Delhi Regional Security Dialogue on Afghanistan and the Shanghai Cooperation Organisation's Afghanistan contact group.[37] The Saudis have not publicly enunciated the measures that the Taliban would have to take to secure its recognition, in effect following the lead of Western nations, notably the United States.

*   *   *

By engaging the Taliban at a relatively early stage of its resumed rule, the UAE and Qatar are seeking a first-mover advantage in pursuing their long-term security and geo-economic interests there. By contrast, Saudi Arabia is held back by the memory of the reputational damage it suffered in the aftermath of 9/11 and subsequent efforts to shed its legacy as the global protector of Islamist causes.[38] Whereas Saudi Arabia runs the risk of being overtaken by its regional competitors in the contest for influence in Afghanistan and Central Asia, the UAE and Qatar court the obverse risk of prematurely committing to the Taliban when its security and governance challenges remain unresolved. Lately, the Gulf Arab states' attempts to align their foreign and security policies on key issues have been generally dismal. Afghanistan is no exception. Their recently released shared vision for regional security – their latest effort to bridge differences – makes no mention of Afghanistan, implying that closer coordination of their respective approaches to dealing with the Taliban remains unlikely.[39]

Notes

1   Email to the authors from former Saudi Ambassador to Pakistan Dr Ali Awadh Asseri, 20 August 2023.

2   See 'Saudi Halts Mediation Between Taliban & Afghan Govt', Alarabiya News, 6 November 2010, https://english.alarabiya.net/articles/2010%2F11%2F06%2F125145.

3   See Carlotta Gall, 'Saudis Bankroll Taliban, Even as King Officially

Supports Afghan Government', *New York Times*, 6 December 2016, https://www.nytimes.com/2016/12/06/world/asia/saudi-arabia-afghanistan.html; Gretchen Peters, 'Haqqani Network Financing: The Evolution of an Industry', Combating Terrorism Center at West Point, July 2012, pp. 27–34, https://ctc.westpoint.edu/wp-content/uploads/2012/07/CTC_Haqqani_Network_Financing-Report__Final.pdf; Don Rassler, 'Multinational Mujahidin: The Haqqani Network Between South Asia and the Arabian Peninsula', in Christophe Jaffrelot and Laurence Louër (eds), *Pan-Islamic Connections: Transnational Networks Between South Asia and the Gulf* (London: C. Hurst & Co., 2017), p. 121; and 'US–UAE Further Cooperation to Disrupt Taliban Finance', 7 January 2010, released by WikiLeaks as Cable 10ABUDHABU9_a, https://www.wikileaks.org/plusd/cables/10ABUDHABI9_a.html.

4   See David D. Kirkpatrick, 'Persian Gulf Rivals Competed to Host Taliban, Leaked Emails Show', *New York Times*, 31 July 2017, https://www.nytimes.com/2017/07/31/world/middleeast/uae-qatar-taliban-emails.html.

5   See '360 Tonnes of Saudi Aid Arrives in Afghanistan from Pakistan', Middle East Monitor, 31 December 2021, https://www.middleeastmonitor.com/20211231-360-tonnes-of-saudi-aid-arrives-in-afghanistan-from-pakistan/; 'Saudi Arabia Sends Humanitarian Aid to Afghanistan', Al-Jazeera, 17 December 2021, https://www.aljazeera.com/news/2021/12/17/saudi-arabia-sends-humanitarian-aid-to-afghanistan;

and United Arab Emirates Ministry of Foreign Affairs, 'UAE Pledges AED184 Million in Humanitarian Support to Afghanistan', 13 September 2021, https://www.mofa.gov.ae/en/mediahub/news/2021/9/13/13-09-2021-uae-afghanistan.

6   See Saudi Fund for Development, 'Saudi Arabia Provides a USD 30 Million Grant to Support the Afghanistan Humanitarian Trust Fund', 9 June 2022, https://www.sfd.gov.sa/en/n316; and Ali Younes, 'UN Receives Hundreds of Millions in Pledges for Afghan Humanitarian Aid', *Arab News*, 13 September 2021, https://www.arabnews.com/node/1928126/world.

7   The move was made all the more significant by the fact that the UAE was the United Nations Security Council joint pen holder with Japan on Afghanistan. See 'Taliban Appoints New Head of Mission for Afghan Embassy in UAE', Afghanistan International, 27 October 2023, https://www.afintl.com/en/202310275319.

8   See Parwiz Karokhail, 'Afghan Taliban Attend Doha Maritime Conference to Increase Engagement with International Community', *Arab News*, 4 March 2024, https://www.arabnews.com/node/2470886/amp.

9   On NATO's watch, the amount of land in Afghanistan used for poppy cultivation almost tripled between 2002 and 2020. In under a year after the Taliban had announced a ban on cultivating opium poppies in 2022, cultivation dropped by 95%. See United Nations Office on Drugs and Crime, 'Drug Situation in Afghanistan 2021', November 2021, https://www.unodc.

org/documents/data-and-analysis/
Afghanistan/Afghanistan_brief_
Nov_2021.pdf.

10   Authors' interview with senior Gulf
     official, 19 July 2022.

11   *Ibid.*; and authors' interview with
     former senior Pakistani official, 18
     September 2022.

12   See IISS, *Iran's Networks of Influence
     in the Middle East* (London: IISS,
     2019), pp. 103–6, https://www.
     iiss.org/globalassets/media-
     library---content--migration/
     files/publications---free-files/
     strategic-dossier/iran-dossier/irans-
     networks-of-influence-in-the-middle-
     east.pdf.

13   'In fact, as the normalisation of diplo-
     matic relations between Saudi Arabia
     and Iran progressively evolves in
     meaningful political and economic
     cooperation, we expect greater
     Saudi–Iranian policy coordination in
     stabilising the humanitarian situation
     in Afghanistan.' Email to authors from
     former Saudi Ambassador to Pakistan
     Dr Ali Awadh Asseri.

14   See Michael Knights, 'The Current
     State of Al Qa'ida in Saudi Arabia',
     CTC Sentinel, September 2008,
     pp. 18–21, https://ctc.westpoint.
     edu/wp-content/uploads/2010/08/
     CTCSentinel-YemenSI-2009.pdf.

15   See ACLED, 'Al-Qaeda in the
     Arabian Peninsula', 6 April 2023,
     https://acleddata.com/2023/04/06/
     al-Qaeda-in-the-arabian-peninsula-
     sustained-resurgence-in-yemen-or-
     signs-of-further-decline/; Elisabeth
     Kendall, 'Death of AQAP Leader
     Shows the Group's Fragmentation
     – and Durability', PolicyWatch
     3263, Washington Institute for

Near East Policy, 14 February 2020,
https://www.washingtoninstitute.
org/policy-analysis/
death-aqap-leader-shows-groups-
fragmentation-and-durability; and
United Nations Security Council,
'Letter Dated 23 January 2024 from
the Chair of the Security Council
Committee Pursuant to Resolutions
1267 (1999), 1989 (2011) and 2253
(2015) Concerning Islamic State in Iraq
and the Levant (Da'esh), Al-Qaida
and Associated Individuals, Groups,
Undertakings and Entities Addressed
to the President of the Security
Council', S/2024/92, 29 January
2024, https://digitallibrary.un.org/
record/4035877/files/S_2024_92-EN.
pdf?ln=en.

16   See Jim Garamone, 'U.S. Drone Strike
     Kills al-Qaida Leader in Kabul', US
     Department of Defense, 2 August
     2022, https://www.defense.gov/News/
     News-Stories/Article/Article/3114362/
     us-drone-strike-kills-al-qaida-leader-
     in-kabul/. See also Bryce Loidolt,
     'How the al-Qaeda–Taliban Alliance
     Survived', *Survival*, vol. 64, no. 3,
     June–July 2022, pp. 133–52.

17   See, for example, Jerome Drevon,
     'The Al-Qaeda Chief's Death and Its
     Implications', International Crisis
     Group, 9 August 2022, https://www.
     crisisgroup.org/asia/south-asia/
     afghanistan/al-qaeda-chiefs-death-
     and-its-implications.

18   See United Nations Security Council,
     'Letter Dated 23 January 2024 from
     the Chair of the Security Council
     Committee Pursuant to Resolutions
     1267 (1999), 1989 (2011) And 2253
     (2015) Concerning Islamic State in Iraq
     and the Levant (Da'esh), Al-Qaida

and Associated Individuals, Groups, Undertakings and Entities Addressed to the President of the Security Council'.

19   See Observatory of Economic Complexity, 'Afghanistan Country Profile', https://oec.world/en/profile/country/afg.

20   See 'Afghanistan Investment Conference in Dubai', *Gulf News*, 26 November 2010, https://gulfnews.com/business/afghanistan-investment-conference-in-dubai-1.718743; and Afghanistan Chamber of Commerce and Industries, '11th Business Match Making Conference', 8 December 2015, https://acci.org.af/en/media/booklets/11th%20Match%20Making%20Booklet%202015.pdf. Following the Taliban's downfall in 2001, Dubai's lucrative real-estate sector become a preferred destination for powerful, wealthy Afghans to park funds. The Kabul Bank scandal which erupted in 2010 unravelled a network of *hawalas* (informal financial intermediaries) and banks that Afghanistan's political elite used to embezzle and launder money, much of which ended up in Dubai's real-estate sector. See Brian George, 'The Kabul to Dubai Pipeline: Lessons Learned from the Kabul Bank Scandal', Carnegie Endowment for International Peace, 7 July 2020, https://carnegieendowment.org/2020/07/07/kabul-to-dubai-pipeline-lessons-learned-from-kabul-bank-scandal-pub-82189; and Hadeel al Sayegh, 'Kabul Bank to Auction Villas on Palm Jumeirah in Dubai', National News, 11 November 2012, https://www.thenationalnews.com/business/kabul-bank-to-auction-villas-on-palm-jumeirah-in-dubai-1.411559.

21   See Emirates Telecommunications Group Company PJSC, 'e& Capital Markets Day 2023', 7 March 2023, https://www.eand.com/content/dam/eand/en/system/docs/financial-quarterly-presentations/2022/etisalat-group-capital-markets-day-2022.pdf; 'Parallel Wireless Announces Partnership with Etisalat to Deliver Central Asia's First O-RAN Implementation in Afghanistan', PR Newswire, 7 April 2021, https://www.prnewswire.com/news-releases/parallel-wireless-announces-partnership-with-etisalat-to-deliver-central-asias-first-o-ran-implementation-in-afghanistan-301262236.html; and Alkesh Sharma, 'Afghan Telecom Relying on Etisalat to Grow Market Share', National News, 26 September 2018, https://www.thenationalnews.com/business/technology/afghan-telecom-relying-on-etisalat-to-grow-market-share-1.774119.

22   See Mohammad Yunus Yawar, 'Taliban to Sign Contract with UAE's GAAC Holding over Airspace Control at Afghan Airports', Reuters, 8 September 2022, https://www.reuters.com/world/asia-pacific/taliban-sign-contract-with-uaes-gaac-holding-over-airspace-control-afghan-2022-09-08/; and 'Taliban in Talks with Qatar, Turkey to Manage Kabul Airport', Al-Jazeera, 31 August 2021, https://www.aljazeera.com/economy/2021/8/31/taliban-in-talks-with-qatar-turkey-to-manage-kabul-airport.

23   See Air Arabia, 'Air Arabia Launches Daily Flights Connecting

Sharjah to Kabul', 27 December 2023, https://press.airarabia.com/air-arabia-launches-daily-flights-connecting-sharjah-to-kabul/; and 'Flydubai Becomes First International Carrier to Resume Kabul Flights', France24, 12 October 2023, https://www.france24.com/en/live-news/20231012-flydubai-becomes-first-international-carrier-to-resume-kabul-flights.

24 See 'UAE, Turkmenistan Issue Joint Statement Marking Visit of Chairman of People's Council of Turkmenistan to UAE', Emirates News Agency, 13 February 2023, https://wam.ae/en/details/1395303127665; and Syed Fazl-e-Haider, 'Revival of TAPI Pipeline Project Brings Serious Geopolitical Implications for Russia', Jamestown Foundation, 6 June 2023, https://jamestown.org/program/revival-of-tapi-pipeline-project-brings-serious-geopolitical-implications-for-russia/.

25 See Khurshid Ahmed, 'Progress on Saudi Aramco Oil Refinery Project Within Two Months – Pakistan Energy Minister', Arab News Pakistan, 15 November 2023, https://www.arabnews.pk/node/2409156/pakistan; and Asif Shahzad, 'Riyadh Eyes Significant Investment in Pakistan, Saudi FM Says', Reuters, 16 April 2024, https://www.reuters.com/business/riyadh-eyes-significant-investment-pakistan-saudi-fm-says-2024-04-16/.

26 See Gulf Cooperation Council, 'Joint Statement Second GCC–Central Asian Ministerial Meeting on Strategic Dialogue', 15 April 2024, https://www.gcc-sg.org/en-us/MediaCenter/NewsCooperation/News/Pages/news2024-4-15-2.aspx.

27 See Amin Ahmed, 'Trans-Afghan Railway to Connect Uzbekistan with Pakistan', Dawn, 18 July 2023, https://www.dawn.com/news/1765398; 'MoU Signed for Start of Trans-Afghan Railway Feasibility Studies', Ariana News, 20 February 2024, https://www.ariananews.af/mou-signed-for-start-of-trans-afghan-railway-feasibility-studies/; Kakar, 'Afghanistan, UAE & Uzbekistan Talk Railroad Project', Pajhok Afghan News, 24 September 2023, https://pajhwok.com/2023/09/24/afghanistan-uae-uzbekistan-talk-railroad-project/; 'Qatar Asked to Assist Uzbekistan with Trans-Afghan Railway', Tolo News, 21 December 2023, https://tolonews.com/business-186590; Republic of Uzbekistan's Ministry of Transport, 'Transafg'on temir yo'li qurilishi loyihasi muhokama etildi' [The project of construction of Trans-Afghan Railway was discussed], 7 February 2024, https://mintrans.uz/news/transafg-on-temir-yo-li-qurilishi-loyihasi-muhokama-etildi; and 'UAE and Uzbekistan Engaged for Railway Network in Afghanistan', Salam Watandar, 25 September 2023, https://swn.af/en/2023/09/uae-and-uzbekistan-engaged-for-railway-network-in-afghansitan/.

28 See Mohammad Yunus Yawar, 'Taliban Seeks Economic Self-sufficiency and Foreign Investment for Afghanistan, Minister Says', Reuters, 3 January 2023, https://www.reuters.com/world/asia-pacific/taliban-seeks-economic-self-sufficiency-foreign-investment-afghanistan-minister-2023-01-02/. See also 'Int'l Conference on Afghanistan's

Economic Development Kicks Off in Kabul', English News, 6 November 2023, https://english.news.cn/202311 06/53897a707d5f4a94844948cfcdc55f6 3/c.html.

29   See Akmal Dawi, 'Afghan Oil Production Jumps with $49 Million Chinese Investment', VOA News, 6 February 2024, https://www.voanews.com/a/ afghan-oil-production-jumps-with-49-million-chinese-investment-/7473728. html; Ayaz Gul, 'Taliban Sign Multibillion-dollar Afghan Mining Deals', VOA News, 31 August 2023, https://www.voanews.com/a/ taliban-sign-multibillion-dollar-afghan-mining-deals/7249135.html; and 'Taliban Sets Up Investment Consortium with Firms from Russia, Iran', Reuters, 22 February 2023, https://www.reuters.com/ world/middle-east/taliban-sets-up-investment-consortium-with-firms-russia-iran-2023-02-22/.

30   The Security Council has passed several resolutions imposing and amending sanctions against the Taliban, including resolutions 1267 (1999), 1988 (2011) and 2082 (2012) among others. For a comprehensive list of Security Council resolutions on Afghanistan and the Taliban, see Security Council Report, 'UN Documents for Afghanistan: Security Council Resolutions', https://www.securitycouncilreport. org/un_documents_type/security-council-resolutions/page/1?ctype=Af ghanistan&cbtype=afghanistan#038;c btype=afghanistan.

31   The Security Council did not extend travel exemptions for Taliban officials in August 2022, over the objections of China and Russia. 'UN Ends Taliban Travel Ban Exemptions', DW, 20 August 2022, https://www.dw.com/ en/un-fails-to-reach-deal-to-extend-taliban-travel-ban-exemptions/ a-62873851.

32   See Antonio Giustozzi, 'The Islamic State in Khorasan Between Taliban Counter-terrorism and Resurgence Prospects', International Centre for Counter-terrorism, 30 January 2024, https://www.icct.nl/publication/ islamic-state-khorasan-between-taliban-counter-terrorism-and-resurgence-prospects.

33   According to a senior Gulf official interviewed by the authors, Saudi Arabia opposed Qatar's push for direct GCC engagement of the Taliban and insisted on engaging the group through the OIC instead. Authors' interview with senior Gulf official, 19 July 2022. See also State of Qatar's Ministry of Foreign Affairs, 'GCC Representatives Meet De Facto Afghan Authorities in Doha', 14 February 2022, https:// mofa.gov.qa/en/qatar/latest-articles/ latest-news/details/1443/07/13/ gcc-representatives-meet-de-facto-afghan-authorities-in-doha; Organisation of Islamic Cooperation, 'CFM in Islamabad Is the Second "Ministerial Meeting" to Promote OIC Efforts in Afghanistan', 20 March 2022, https://www.oic-oci.org/topic/?t_ id=33896&t_ref=22671&lan=en; and 'Pakistan Thanks Saudi Arabia for Helping Convene OIC's Emergency Meeting on Afghanistan', Arab News, 17 December 2021, https://www. arabnews.com/node/1915856/pakistan.

34 See Organisation of Islamic
Cooperation, 'A Delegation of Muslim
Scholars Begins a Visit to Afghanistan
and Meets the Foreign Minister and
Afghanistan Scholars', 1 September
2023, https://www.oic-oci.org/topic/?t_
id=39446&t_ref=26590&lan=en;
'Muslim Scholars Delegation to
Afghanistan Continues Meetings with
Afghan Officials', 9 April 2023, https://
www.oic-oci.org/topic/ampg.asp?t_
id=39461&t_ref=26595&lan=en; and
International Islamic Fiqh Academy,
'Ummah Delegation Concludes Visit
by Meeting Afghan Minister of Higher
Education', 6 September 2023, https://
iifa-aifi.org/en/45303.html.

35 See 'Taliban Urges Pakistan & Iran
to Stop Forced Deportations of
Afghans', Afghanistan International,
1 November 2023, https://www.
afintl.com/en/202311011990; and
'Why Is Pakistan Deporting Over
a Million Undocumented Afghan
Immigrants?', Reuters, 2 November
2023, https://www.reuters.com/world/
asia-pacific/pakistans-plan-expel-over-
1-million-afghans-living-country-
illegally-2023-10-31/.

36 Abid Hussain, 'Taliban's Ties with
Pakistan Fraying amid Mounting
Security Concerns', Al-Jazeera,
17 August 2023, https://www.
aljazeera.com/news/2023/8/17/
talibans-ties-with-pakistan-fraying-

amid-mounting-security-concerns;
and 'Pakistan–Taliban Attacks
Updates: Exchange of Fire at Border
After 8 Killed', Al-Jazeera, 18 March
2024, https://www.aljazeera.com/
news/liveblog/2024/3/18/pakistan-
taliban-attacks-live-exchange-of-fire-
at-border-after-8-killed.

37 See Ministry of Foreign Affairs of the
Russian Federation, 'Press Release on
the Moscow Format Consultations
on Afghanistan', 16 November 2022,
https://mid.ru/en/foreign_policy/
news/1838964; and Ministry of Foreign
Affairs of the Russian Federation,
'Press Release on a Meeting of the
Moscow Format of Consultations
on Afghanistan Held in Kazan', 29
September 2023, https://mid.ru/en/
foreign_policy/news/1907018/.

38 Authors' interviews with two former
senior Afghan and Pakistani officials,
17–18 September 2022.

39 See Gulf Cooperation Council,
'Gulf Cooperation Council Vision
for Regional Security', 2024, https://
gcc-sg.org/ar-sa/CognitiveSources/
DigitalLibrary/Lists/DigitalLibrary/%D
8%A7%D9%84%D8%B4%D8%A4%D9
%88%D9%86%20%D8%A7%D9%84%
D8%B3%D9%8A%D8%A7%D8%B3%
D9%8A%D8%A9%20%D9%88%D8%
A7%D9%84%D9%85%D9%81%D8%A
7%D9%88%D8%B6%D8%A7%D8%AA/
GCCPOL%20EE.pdf.

Changing the Way We Think About Europe

Erik Jones

The Origins of European Integration: The Pre-history of Today's European Union, 1937–1951
Mathieu Segers. Cambridge: Cambridge University Press, 2023.
£22.99. 244 pp.

Mathieu Segers wanted to change the way we think about Europe. Specifically, he wanted to explain why Europeans define their common project in terms of shared values rather than something more concrete, like fixed geographic boundaries. He wanted to explain how this notion of Europe came together in reaction to the Americanisation of the world economy during the years immediately following the Second World War. And he wanted to shed light on how this value-centred, non-American European project came to focus on the creation of a mixed economy that consisted not just of market elements and welfare-state institutions, but also of a healthy dose of planning. Segers argued that the planning element is particularly important, both for understanding Europe's past and for anticipating its future. 'The European Republic of Planning', Segers believed, 'remains at the epicentre of the struggle for survival of the free world, as a powerhouse for peace in European history and a source of learning' (p. 209).

Erik Jones is director of the Robert Schuman Centre for Advanced Studies at the European University Institute.

Survival | vol. 66 no. 3 | June–July 2024 | pp. 159–166   https://doi.org/10.1080/00396338.2024.2357488

The sentences above are in the past tense because Segers tragically passed away on 16 December 2023 at the age of 47. He was an accomplished historian, university administrator and policy adviser who taught at the University of Maastricht. He was also a friend whose strong commitment to Europe and profound desire to make the world a better place was an inspiration to many of us. His vision of Europe resonates closely with the themes set out in the speech on Europe given by French President Emmanuel Macron at the Sorbonne on 25 April 2024.[1] Repeatedly in that speech, Macron called for a paradigm shift in thinking about Europe, advocating for greater

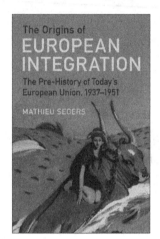

emphasis on European power, prosperity and humanism. Like Segers, Macron stressed the importance of planning – for defence, industry, trade, agriculture and finance. Such planning is essential for the preservation of Europe's mixed economies, because only through planning can Europe resist destructive forms of market competition and so protect the ability of Europeans to produce the value-added that can be used for redistribution. Also, like Segers, Macron emphasised the importance of shared values as the glue that binds Europeans together and as the purpose for their collective action. Being European is not about where a person lives, Macron argued, 'it is to defend a certain idea of humanity which places the free, rational and enlightened individual above all else'.[2]

The paradigm shift Macron is calling for is not a new vision of Europe. In many ways, it is a reprise of the original vision Segers identified that inspired the European project. That similarity stems from the wider context. Then as now, Europeans faced overlapping threats, both foreign and domestic. They also needed to re-engineer their economies in a fiercely competitive global environment. They could only succeed by finding some formula for working together in the absence of the United Kingdom and without relying too heavily on the United States. The formula they found lay in an 'ideology of non-ideology' that focused on the development of 'practical policy solutions' to 'deep seated problems' that no national government could address in isolation (p. 112). That formula also constituted a rejection of 'unification' as in a 'United States of Europe' in favour of 'integration', which worked better because 'nobody knows what it means' (p. 177). That remains true today. As Macron explained, 'Europe is an unending conversation' because there is an aspect of 'ambiguity' around it. 'The time has come', Macron suggested, 'for Europe to ask itself what it intends to become'.[3]

Plus ça change

Segers makes the fascinating point in his account of the pre-history of European integration that 'Europe' was not the first choice for most Europeans. Instead, they were beguiled by the example of America and the prospect of forging an Atlantic partnership within a wider global economy. Moreover, it was the Americans who pushed the Europeans to engage in planning (p. 21). Most prominent European economists were more interested in promoting free markets and market competition. They embraced a strongly liberal world view and saw state intervention as both inefficient and destructive (p. 192). By contrast, the Americans focused on the success they'd had organising a wartime economy. They also worried that European economic performance would not improve quickly enough to stave off social unrest.

'Europe' and 'planning' came together when the US government realised that it would need to bankroll European reconstruction with the Marshall Plan. This realisation dawned as the threat from the Soviet Union grew to overlap with the threat of domestic political instability. American policymakers recognised that European governments would need to coordinate their reconstruction efforts if they were to avoid wasteful and destructive competition among them. They also recognised that such coordination could not take place via the United Nations Economic Commission for Europe because of the Soviet Union's influence over that organisation. So, they pushed for coordination to take place via the Organisation for European Economic Cooperation (OEEC) instead (pp. 136–7).

According to Segers, this change of venue represented a decisive shift in emphasis from the global to the regional. Moreover, it coincided with the breakdown of talks over the creation of an International Trade Organization (ITO). Worse, the US government was responsible for the ITO's failure. By implication, any prospect for forming an Atlantic partnership in a wider global economy was diminished, because the United States preferred to act on its own. This left the Europeans little choice but to focus on finding a European solution to the challenge of planning for their own reconstruction in a manner that would avoid destructive competition (pp. 137–8).

Segers believed that the first concrete step in forging a European solution lay in the creation of the European Payments Union – a multilateral clearing house for dollar-denominated deficits and surpluses on the balance of payments (pp. 202–3). European governments needed such an arrangement because their bilateral relationships with the United States were uneven and hard to manage, and because each country preferred to export to the US (which paid in dollars) rather than trade with other European countries (which tried desperately to hold on to their dollar reserves).

The great strength of this arrangement was that it brought West Germany into the fold. West Germany was one of Europe's largest economies and so offered an important market for firms from other countries. Another strength was that it left out the British, who sought to manage the relationship between the dollar and the pound sterling on their own terms. The British proved to be problematic partners in the OEEC, and in many ways prevented it from functioning efficiently. Their absence from the European Payments Union made that organisation more effective in balancing West German balance-of-payments surpluses and deficits in other countries, notably France (pp. 179–84).

The inclusion of West Germany in 'Europe' as a regional project set the stage for the first major initiative aimed at Franco-German reconciliation – the European Coal and Steel Community that French foreign minister Robert Schuman proposed on 9 May 1950. It also marked a sharp break with the rival, British conception of Western Union that Ernest Bevin hoped to build on the back of the 1948 Brussels Treaty, which was a collective-security agreement between Britain, France and the Benelux countries against the threat of German remilitarisation (pp. 154–7). Segers used the existence of this British alternative to underscore that there was nothing inevitable about the 'Europe' that emerged from the early post-war period. Still, there was something functional about the post-war vision – at least insofar as Europe could never be prosperous without a vibrant West German economy, and West Germany could never be trusted (even by the Germans) so soon after the Second World War without a robust European arrangement to contain it.

These elements appear again in Macron's argument. Europeans may prefer to live in a global economy governed by strong multilateral institutions, but that option is no longer on the table. China and the United States have changed the 'rules of the game'.[4] Within this new environment, Europeans will have to pull themselves together, including France and Germany. They will have to plan for their industrial future and pay particular attention to how they conduct trade with the outside world. The efficient use of capital will also be important. This will involve more than just improvements in the way savings translate into investments within Europe's Capital Markets Union, which is the framework of rules that make it easier for money to move across national borders within the European Union. Macron insists more could be done on that front, but it will not be enough. Instead, European countries will have to focus on raising funds with the issuance of common debt – as they did in response to the pandemic – to pay for 'important projects of common European interest' and to deliver a new 'shock of common investment'.[5] The question is how to rally the necessary political support.

European ecumenism

The challenge for Macron is to tell the story of Europe in a way that will attract people's attention at this 'decisive moment' in the history of the continent. Unfortunately, so many others offer competing narratives about the disappearance of national identities and the threats posed by European institutions. 'Our Europe could die', Macron warned, 'through a kind of historical sleight of hand'.[6]

The competing narratives at the end of the Second World War were if anything more pernicious because they centred on the horrific violence done by Europeans to one another. Hence the challenge for policymakers was to find some way to frame the existence of a common 'European' identity or purpose. Segers found the solution in the actions of the ecumenical World Council of Churches and their political allies in the Christian Democratic parties. Importantly, these voices existed on both sides of the Atlantic, and many, like Reinhold Niebuhr and John Foster Dulles, had significant influence in the US government (pp. 88–93). Hence, they were able to shape both the narrative of Europe and the policies that flowed from it. The mixed or social-market economy is a natural outgrowth of this influence, softening the edges of German liberal thought by adding concern for social protection.

Segers underscored the role of Christian churches, both Catholic and Protestant, but the Christianity they promoted is hard to distinguish from what Macron identified as the characteristically European form of humanism. The reason for this lies in ecumenical activism. The World Council of Churches promoted human rights and respect for individual freedom together with a sense of social obligation and solidarity (p. 96). It also promoted democracy and the rule of law (p. 93). To the extent that the different churches identified these values as important shared commitments, they could also tell a story of what it means to be 'European' – a peaceful, aspirational story rather than a nihilistic and violent one. In this way, religion – in a soft, ecumenical form – offered not only an escape from nationalism, but also an alternative to other secular ideologies, such as communism or fascism (pp. 99–100).

Most important, this narrative of Europe could legitimate the project of reconciling France and Germany, and binding Germany to the West. As Segers explained, the appeal to common values as the essence of Europeanness 'combined realpolitik with an appeal to the zeitgeist' (p. 101). It captured the popular imagination, appealed to popular emotion, and then focused both elements on tackling the challenges to be faced.

Macron clearly hopes to do something similar. That is why he stated so often in his speech that Europe is mortal, and therefore can die. Europeans need to confront the fear and anger that comes in those shocking moments when they sense that they could disappear. 'The response', Macron insisted, lies 'not in timidity, but in audacity'.[7] Europeans must choose their future. To do so, they need to understand what is at stake. Europe is the values that define Europeans. That realisation is an essential part of the pre-history of today's EU, as Segers argued. The EU only exists because Europeans recognised its value and theirs.

Now Europeans face a challenge as great as the one they confronted at the end of the Second World War. That challenge is not just to strengthen the existing EU. Macron made clear toward the beginning of his speech that the Russian war against Ukraine has forced Europeans 'to reconsider [their] geography in the limits of their neighbourhood' and to affirm that 'Ukraine and Moldova are part of the European family', as are 'the countries of the Western Balkans'.[8] The EU must respond by ensuring those countries are anchored to Europe, supporting them in making the necessary reforms, and working in parallel to prepare the Union to receive them.[9] This challenge is fundamental to what Europe means for Europeans. As Segers explains in the last sentence of his book: 'The present times confront this Europe with the test of inclusiveness, the promise that is at the very heart of the ideas and programme on which the Europe of European integration has been built' (p. 215).

Notes

[1] Emmanuel Macron, 'Discours du Président de la Republique sur l'Europe à la Sorbonne', Élysée, 25 April 2024, https://www.elysee.fr/front/pdf/elysee-module-22625-fr.pdf.

[2] *Ibid.*, p. 17.

[3] *Ibid.*, p. 21.

[4] *Ibid.*, p. 4.

[5] *Ibid.*, pp. 12, 16.

[6] *Ibid.*, p. 21.

[7] *Ibid.*, p. 21.

[8] *Ibid.*, p. 3.

[9] This is a very close paraphrase of Macron's original text. *Ibid.*, p. 3.

Review Essay

The Western Forces' March to the Sea

Jonathan Stevenson

Civil War (American–British film)
Alex Garland, director and writer. Distributed by A24 (United States) and Entertainment Film Distributors (United Kingdom), 2024.

Civil War is a beautifully shot and stealthily clever film. For the most part, it is a well-acted one, featuring a superb Kirsten Dunst as stoic photojournalist Lee Smith, a scarred and noble legend, though marred slightly by Wagner Moura's woefully broad caricature of an adrenalised war correspondent. The movie is perhaps too contrived and schematic to be great cinema. But it remains a timely and suitably jarring public-service announcement and a kind of strategic warning about an American political outcome that is no longer beyond imagining.

Historical credibility

In combat action close and pounding enough to be merciless but so succinct as to avoid gratuitousness, the film illuminates the brutality and gore that large-scale civil breakdown could eventually produce. Writer-director Alex Garland, who is British, is keenly attuned to the singular value of a government that honours and enforces the rule of law in terms of ensuring stability,

Jonathan Stevenson is an IISS Senior Fellow and Managing Editor of *Survival*.

Survival | vol. 66 no. 3 | June–July 2024 | pp. 167–174   https://doi.org/10.1080/00396338.2024.2357489

safety and a baseline morality. In his United States, the Constitution has been comprehensively suspended, the government and rebels alike resort to summary execution, the main forces have discarded the laws of armed conflict and the Geneva Convention, and marginal players torture and kill their enemies in their backyards with impunity.

As for the general credibility of these phenomena, consider the century spanning the end of the American Civil War in 1865 to the 1960s, when legal authorities tolerated the Ku Klux Klan and other white supremacists, who lynched more than 6,000 people, mainly African Americans.[1] These

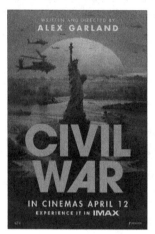

atrocities were validated in the popular culture of my grandparents and parents – for example, in D.W. Griffith's acclaimed 1915 silent film *The Birth of a Nation*, which glorified the Klan's campaign of terror during Reconstruction, and Victor Fleming's 1939 movie *Gone with the Wind*, which promulgated the 'lost cause of the Confederacy' myth of Southern rectitude and gentility and, adjusted for inflation, remains the highest-grossing film in history.

Historians and social critics such as Jamelle Bouie have pointed out that the current age of Donald Trump is actually an era of less political violence than many periods in American history. Yet Bouie is hardly complacent about future consequences of the ongoing, acrimonious unravelling of American comity. In a recent *New York Times* podcast, he commented: 'I do think that there are reasons to worry about the near future of American politics and the integrity of constitutional government in this country.'[2] If constitutional government were dissolved, many untoward things could happen, and not just those that are easiest to conceive, or film.

In its incidental particulars, *Civil War* broadly observes both historical and cinematic precedent. Quite sensibly, the conflict's epicentre is the northeast and mid-Atlantic region, and its strategic focal point Washington DC. Some citizens in areas off the beaten track of warfare opt for blinkered neutrality, treating nearby fighting as a transient inconvenience. Entire states – Colorado and Missouri are mentioned by name – avoid open hostilities.

Still others form alternative coalitions, one led by Florida. But the fabric and infrastructure of the entire country are denatured. Hyperinflation kicks in, à la Weimar Germany and conflict-ridden post-Cold War Yugoslavia, making the Canadian dollar the currency of choice. Electricity is sporadic and rationed, Teslas are stranded. Gasoline is a precious commodity lethally guarded, as in *The Road Warrior*.

Garland likewise thrusts the audience right in scene, choosing not to articulate precisely why or how the civil war, under way for several years, might have arisen. The root 'why' is presumed to be understood by audiences who have watched bedrock norms of political civility trashed in a toxically divided America.[3] The side that has done most of the trashing, moreover, has access to an abundant and effectively unregulated domestic weapons bazaar. American liberals have lamented that it is mainly one side of the current divide that possesses these weapons, but in the event of a real breakdown, reciprocal stockpiling on the part of adversary resistance groups would only be logical.

The 'how' is at least not utterly opaque. Local pockets of unrest could coalesce into geographically larger occupations, enabled by partisan or acquiescent law-enforcement personnel, which become more prevalent as societies fracture. Substantial lawlessness, including ethnic cleansing – a bilious taste of which Jesse Plemons provides as a terrifyingly placid and resolutely nativist mass murderer – would take hold. The grassroots surge could in turn galvanise increasingly formal and operational coordination up the chain of government to the state level, such that states themselves could form rebellious coalitions. This is the rough arc of many civil wars. The path to conflict could also entail more top-down dynamics, such as contested secession, as the American Civil War did.[4] Violent usurpation, especially in a country where democracy was once entrenched, would likely give rise, eventually, to counter-revolution.

Political and military plausibility

Garland has reasons in addition to knowing presumption and dramatic tension for eschewing ideological exposition. Initially, he keeps the political dispositions of the respective combatants unclear. Everyone commits atrocities, and each main side boasts mixed ethnicity. The narrative approach, it seems, is to jolt viewers of all partisan stripes with the shock of civil war's undiscriminating perilousness and depravity – universalising the tragedy of war – before alienating anyone through narrative judgement. If so, it works well.

In an exquisitely enigmatic scene at a ravaged rural spread decorated for Christmas even though it's summer, journalists under vicious sniper fire from a hilltop take cover with two fighters who are trying to get a bead on their enemy. When one of the reporters tries to ascertain the affiliations of the combatants, a sarcastic spotter elides the question and wryly observes that the gunman is trying to kill them, so they are looking to kill him. The patter suggests both the mutual ignorance that presumably caused the war and the irrelevance of politics to those merely seeking to survive under fire. Thomas Hobbes meets Charles Darwin. The Christmas paraphernalia is at this point a cruel joke, signifying social and moral bearings now lost, a distant season. There do appear to be atheists in foxholes after all.

Good storytelling is the art of delay

Garland does eventually identify the sides, but good storytelling is the art of delay. The opening scene has the sitting president – an impressively subtle Nick Offerman – rehearsing a purported victory speech that, it becomes clear, is utterly at odds with facts on the ground. The Secret Service, it transpires, has been executing journalists on the South Lawn of the White House. The administration has disbanded the FBI, the main muscle in our real world of Trumpists' despised 'deep state'. Black soldiers hold command positions in the main rebel army, which welcomes embedded reporters. And, in the end, the president proves to be a craven narcissist happy to sacrifice underlings to save himself. Now we know.

Garland thus leaps forward along the standard timeline, and – insofar as the future-civil-war genre is predominantly an inspirational vehicle of the far right[5] – subverts informed expectations. While it may be tempting to label this a cop-out, the deeper read is that Garland is thinking more strategically than others, credibly extending the familiar scenario farther out to show just how hard it is to contain abject chaos once it breaks out and how elusive victory is for anyone. As the *New York Times*'s Manohla Dargis put it: 'The very premise of Garland's movie means that – no matter what happens when or if Lee and the rest reach Washington – a happy ending is impossible, which makes this very tough going.'[6] As it should be.

Whereas the 6 January 2021 insurrection has tended to prompt public discussion contemplating a rebellion by MAGA Trump supporters against a Democratic government, in the movie's world, that rebellion has been provisionally successful. The president faces a counter-rebellion by the so-called Western Forces – an alliance between California and Texas, which appear to be essentially centrist insurgents. The two states are, of course, iconic near-opposites on the American political spectrum, and many have noted that they would be very strange political bedfellows.[7] Yet the plot device, however counter-intuitive, seems improbably credible. California and Texas actually do have the two largest separatist movements in the United States.[8] It isn't terribly far-fetched to imagine that maximal Trumpism could awaken Texans to the folly of supporting a populist, nativist autocrat and move the state – perhaps having first seceded on its own, given its peculiar history – to form an alliance of necessity with the nation's other pre-eminently powerful and well-resourced state. Beneath Texas's gerrymandered red legislative top cover, it is complicatedly purple.[9] Faced with the federal government's violent seizure of dictatorial power, a state's dominant ideology might well yield to more fundamental concerns about the future of the country.

Garland indulges a sense of historical mischief in portraying the Western Forces staging from Charlottesville – site of the lethal 'Unite the Right' rally in 2017 that Trump notoriously sanitised – to take Washington when Robert E. Lee's Army of Northern Virginia never could. It may seem dubious that the Western Forces could vanquish the US armed forces, but on this, too, Garland is cagey and, on balance, sussed. He makes it clear that the group has ample heavy military equipment, including high-end aircraft and main battle tanks. It is thoroughly trained if ruthless, and strategically as well as tactically duly schooled in the operational art. The Western Forces are not remotely a ragtag guerrilla insurgency, but rather operate like a sophisticated and highly motivated professional state military force, complete with full web gear and 'WF' patches neatly stitched onto their camo uniforms.

The film strongly suggests that the Western Forces have absorbed the bulk of US military personnel and kit. It's certainly plausible. WF leaders might indeed be able to secure most of the US military assets housed in California and Texas, which are considerable. California hosts more than 40 US military installations, more than any other state, and Texas is a close third (after Virginia) with almost 30.[10] Notwithstanding the slightly disproportionate membership of veterans and serving military in the right-wing groups involved in 6 January, the WF could well gain the loyalty of many if not most active US military personnel who, in the end, might align with the side they considered the most faithful to the US Constitution.[11]

*   *   *

It's well-nigh impossible for a sentient American to watch *Civil War* without considering how Garland's provisionally fictional conflict resonates with the American Civil War. In 1865, the southeastern United States was devastated, lanced and shredded by Union General William Tecumseh Sherman's pitiless 'March to the Sea'. He believed in total war, which meant war as terror, waged not only to militarily subdue opposing forces but also to break the political will of the people who supported them. He took 'war is hell', the quip he made famous, dead seriously, and Garland takes it to heart. On the screen, Washington burns as Atlanta did, and the Western Forces are less forgiving of the enemy head of state than Abraham Lincoln was of Confederacy president Jefferson Davis. In the moment, the vengefulness will be gratifying to some. And the March to the Sea requited much of the United States' Northern population. But, in the South, it also conditioned the deep resentment that fuelled the lost-cause myth and prompted the government's acceptance of Jim Crow as the quid pro quo for Southern quiescence and loyalty.[12]

How'd that go? As 150-plus years of post-slavery racial injustice and the very marketability of *Civil War* – as of 7 May 2024, it was the year's eighth-highest-grossing film in North America[13] – attest, not so well. Garland is not, of course, endorsing civil war or its lethal vindictiveness. Rather, he is thinking the unthinkable out loud in hopes of motivating people to avoid it, much as Stanley Kubrick made *Dr. Strangelove* and Sidney Lumet made *Fail Safe* to entrench the moral compulsion to avert nuclear war in the early 1960s, and Christopher Nolan revived the effort with *Oppenheimer* last year.[14] This admonitory imperative may be one reason that, in certain parts of the film, the tail of journalistic commitment, integrity and ambition wags the dog of civil war, especially towards the end. Metaphorically, Garland seems to be urging Americans that their participation at some risk is required to thwart the dark forces that have benighted their country, and that blithe acquiescence in lies and demagoguery as mere jokes or natural incidents of politics on the view that American democracy is self-regulating is naively and dangerously sanguine.[15]

As vocational horror transforms Lee's protégé from inquisitive to impassioned, the elder journalist tries to calm her: 'We record so others can speak.' It's a calculatedly grudging and dispirited remark. At this crucial historical juncture, Garland suggests, that brand of passivity may not be enough. It seems he is looking to prepare the next generation for a protracted struggle even if it does not descend into full-blown civil war. Here *Civil War* dovetails nicely with the captivating television miniseries *Manhunt*, which unearths the fraught political background of Lincoln's assassination shortly after the American Civil War and chronicles secretary of war Edwin Stanton's iron-willed pursuit of John Wilkes Booth and his accomplices.[16] In the epilogue, four years have passed, political support for Reconstruction is collapsing and a fatefully frail Stanton has been confirmed as a Supreme Court justice. 'We finish the work now', he says, notionally to the deceased Lincoln. 'We have to.' Stanton died before he could don the robe.

Notes

1   See, for example, Equal Justice Initiative, 'Lynching in America: Confronting the Legacy of Racial Terror', 2017, https://eji.org/wp-content/uploads/2005/11/lynching-in-america-3d-ed-110121.pdf.

2   Jamelle Bouie, 'How Does Trump's Violent Rhetoric End?', *New York Times*, 26 April 2024, https://www.nytimes.com/2024/04/26/opinion/trump-political-violence-civil-war.html?showTranscript=1.

3   See Steven Simon and Jonathan Stevenson, 'These Disunited States', *New York Review of Books*, 22 September 2022, pp. 51–4.

4   See generally Barbara F. Walter, *How Civil Wars Start – and How to Stop Them* (New York: Crown, 2022), pp. 161–93.

5   See Stephen Marche, *The Next Civil War: Dispatches from the American Future* (New York: Avid Reader Press, 2022), pp. 21–3.

6   Manohla Dargis, '"Civil War" Review: We Have Met the Enemy and It Is Us. Again', *New York Times*, 11 April 2024 (updated 15 April 2024), https://www.nytimes.com/2024/04/11/movies/civil-war-review.html.

7   See, for example, Justin Chang, 'Snap Judgments', *New Yorker*, 22 and 29 April 2024, pp. 78–9; and Michelle Goldberg, '"Civil War" and Its Terrifying Premonition of American Collapse', *New York Times*, 12 April 2024, https://www.nytimes.com/2024/04/12/opinion/civil-war-movie.html.

8   See Walter, *How Civil Wars Start*, pp. 187–91, 201.

9   See, for instance, Lawrence Wright, 'America's Future Is Texas', *New Yorker*, 10 July 2017, https://www.newyorker.com/magazine/2017/07/10/americas-future-is-texas.

10   See 'Military Bases by State', https://www.militarybases.us/by-state/. A full analysis would have to field other critical issues – in particular, the status of ground-based nuclear forces – though it's a fair presumption that in a civil war on US soil, all combatants would be substantially self-deterred.

11   Stephen Marche speculates that 'soldiers would serve a constitutionally elected government whether they considered it legitimate or not', but he is thinking about right-wing soldiers facing a right-wing rebellion and thus underlining the same professionalism and constitutionalism that could induce soldiers serving a right-wing government they deemed illegitimate to turn against it. See Marche, *The Next Civil War*, p. 162.

12   See, for example, Jonathan (Yoni) Shimshoni, 'Swords and Emotions: The American Civil War and Society-centric Strategy', *Survival*, vol. 64, no. 2, April–May 2022, pp. 141–66.

13   The Numbers, 'Top 2024 Movies at the Domestic Box Office', https://www.the-numbers.com/box-office-records/domestic/all-movies/cumulative/released-in-2024.

14   The filmmaker thus answers an exhortation that Steven Simon and I lodged a couple of years ago. See Steven Simon and Jonathan Stevenson, 'We Need to Think the Unthinkable About Our Country', *New York Times*, 13 January 2022, https://www.nytimes.com/2022/01/13/opinion/january-6-civil-war.html. On *Oppenheimer*, see Jonathan Stevenson, 'Oppenheimer: The Man, the Movie and Nuclear Dread', *Survival*, vol. 65, no. 5, October–November 2023, pp. 153–60.

15   See Fintan O'Toole, 'Laugh Riot', *New York Review of Books*, 21 March 2024, pp. 51–4; and Jeffrey Toobin, 'Donald Trump Is Going to Get Someone Killed', *New York Times*, 23 October 2023, https://www.nytimes.com/2023/10/19/opinion/trump-gag-order-violence.html.

16   *Manhunt* (limited TV series), created and written by Monica Beletsky, directed by Carl Franklin, John Dahl and Eva Sørhaug, AppleTV+, 2024.

Book Reviews

Culture and Society
Jeffrey Mazo

How Data Happened: A History from the Age of Reason to the Age of Algorithms
Chris Wiggins and Matthew L. Jones. New York: W. W. Norton & Co., 2023. $30.00. 367 pp.

The declared aim of Chris Wiggins and Matthew Jones – the first a Columbia University professor of applied mathematics and chief data scientist for the *New York Times*, and the second a historian of science and technology at Princeton – is to provide 'an actionable understanding' (p. xiii) of the history of the role of data in rearranging corporate, state and popular power. By 'data' they do not mean a mere collection of facts or information; the term is shorthand for the algorithmic decision-making systems, driven by data in that mundane sense, that are so ubiquitous today.

Taking as their starting point the late eighteenth century, the authors first discuss the development of statistics as a tool of state-building, from knowledge as power to the invention of the 'average man' and the science of 'social physics'. In particular, they focus on the negative aspects, not out of any anti-data agenda but because such examples provide the best lessons, many of which are still to be learned. Thus, Wiggins and Jones cover biometrics, IQ testing, eugenics, scientific racism and classism, and other fraught topics. Part II covers the post-Second World War shift to large-scale digital data processing, the shifting, boom-and-bust quest for artificial intelligence (AI) in various forms, and tensions between state and popular power. In the concluding chapters, they discuss the further shift to big tech and related social and ethical issues. But this is not a reductionist approach; throughout they take pains to point out the deep

 https://doi.org/10.1080/00396338.2024.2357490

roots and myriad branches of the trends they discuss, and the overlaps and interconnections among them.

In their final chapter, Wiggins and Jones discuss how data in the broad sense can be kept, or made, compatible with democracy and a just and equitable society; in other words, why all this matters. This, they argue, will require a certain balance between corporate power, state power and people power. Both big tech and governments recognise the problems, and are not inherently opposed to power-sharing and ethical actions, but there are systemic barriers to unilateral action. However, both are made up of people, and people power can be harnessed both within and outside such institutions, even at boardroom or cabinet level. Still, the authors decline to make either predictions or specific proposals. 'The work will be granular', they say (p. 306). There are no quick fixes. 'It's likely to involve strange and sometimes cynical, even uncomfortable, alliances ... It takes decades for a technology to get integrated into society before it comports with our values and norms – if it does at all' (pp. 306–7).

Despite a necessary focus on the negative at times, *How Data Happened* is at its core an optimistic book. As Wiggins and Jones put it, 'a historical view makes the present strange, as it shatters the fallacy ... that technology causes social, economic and cultural transformation' (p. 306). These effects must be enabled by society writ large – by deliberate social decisions. A historically informed view like this one will make it easier to avoid repeating the past, or at least the more pessimistic predictions of the future of data. So much the better for us that Wiggins and Jones have given us such a clear and detailed grounding in that history.

Guardrails: Guiding Human Decisions in the Age of AI
Urs Gasser and Viktor Mayer-Schönberger. Princeton, NJ:
Princeton University Press, 2024. £22.00/$27.95. 240 pp.

With the recent boom – over the last decade or so – in AI research and applications based on neural networks and deep learning, AI is increasingly seen as either an impending problem or a panacea (or sometimes both). But such hopes and fears reflect the more general issue of how society structures itself. In *Guardrails,* two experts in governance and innovative technology use AI as a hook to explore this broader question. Guardrails are the external social forces shaping an individual's decision-making, from what information is available to the rules and norms that govern the selection of acceptable choices. They can range from formal rules and tools to institutional cultures and 'ways of thinking'. Urs Gasser and Viktor Mayer-Schönberger argue that modern society overemphasises narrow technological guardrails (including but not limited to

AI) at the expense of broader social ones. The problem, they say, is that 'the real issue is not the nature of the decision guardrails – whether they are technical or social – but the principles underlying their design' (p. 3). Good guardrails allow society, in their words, to split the difference between *Atlas Shrugged* and *1984*.

After setting the scene with a discussion of the emergence of internet governance in the 1990s, the authors explore three governance challenges which resisted or challenged traditional guardrails and provoked technical solutions: disinformation, misinformation and fake news; cognitive 'deformations' such as confirmation, recency and loss-aversion bias; and uncertainty, ambiguity and unpredictability. These led to such 'solutions' as AI-enabled screening of online posts, Russia's autonomous, computer-contolled *Perimetr* nuclear-launch system and blockchain-enabled 'smart contracts' – all of which give rise to problems of their own. The authors' analysis of these three main governance challenges seems, they say, to offer only a choice between guardrails that mindlessly mandate decisions that worked in the past, and a set that allows flexibility and trial-and-error. But, they argue, replacing the latter with the former is not an option. Subsequent chapters outline some general principles underlying guardrails: rather than privileging consistency and coherence, guardrails should empower individuals, be rooted in social institutions and encourage both individual and societal learning. They should embody self-restraint and constraint. And technical tools or guardrails should be embedded in, not substitute for, social ones.

Gasser and Mayer-Schönberger conclude with an unexpected analogy. Rather than look to the recent past as a guide to guardrails for emerging challenges such as the metaverse, they cite the sixth-century Rule of Saint Benedict that kick-started Western monasticism and governs many religious communities around the world to this day. Even before the information age, guardrails were trending towards the rigid and specific, but what gave the Benedictine Rule legs was the same set of attributes the authors recommend for contemporary guardrails: diversity, variability and plasticity. Guardrails that vest power in processes, institutions, practices and culture produce better results, and those that don't lack legitimacy. Despite the risk of human frailty or corruption, 'guardrails *are* social constructs – take the human element out of the equation and they will fail. There is no shortcut to avoid facing … the messiness of human involvement' (p. 190).

Guardrails is meticulously researched, insightful and cleanly argued. But it does raise some further questions the authors don't address – although one could fruitfully extrapolate their analysis. How do guardrails function in, for example, international relations or a clash of normative systems, and are the authors' guidelines applicable in those contexts? What about autonomous military systems, or an AI arms race? At several points the authors invoke Neal Stephenson's prescient 1992 sci-fi novel *Snow Crash*, in which he predicted and named the idea of the metaverse. They might have done better to call on his 1999 *Cryptonomicon*, which explored digital currencies and their international governance a decade before Bitcoin and blockchain. When the processes, institutions, practices and culture are themselves the foci of power struggles, who then are the guardians?

The Will to Predict: Orchestrating the Future Through Science
Eglė Rindzevičiūtė. Ithaca, NY: Cornell University Press, 2023.
£54.00/$59.95. 306 pp.

It was Francis Bacon who wrote, in 1597, that '*ipsa scientia potestas est*' – 'knowledge itself is power'. He would know; he was one of the founders of modern science and later lord chancellor and regent of England. In *The Will to Predict*, political sociologist Eglė Rindzevičiūtė argues that it is the ability to predict – to deploy knowledge – that generates and amplifies power. 'Deploying scientific predictions in planning for the long term … is central to the legitimacy and power of government itself' (p. 1). But this power is not a given: 'scientific prediction is at once technical, political, social and institutional'.

The bulk of the book is concerned with the specific case of scientific prediction as an instrument of power in the Soviet Union and post-Soviet Russia. The author explores the origins and development of a distinctive Russian approach to the question that evolved parallel to and in conversation with Western epistemology, as well as how this approach influenced, was in tension with or was co-opted by Soviet planners and policymakers. The discussion touches on early five-year plans and 'prospective reflexivity' (a form of collective and iterative decision-making involving both means and goals); early calls for glasnost in the 1960s and the principle of 'reflexive control' (a form of game theory devoted to manipulation and deception of an opponent that underlies post-Soviet economic, military and management thinking); and questions of global environmental governance such as nuclear winter or climate change. Her critique of the intellectual history and current practice (especially in the context of Russian foreign policy and the Ukraine conflict) of reflexive-control theory in chapter 6 is alone worth the price of admission.

Rindzevičiūtė concludes that prospective reflexivity, reflexive control and global governance 'paved the way for the contemporary Russian governmental imagination' (p. 187) that is at odds with the Western world view in its intellectual roots, normative behaviour and anticipation of future trends. More broadly, she draws some general lessons that appear to be applicable to Western and Chinese as well as to Russian epistemologies. Firstly, societies and politics that are perceived as unpredictable, such as Russia's Ukraine policy, Britain's Brexit referendum or the rise of Donald Trump, are of particular concern and accompany conspiracy-theoretical world views, or can lead to a reversion to reliance on pre-scientific methods such as astrology or witchcraft. Secondly, politicians and the public see the unpredictability of negative events as the problem, whereas academics are as concerned with failures to predict positive events, such as the collapse of communism. Finally, the human will to predict is one with the need to make sense of the past, or the present, where historical causal explanations can be seen as a form of retrospective prediction.

The Gutenberg Parenthesis: The Age of Print and Its Lessons for the Age of the Internet
Jeff Jarvis. London: Bloomsbury Academic, 2023.
£20.00/$27.00. 328 pp.

The expression 'Gutenberg Parenthesis', coined in the mid-1990s, refers to the theory that the 'Age of Print', from Johannes Gutenberg's invention of moveable type in the fifteenth century to the rise of the internet in the twenty-first, was exceptional – not in the sense of 'superlative', but in that it was a sort of hiccup in the continuity of culture. While there are obvious differences between mediaeval manuscript culture and cyberspace, there is also a marked continuity; we are seeing not so much a new phase but a return, with some variation, to an older one. (For US readers, the expression relies on the British meaning of 'parenthesis' as an aside, or that which is enclosed within the punctuation marks Americans denote with the word.)

The theory relies first on the assumption that we are in the midst of a major, global cultural transition, from the Age of Print to something new. Whether that something new is also old is another question. Jeff Jarvis, a journalist with an academic bent, takes both as givens, or as trivially demonstrated, and explores the opening of the Gutenberg Parenthesis and the developments within it in granular and compelling detail to better understand its closing. He does not try to predict; not only does he show that, for example, the death of the book has been repeatedly and incorrectly forecast for a century and a half, he argues that these transitions are gradual rather than abrupt. The metaphor of a parenthesis with two definite brackets is somewhat misleading. As he puts it, 'Gutenberg himself did not live in his own age; he lived in the scribes' time, which did not end until long after his death … It was Gutenberg's descendants who created the next age at the opening of the Parenthesis. It will be our descendants who build what succeeds it' (p. 9).

Nevertheless, in Part III, 'Leaving the Parenthesis', he looks toward the future in broad themes: a shift from media-controlled content to popular conversation, a renaissance in expressive creativity, a weakening of gatekeepers. Most important is what he calls 'institutional revolutions', with institutions broadly conceived. Among them he lists copyright, authorship, news, privacy, currency work, welfare, warfare, policing, capitalism, democracy and even the nation-state – the Westphalian state itself was born inside the parenthesis. New, unforeseen institutions might be needed, or in any case might emerge. Some of this is speculative, some may be driven by wishful thinking, but it is not superficial. The form these revolutions will take, moreover, is in some ways less important now than which institutions are in play. This is one of Jarvis's strengths. Only through understanding how, why and which institutions were affected by the opening of the parenthesis can we get a feel for the changes that are to come. As a whole, *The Gutenberg Parenthesis* is an outstanding and engaging analysis of a complex and wide-ranging subject.

A City on Mars: Can We Settle Space, Should We Settle Space, and Have We Really Thought This Through?
Kelly Weinersmith and Zach Weinersmith. London: Particular Books, 2023. £25.00/$32.00. 448 pp.

This year marks the 50th anniversary of the publication of Gerard K. O'Neill's seminal paper 'The Colonization of Space', the founding document of a growing movement. With more and more newcomers to the ranks of spacefaring nations and the emergence of private spaceflight companies as players in their own right, rather than just contractors to the stars, the dream of large-scale human settlement off Earth appears less of a pipe dream than ever before, beginning perhaps as early as 2050. The motivations for such settlement are many and overlapping: to create a back-up or Plan B in case of global environmental disaster or war; to create a new (and usually libertarian) utopia; to access vast new resources; to feed the human spirit. As Kelly and Zach Weinersmith put it in *A City on Mars*, 'there's no political corruption on Mars, no war on the Moon, no juvenile jokes on Uranus' (p. 1).

This last bit is emblematic of the Weinersmiths' approach. This is not, in style and presentation, a serious book. But it is very much so in content and contention. As a scientist and a social critic – or, as they describe themselves, 'a guy who draws funny pictures for the internet and … the president of a regional society for the study of parasitic worms' (p. 384) – this wife-and-husband research team have produced a comprehensive overview of the promises, problems and policy issues related to space settlement. It is particularly important in that most of what is written about the topic is essentially boosterism; the Weinersmiths began their research with the same attitude, but gradually brought their vision back down to Earth. If you are already an advocate of space settlement, this book may be sobering (the Weinersmiths point out that making booze in space – or space simulations like Biosphere 2 – is an outrageous waste of resources, but the people in Biosphere 2 did it anyway).

Sections on how people might thrive, or at least survive, in space on a day-to-day basis, and what off-Earth colonies might look like in physical terms, are absorbing in themselves, but for readers of *Survival* it will be the sections about legal and governance regimes, 'astropolitics', state formation, colony–metropole relations, security and war that will be of greatest interest. The authors show that advocates of off-Earth settlement tend to be technically *au fait* (if somewhat optimistic) but politically and socially naive. On balance, they conclude that the arguments for space settlement fall short – even with the worst projections for catastrophic climate change, for example, Earth will still beat space as a living environment by orders of magnitude. We are likely to take deep-rooted social, political, economic and cultural conflicts with us, not escape them. And it might not be cost-effective, for those who keep score that way. But settlement might be inevitable; if that's the case, the Weinersmiths advocate not just more biological and ecological research, but getting international space law and sociopolitical issues sorted first.

Experts in particular areas may find the book lacking in depth in their baili-wicks; it is, after all, 'designed for a general audience who doesn't want to read texts that weigh more than they do' (p. 386). But from a global (solar-systemic?) perspective, *A City on Mars* will tell you everything you need to know. For those who like the Weinersmiths' light-hearted style and quirky humour, this is a must-read. For those who can just tolerate them, it's a should-read. For those who find this approach off-putting, it's a read-it-anyway.

Politics and International Relations
Chester A. Crocker

Shame: The Politics and Power of an Emotion
David Keen. Princeton, NJ: Princeton University Press, 2023.
£30.00/$35.00. 360 pp.

This volume explores how shame and related emotions can be weaponised and manipulated by those with an interest in doing so. David Keen illustrates how shame often morphs into shamelessness as leaders and other officials convert feelings of shame into successful political narratives and tools. Citing Hannah Arendt (to whom there are nearly 30 references in the index), he argues that people tend to descend into 'magical thinking' and 'alternative facts' to maintain their self-image and avoid the impression of failure or defeat (p. 243). A professor of conflict studies at the London School of Economics and Political Science, Keen deploys a wide range of knowledge and literature, drawing on the work of thinkers such as Frantz Fanon and Saint Thomas Aquinas, and the fields of psychology and psychoanalysis, political theory, and conflict and development studies to bolster his arguments.

The book features ten cases ranging across criminal justice, Sierra Leone (one of Keen's specialties), Adolf Eichmann, Donald Trump (two chapters!), Brexit, colonialism, economy and development, mass violence, and the West. Along the way, the author discusses individual leaders, regimes, systems and rebel movements, and the myriad ways in which they all experience and use powerful emotions. Chapter 4 on 'Shame and Shamelessness' offers persuasive insights on how shame – about loss, weakness, humiliation, disrespect or 'invisibility' – can be overcome by the shameless use of toughness, insensitivity and raw power, deflecting insults or criticism onto others. A leader like Trump exploits others' shame by promising an escape 'from the shame of poverty, from the shame of holding certain opinions and having certain feelings, and from the shame of being invisible and unheard' (p. 133). Shaming his supporters, on the other hand, plays right into his hands. Boris Johnson likewise 'seemed to embody an escape from shame, making a show of independence from haircuts, suits, and social conventions' (p. 147).

Readers' interpretation of the findings of chapter 11 ('Shame and Colonialism') may vary according to their degree of sympathy for Keen's progressive politics. The US experience of expansion, conquest, empire and modern warfare is fully aired: 'We can see here how shame – whether over harm done or weakness – can be harnessed to some very toxic kinds of politics' (p. 167). For Britain, France and the United States, shame around past abuses is weaker than shame around weakness or loss of empire or status, a tendency Keen believes often produces an assertive reflex. This can be seen, for example, in Tony Blair's 1997 remark: 'Century upon century it has been the destiny of Britain to lead other nations … We are a leader of nations or nothing' (p. 174). Chapter 13 offers useful findings on the relationship between shame and mass violence, drawing on examples of starvation, rebellion and atrocities in China, Guatemala, Rwanda, Sierra Leone and Sudan.

Readers of *Survival* may (or may not) be amused by Keen's brief recap of his experiences as a fellow at the International Institute for Strategic Studies in the late 1990s, which included having his research plans 'ruthlessly torn apart' by 'intelligent' and 'well-dressed' but 'emotionless' security experts, whose views on NATO expansion, the Cold War and Russia he found lacking (p. 248). This leads into a discussion of how Russia's humiliation at having lost great-power status and sense of being disrespected by the West following the end of the Cold War should not be overlooked in explaining the contemporary behaviour of Vladimir Putin. Elsewhere Keen notes that while 'Putin has brought more shame on himself – and by extension Russia – through his actions over Ukraine in particular … we have seen many times … that shame-for-abuse tends not to deter those who are pushing back against shame-for-loss-of-power' (p. 179).

Shame offers an important inquiry into the power of emotions in international relations and comparative politics. It doesn't hurt that the author is himself emotional about his subject.

Fragile Victory: The Making and Unmaking of Liberal Order
James E. Cronin. New Haven, CT: Yale University Press, 2023.
$40.00. 346 pp.

Readers face no shortage of books and articles about the decline of the liberal-international order, commonly referred to as the 'rules-based order' by Western scholars and dismissively described as 'Western hegemony' by authoritarian critics. James Cronin, a research professor in history at Boston College, introduces this vastly ambitious book by quickly acknowledging that he is entering definitional quicksand. He aims to tell the story of how the victorious Allies during and after the Second World War sought to build international structures that would prevent a return to the chaos of the 1930s; how the emerging system did fairly well within the context of the Cold War rivalry until the economic shocks of the 1970s; and how the quest was renewed on an expanded global playing field after 1989. Since then the roof has fallen in due to a combination of domestic political fragmentation and polarisation within the leading Western states, and several 'external' shocks and challenges, notably trade, immigration, terrorism and resurgent geopolitics. The nadir for Cronin, unsurprisingly, was 2016, the year of Brexit and Donald Trump in the two countries he considers most central to the story of liberal order.

Cronin manages this sweeping tale by acknowledging in the opening pages that the notion of a liberal order must be heavily qualified due to the imperfect liberalism of the leading Western states and their evident determination to build an order consistent with their own interests. That order was also geographically limited during the Cold War and was only briefly (say from 1989 to 2001) in any sense global. What makes the book refreshingly different from much other writing on these topics is that Cronin is a historian, not an international-relations scholar. This means we are spared yet another dive into the conceptual debates between realists, liberal-internationalists and constructivists. Instead, we are introduced to Cronin's own mega-theoretical framing: 'A liberal international order is almost by definition to be built on liberal politics within states and commitments to foster democratic norms within and across states' (p. 4).

This theory is the analytical crux of the book, rooted in assumptions about what kinds of states, with which kinds of domestic social contracts, are likely to build and maintain a liberal-international order. Cronin's commitment to this framing leads to nuanced argumentation:

> The history of liberal order was extremely complicated and in no way a linear or logical progression. Its creation was not easy or automatic but required unique conditions; its maintenance was not assured, but very much depended on prosperity and on political systems whose effective functioning was by no means guaranteed. (pp. 5–6)

Hence the title, *Fragile Victory*. Accordingly, Cronin's three goals are 'to chart the creation of liberal order ... to investigate the conditions and choices that made it more or less stable ... and to examine and explain what happened to weaken liberal order' (p. 11).

Cronin's primary focus throughout is on domestic politics and economics, and on the resulting social contracts. There is much less discussion about how these shaped foreign policies and international relationships. Chapters unfold chronologically, starting with the collapse of the post-Versailles order in the 1930s and the wartime planning process that laid the foundations for a liberal order through key milestones such as the Atlantic Charter, the 1942 United Nations Declaration and Bretton Woods. Cronin sums up the emerging order as being 'more or less liberal in three senses' by creating a 'more open world economy'; embracing Franklin Roosevelt's Four Freedoms and the Atlantic

Charter; and favouring democracy and self-determination. This 'framework' was contradicted by the persistence of empires and the emergence of the Soviet system, now imposed on much of Europe. Hence, the order established after 1945 was 'incompletely liberal', or 'liberal in theory but not always in practice' (p. 75). The third chapter concisely describes how the wartime alliance collapsed and the Cold War emerged, creating 'a smaller but more manageable' order within a Cold War balance of power; this embryonic liberal order was 'still a project, an aspiration' that, whatever its flaws, was more attractive than the situation in 1939 or the order that might have resulted if the Axis had prevailed (p. 103).

Chapters 4–6 take the reader through the 'search' for political and economic stability; its achievement in the 1950s, 1960s and early 1970s; and its arguably substantial modification in the 1970s and 1980s. Much of this tale is familiar, but key themes centre on the ingredients of a 'golden age' of capitalism, including trade expansion, population growth and migration, and equitable income distribution. According to Cronin:

> The reform and refounding of capitalism after the war and the elaboration of social protections that occurred in almost every [Western] country led to an era of prosperity that made it possible to build democratic polities that provided the liberal international order a distinctive and attractive domestic content and a solid political anchor. (p. 134)

To this, Cronin adds 'the centering effect of the Cold War', which helped to reduce political extremism even in the face of political challenges such as trade, immigration, race relations and decolonisation.

Inevitably, *les trente glorieuses* came to an end due to economic shocks and policy shifts that transformed the role of the state and glorified the role of markets. Margaret Thatcher and Ronald Reagan come in for predictable attention as champions of free markets and 'a revolt of the wealthy against the welfare state and the compromises of the early post-war period' (p. 183). For Cronin, the neo-liberal turn represented 'a repudiation, a ripping up, of the implicit [social] contract that underpinned the postwar order' (p. 185).

Chapter 7 casts a sceptical eye on talk of establishing a new, expanded liberal order after 1989. In the lands of the former Soviet Union, the order constructed in the 1990s was at best 'liberal in form and in rhetoric' – neither economic reforms nor political institutions were solid. It is disappointing that the book tells us very little about how the post-Cold War order dealt with challenges to regional and global security – surely a key topic for any study of the liberal-international order. Instead, Cronin looks at how this new order fundamentally changed the role of the state, which would de-emphasise the earlier norms of 'reformed capitalism' and shift toward constraining states from interfering with markets, both at home and internationally (pp. 213–14).

Cronin's history ends with the collapse of the political centre in Western politics, especially in the United States and United Kingdom. Parties of the centre-left lost much of their socio-economic base, while centre-right parties gradually moved further right in the absence of the Cold War's discipline. Rehearsing US and UK domestic politics at length, Cronin underscores the seminal role played by right-wing ideologues such as Newt Gingrich and Patrick Buchanan in focusing on divisive cultural threats and domestic enemies. Two factors, he argues, weakened the liberal order: its extension across a vast range of diverse states and societies, many only nominally wedded to liberal norms; and the gradual collapse of coherent attachment to liberal norms in the domestic politics of the West. To these factors, he adds the impact of 9/11 and the ineffective US interventions in Iraq and Afghanistan, plus the growing geopolitical assertiveness of Russia and China – all of which contributed to a loss of US leadership.

Returning to the theme in his title, the author is at pains to underscore that advancing a liberal-international order and liberal domestic politics within states is a 'continuing quest'. Yet he also writes that 'the successes of the liberal project required specific historical conditions that will not be replaced' (p. 299). If specific historical conditions are required, readers may ask themselves if Cronin's meta theory – that 'any liberal order in international relations that is at all robust and durable is necessarily linked to the existence and promotion of liberal democracy' (p. 243) – is over-determined and its conditions under-specified. Unique historical correlations may be just that, but they may still yield important lessons and reminders of what's been lost.

The Geopolitics of Shaming: When Human Rights Pressure Works – and When It Backfires
Rochelle Terman. Princeton, NJ: Princeton University Press, 2023. £25.00/$29.95. 216 pp.

This is a courageous book, taking on many policy assumptions and academic arguments. It is largely persuasive in 'proving' the obvious about the importance of political–diplomatic relationships when trying to apply human-rights norms. Rochelle Terman uses empirical and experimental political-science methods to test her theories and answer basic questions about why and when states shame other states over human-rights issues; why this either works or backfires; why states shame their targets even when they expect backlash and resistance; and why some states redouble their commitment to violations while others comply with pressure to change their behaviour.

Terman's core insight is to focus on the 'relational context' between the shamer and the target. Joining other scholars of 'relationalism', Terman argues that shaming is fundamentally shaped by the political relationship between shamer and target. She argues that 'shaming can be rational even when it fails to promote compliance', and that 'states will shame their geopolitical rivals more often, and more harshly, than their strategic partners' (p. 28). Shamer-states are motivated by three potential benefits: achieving changes in behaviour; pleasing or impressing indirect audiences both at home and abroad; and doing damage to the target's standing and legitimacy. Terman focuses on the latter two as components of 'weaponized shaming' (pp. 34–41). The importance of the first benefit – achieving compliance – differs depending on relationships; states often shame hostile targets that are unlikely to change because the goal is punishment, not compliance (pp. 42–3).

Shaming by a strategic partner is more effective because it is costly for the shamer and therefore more 'credible'. Shaming by an adversary has less effect because the relationship is less valued, the signal is less credible and the target suffers less reputational damage. Targets react by focusing on the source of rebukes, not the content (pp. 54–5). Moreover, shaming affects the target's behaviour mainly by 'unleashing political forces *within* the target state, changing the domestic political game' (p. 55). Terman rebuts the view that outside pressure reliably 'mobilizes domestic movements for human rights'. Rather, foreign shaming often 'threatens citizens' national attachments, reinforcing positive views about their country and diminishing support for activism or political mobilization in defense of human rights' (p. 96).

Terman explores two real-world case studies to illustrate these dynamics: the murder of Jamal Khashoggi by Saudi agents in 2018 and the 2010–11 campaign to save Sakineh Mohammadi Ashtiani from execution by stoning in Iran. In the former case, both Donald Trump and Joe Biden declined to impose serious normative pressure on Riyadh because there was insufficient 'political will to prioritize HR [human rights] over strategic cooperation' (pp. 137–9). In the latter case, Iran pursued a strategy of 'deflection' – it rejected and doubled down against Western pressure, but reacted differently to an appeal by Brazilian president Luiz Inácio Lula da Silva, who offered Ashtiani asylum (p. 148).

In the concluding chapter, Terman debunks the notion that human-rights shaming is just 'cheap talk'. Her guidance for governments is to focus on states with which they have friendly relations, where relational benefits can be withheld if compliance is not forthcoming. With rivals or adversaries, she suggests that 'a strategy of engagement, not isolation, provides the best chance for promoting HR in the long term' (p. 166).

Nation Branding and International Politics
Christopher S. Browning. Montreal and Kingston: McGill-Queen's University Press, 2023. £29.99/C$39.95. 240 pp.

As the title suggests, this book explores the significance of 'nation branding', the practice by which states seek to define and establish their reputation for both external and domestic audiences. This practice is not new, but has intensified in the post-Cold War era as states seek to position themselves in an increasingly competitive global landscape characterised by anxiety about status and identity. Christopher Browning's study has several goals, pulling together themes and case studies he has developed over the years (the bibliography lists 14 previous works on related themes). One primary goal is to situate nation branding as an important field of inquiry in the field of international relations. Rejecting the idea that it is a superficial phenomenon, Browning asserts that it is linked to the core concerns of international relations – geopolitics and security, community and identity, competitive markets and trade flows (pp. 6–7).

Browning argues that nation branding – which he distinguishes from everyday activities such as public relations, propaganda and marketing – comes in two types: cosmetic and institutional. Examples of the latter, in which 'nation branding becomes embedded more centrally into national policy and becomes significant to how the country is run and organized' (p. 15), include building a new capital city (Kazakhstan) or establishing an educational hub (Qatar). States may decide to stress their cultural, diplomatic/geopolitical or commercial/economic identity.

Readers are introduced to the denizens of the nation-branding 'industry' comprising consultants and academics who specialise in helping states up their reputational game. Developed largely in the 1990s, the industry urged its prospective clients to forget about their territorial identity and to focus on their comparative competitive placement in the international system. The logic of globalisation and a borderless world obliged states to redefine themselves for the global market, with an emphasis on economic rather than military assets. The goal was to become 'fit for business in a context of unbridled capitalist competition for footloose capital and increasingly transnational firms' (p. 55). The problem with the industry, according to Browning, is that it is 'inherently anti-democratic in orientation', and tends to commodify national cultures and homogenise attributes perceived as desirable to 'affluent Western markets' and the liberal global order (pp. 76–7).

Browning's book is peppered with an impressive range of examples that includes parts of Africa (especially South Africa, home of the 'Brand Africa' movement), Bhutan, Colombia, Kazakhstan, the Koreas, Lithuania, the Nordic countries, Romania, Russia and Thailand. These can be divided into three sub-types: 'good states', 'peaceful states' and 'stigmatized states'. Good states stress 'altruistic components' in their branding, positioning themselves as 'moral actor[s] selflessly addressing commonly held problems' in fields such as peace and conflict resolution, the environment, education and health. Browning calls this 'nation branding as conspicuous do-goodism' (pp. 87–8). Examples include the Nordic countries, which are discussed in detail.

Browning looks at claims that nation branding can contribute to more 'peaceful states' and greater understanding between states (chapter 5). On the contrary, he argues, branding can be co-opted in the service of traditional geopolitics. Countries such as Russia and North Korea use nation branding as a 'mechanism for manufacturing political legitimacy for existing regimes', rather than for supporting democratic transitions (p. 122). Moscow's obsession with bidding for and hosting mega events to signal its 'return to the "premier league" of world politics' is exhibit A (p. 130), but countries such as Colombia and South Africa also come in for scrutiny for their efforts to gild the lily on behalf of incumbents.

The final category – to which many post-Soviet and African states belong – is 'historically stigmatized states at the wrong end of global geopolitical and geoeconomic hierarchies' (p. 154). The core challenge they face is overcoming entrenched and distortive stereotypes. In an amusing discussion (pp. 159–63), Browning identifies four branding strategies they might adopt: accept and embrace negative images ('dark tourism' in Romania); replace negative images with positive ones (Estonia as 'Nordic'); assert the state's geopolitical standing (Turkiye as a 'crossroads', South Africa as a 'gateway'); and overcome stigma by redefining the state's standing and asserting agency over its destiny (Thabo Mbeki's 'African Renaissance'). For Browning, these branding efforts all seem to point toward repositioning the state within the existing geopolitical and economic order rather than modifying (let alone overturning) it. Mbeki's approach could, however, point the other way.

Global Policymaking: The Patchwork of Global Governance
Vincent Pouliot and Jean-Philippe Thérien. Cambridge:
Cambridge University Press, 2023. £26.99. 280 pp.

The Canadian authors of this ambitious study focus on what they term 'global policymaking' – a process they consider 'incredibly complex, intricate, and messy' (p. 3). They aim to provide an analytical methodology for examining how global governance actually works. Vincent Pouliot and Jean-Philippe Thérien summarise their approach as follows: 'We revisit the conventional wisdom that conceives of global policymaking as the delivery of global public goods, and instead argue that the process is best construed as a *bricolage*, or patchwork, of competing value claims and politically charged governing practices' (p. 3). Their approach eschews functionalism and rational-choice approaches to optimising policy decisions; instead, they stress 'social conflict, value cleavages, and power dynamics as inherent conditions of global policymaking' (p. 12). The problem with the 'global public goods' mantra, they argue, is that it sweeps political conflict under the rug. Instead, *bricolage* captures the improvised nature of global governance by concentrating on the informal political processes by which decisions occur (that is, the dynamics of inclusion and exclusion) and the value debates that shape those processes, often by means of compromises that paper over basic cleavages (pp. 15, 20).

This analytical framework is applied to the negotiating history and institutional adaptation of three United Nations-based activities in the fields of development (the Sustainable Development Goals or SDGs), human rights (the UN Human Rights Council or HRC) and peacekeeping (the protection of civilians or PoC). In each case, the book seeks to demonstrate how process and values have interacted to produce messy compromises. The SDG process leading to the 2030 Agenda adopted in 2015 is deemed one of the most inclusive – of member states, regions and civil society – in UN history, even though powerful states exercised closed-door control at key points (p. 86). The result showed the 'supremacy of goal setting' in contrast to rule-making or the adoption of new norms (p. 91). Abundant value cleavages had to be managed on issues such as the sources of poverty and inequality; economic growth versus climate, governance and human rights; and national versus international responsibilities. Creativity and improvisation played key roles, but in the end Agenda 2030 should be viewed as 'full of ambiguities … that barely paper over a wealth of normative cleavages that are too easily dismissed by recourse to the notion of "public goods"' (p. 104).

Pouliot and Thérien view the development of the HRC after the 2005 World Summit as 'an exemplary case of incremental institution-building in global governance' (p. 106). The story reveals how minimal guidance from the summit's outcome document evolved into a 2007 resolution with detailed structural and procedural provisions, principally through the efforts of member-state diplomats and UN officials in New York and Geneva. Continuing internal reviews and revisions have incrementally reformed the committee's processes ever since, say the authors. They show how the HRC – created to replace an earlier Commission on Human Rights that was widely blamed for 'politicising' human rights – has managed inescapable political and normative conflicts in often innovative ways. Still, 'deep rifts in the normative underpinning of global public policymaking continue to structure the politics of human rights to this day' (p. 135).

The authors' last case describes the emergence of PoC as the 'primary goal of UN peace operations' over the past 25+ years, a process that has not reflected a 'rational design' but rather 'the shifting balance of global power relations and the vagaries of international circumstances' (p. 137) It is a bewilderingly complex diplomatic tale, featuring a leading role by civil society and a critical link established in UN Security Council Resolution (UNSCR) 1265 (1999) between civilian protection and international peace and security. The PoC doctrine is closely linked to other key milestones: the adoption of UNSCR 1325 (2000) on women, peace and security, the Brahimi Report on peacekeeping that same year, and the World Summit's endorsement of the Responsibility to Protect doctrine in 2005. The book recounts how an early doctrinal consensus was increasingly eroded by mounting polarisation in the Security Council, especially after the Libya fiasco. It is a gripping tale of the unravelling of an ambitious exercise in global policymaking as a 'deep ideological cleavage' opened between 'those who promote a liberal humanitarianism and those who fear that such humanitarianism could be used to justify interventionist policies' (p. 156). Looking ahead in a concluding chapter, they see evidence that 'sovereigntists' of the Right are demonstrating greater vigour than their 'globalist' rivals who held sway in previous decades (p. 215).

Some readers will find value in the book's theoretical material, while others may be especially interested in the three UN case studies. The authors' analysis of these cases might have been helpfully complemented by parallel work on the global policy processes of other international entities such as the G20 or the World Bank.

Europe
Erik Jones

Sacred Foundations: The Religious and Medieval Roots of the European State
Anna M. Grzymała-Busse. Princeton, NJ: Princeton University Press, 2023. £25.00/$29.95. 235 pp.

The modern European state is a huge bureaucratic enterprise that derives its legitimacy from some mixture of representation and effectiveness. In many ways it has set the model for states elsewhere: now, every state is run by a giant bureaucracy that strives (or pretends) both to represent and to provide for the people it governs. Where did these notions of representation and effectiveness come from, and how did people figure out that a giant bureaucracy could meet their needs? The prevailing theoretical wisdom on 'state formation' points to the importance of warfare. Only a formidable bureaucracy can raise the armies and finances necessary to prevail in armed conflict. But this explanation leaves too many unanswered questions about how people learned to make bureaucracies function, how these structures in turn learned to raise revenues, and why the notion of representation is relevant.

Anna Grzymała-Busse finds answers to these questions in the Catholic Church. Drawing on a vast historical literature about the role of the church in the Middle Ages and early Renaissance, supplemented with statistical analysis related to the growth and spread of higher education, Grzymała-Busse pushes back against the war-fighting (or 'bellicist') theory of European state formation by showing how mimetic competition between secular and religious authorities offers a better explanation. Specifically, she shows how secular authorities relied on church personnel and a blend of canon and Roman law to create bureaucracies; how they built universities to train lawyers to make bureaucracies more rational and effective; and how they relied on abstract notions of collective representation to ensure that the people would embrace state institutions as the best way to achieve predictable dispute resolution and so avoid unnecessary violent conflict.

Grzymała-Busse's argument is compelling because it seems so obvious after the fact. The medieval church had a virtual monopoly on literacy and so provided the secretaries or chancellors for secular rulers. In turn, these church officials in their secular guise became the focus for the many petitions that were presented to royal or aristocratic courts. When disputes went unresolved because secular rulers did not have enough literate personnel to answer all the petitions, the petitioners took their claims – and the fees that went with them – to the Catholic Church. Secular rulers realised they were missing out on important revenue and so expanded their staff of literate retainers. When the church could not provide enough people, it founded universities to train secular lawyers to fill the gap. Relatively soon, those lawyers came to replace clerics as the main officers of government.

Grzymała-Busse does a terrific job showing how secular authorities borrowed templates and procedures from the church, including notions of collective representation to give the appearance of assent to new taxes, legislation and judicial interpretations. The church played an active role in spreading bureaucratic practices, particularly to those places where the church needed powerful allies, like Britain and France, or where it wished to create some kind of order, like Scandinavia. The church was less benevolent in its dealings with the Holy Roman Empire, where church leaders were more fearful of competition from secular authorities. There, church officials spread conflict instead of bureaucratic practice. In effect, Grzymała-Busse turns the bellicist tradition of state formation on its head: war was used to prevent the state from building a vast, effective and representative bureaucracy, not to encourage it. Only too late did the church realise that its allies and protectorates outside the Holy Roman Empire would use their bureaucratic skills to displace religion as the focus for political organisation with something that looks more like the modern European state.

Goodbye Eastern Europe: An Intimate History of a Divided Land
Jacob Mikanowski. London: Oneworld Publications, 2023.
£22.00. 375 pp.

'Eastern Europe' is the region sandwiched between Western Europe, Russia and Turkiye. The people who live there display influences from all parts of the continent. They also reflect the experience of having been a permanent site of great-power competition. Yet these shared influences and experiences do not give Eastern Europeans a common sense of identity or solidarity. Eastern Europe is not and was never a 'place' in that sense – the mixture and timing of influences was simply too different from one part of the region to the next. What Eastern Europeans do share, however, is a characteristic sense of creativity, passion, cynicism, insecurity and fatalism. Eastern Europe is a 'divided land' and yet somehow East Europeans exist.

Jacob Mikanowski does a brilliant job bringing the history and people of Eastern Europe to life, even those – like vampires and werewolves – who 'forgot to die' (p. 21). In doing so, he opens a different perspective on a region that has been the site of genius and nightmare in equal measure. Mikanowski does not dwell on nationalism, unlike most histories of the region. He explores the paradoxical nature of national-identity formation in a region constantly traversed by invaders, migrants, nomads and adventurers. More than this, he focuses on extraordinary groups or individuals that illustrate the uniqueness that a constant swirl of ideas, norms, values and passions can generate. The Bogomils in Bosnia, named after their founder, were a gnostic sect of Armenian heretics who were banished to Bulgaria by the Orthodox Church. They fled from persecution to Bosnia, where they inspired the local church to seek greater independence from Rome. What made them attractive to the Bosnians, Mikanowski argues, is 'how *different* they were from the rest of Europe' (p. 64).

This embrace of difference extended to the groups of dervishes found in Muslim Europe who dressed in animal skins and shaved off all their hair; the minstrels in Ukraine and Belarus whose guild insisted they 'had to be blind' (p. 135); and the Roma who arrived as 'converts from Islam' (p. 138) on a pilgrimage to Christian Europe – with signed, sealed documents to prove it – and sought food and shelter from any town or village that would receive them. Mikanowski's reason for dwelling on these groups is not so much to exoticise the region as to underscore the powerful differences between our world of technology, transport and communication, and a past in which people who lived a more isolated existence craved both inspiration and entertainment.

That craving did not diminish as the different parts of Eastern Europe modernised. It intensified, sometimes with horrific results. Mikanowski tells how citizens of the Habsburg Empire enlisted in the First World War seeking adventure, only to be led to slaughter. Along the way, many were drawn to Leninist Marxism, which would have its own disastrous consequences. But genius emerged as well – as can be seen in the paintings of Marc Chagall or the writings of Kazimir Malevich. Some of that genius is difficult to categorise. The millenarian prophet Elijah Klimowicz, who built the city of Wierszalin in eastern Poland, is one illustration among several.

These stories come together in the Second World War and its aftermath, as Eastern Europe emerges as a coherent region for the first time under Soviet communism. Mikanowski describes how the unprecedented violence and totalitarian institutions of this era collided with the differing aspirations of the people who experienced them. When the Cold War ended, the peoples of the region reached back to their pre-communist cultures and traditions, dissolving any notion of a monolithic Eastern Europe. The results have not always been positive, as Russia's full-scale invasion of Ukraine attests. Mikanowski ends with a plea for a more peaceful coexistence.

**Divided They Fell: Crisis and the Collapse of Europe's
Centre-left**
Sean McDaniel. Newcastle upon Tyne: Agenda Publishing,
2023. $95.00. 224 pp.

The global economic and financial crisis challenged the fundamental assumptions underpinning the liberalisation of cross-border capital flows and the development of global financial markets. Those assumptions included the priority given to stable money, sound public finances and competitive labour markets. This cocktail of policies was meant to ensure growth would function as the rising tide that lifts all boats. Instead, the threat of financial collapse exposed huge inequalities both in how people were living and in how much risk they faced. Wall Street was saved but Main Street was not. Yet somehow, the policy consensus around free markets and fiscal consolidation (austerity) remained in place – even on the centre-left.

Sean McDaniel seeks to explain why centre-left parties have not made a more decisive break from the pre-crisis consensus. To do so, he focuses on the British Labour Party under Ed Miliband and the French Socialist Party under François Hollande. Miliband and Hollande should have had a free hand to rewrite the economic playbook and a strong incentive to push for extended state protection for those hit hardest by the crisis. Whether they sought to pay for such support by borrowing on the markets or taxing the rich is less important than the fact that they acknowledged market failure and insisted that only the state could fix it. But that is not what happened. Instead, both Miliband and Hollande fell back on policies that hewed closer to the pre-crisis consensus. They insisted on balancing government accounts, even if that meant shrinking social programmes. And they used rhetoric that showed their confidence in the functioning of the markets.

McDaniel explains this persistence as coming from rigidities in the way political parties develop and use policy ideas. He argues that parties do not like to change their economic policies because they worry this will tarnish their reputations by suggesting they made mistakes in the past. Even if they do want to change, those policies are rooted in how party officials understand the role of states and markets – and that understanding determines which policies are deemed appropriate and which are not. The way the electorate responds to economic ideas is even harder for political parties to manipulate, which means a good idea in practical terms may not land politically. Hence it is safer to stick with a formula that is consistent and popular, even if there is reason to believe it might not work in fixing the economy.

The story McDaniel tells about Labour while in opposition and the Socialists in government demonstrates these patterns. The consequence was not only to weaken support for the centre-left in both countries, but also to expose the two parties to competition from the extremes. Jeremy Corbyn attacked Miliband from the left to take over the Labour Party; Jean-Luc Mélenchon rallied French voters against Hollande's Socialists. Neither extreme succeeded in mobilising enough support to transform the broader consensus about what to do in economic terms. If anything, they created opportunities for more right-wing politicians to turn back the clock in economic thinking.

Then again, McDaniel may be calling the contest too early. Despite any inertia it might have faced, the Democratic Party in the United States has moved in a more radical direction. Its 'foreign policy for the middle class' not only challenges the basic tenets of global free markets, but also lays the foundation for more ambitious forms of state intervention via redistribution and industrial policy. In turn, the US example reinforces debates in Europe about how to recalibrate the economic role of the state. These new policy ideas have their roots in the global crisis. Now they are mainstream, at least on the centre-left, on both sides of the Atlantic.

Deserved: Economic Memories After the Fall of the Iron Curtain
Till Hilmar. New York: Columbia University Press, 2023.
£30.00/$35.00. 272 pp.

US President Joe Biden is struggling to get voters to pay attention to his economic accomplishments. Despite having delivered massive investments and record-low unemployment, polling shows that voters think they were better off under Donald Trump. Even the economic turmoil caused by the pandemic cannot dent that impression. Neither can a wealth of statistics. Somehow, the economic memories of voters are disconnected from 'economics'.

The explanation is social, not technocratic. As Till Hilmar shows through a comparison of economic memories in the former East Germany and the Czech Republic, people do not think in terms of the ups and downs of statistical aggregates. Instead, they remember economic performance as a personal story of hardship and perseverance, solidarity and isolation, justice and unfairness. This is true particularly when the goal is to see merit rewarded in the market.

Within this meritocratic framing, unearned success is a strong indication of market failure – the product of corruption or nepotism. But unfought adversity and unrecognised contributions are even worse. Individuals who fail to fight back against hardship and prove their worth through persistent effort have broken with meritocracy and so betrayed the shared ethic. The society that fails to recognise the value of an individual's skills and determination is unjust.

The Czech Republic and East Germany are good laboratories in which to observe how economic memories work. These countries were leading industrial centres under communism. When the Iron Curtain fell, however, they lurched in different directions. The Czech Republic preserved most of its manufacturing base, and so workers with engineering skills had a good chance to hold onto their jobs or, better, go into business for themselves. They might complain about corruption – particularly resulting from privatisation – but the successful were more likely to break with those whose inability to stay afloat might be blamed on a lack of self-discipline.

The situation in East Germany was different. There, fast-paced privatisation destroyed the territory's manufacturing base even as German reunification exposed highly skilled East German engineers to the scorn of their West German counterparts. The Wessies unjustly assumed that Ossies lacked the skills to match West German accomplishments.

The economic memories of these two parts of Central and Eastern Europe reflected two different perceptions of what was 'deserved'. Czech workers built a world view that prized flexibility and hard work in the face of corrupt adversaries in domestic politics and European institutions. East German workers perceived the whole German economic system as biased. Small wonder, therefore, that so many Czechs have rallied around an anti-EU, pro-market populism, while East Germans have been attracted by some very different messages from the far right.

Hilmar's fascinating case studies force us to ask what kind of framing Trump supporters are using in interpreting their own memories of economic performance. In doing so, Hilmar insists that collective memory and collective experience are likely to play a predominant role in shaping what individuals recall and how they think and feel about it. If the Biden campaign wants to improve its standing among voters disenchanted with the president's economic record, they would be wise to rely on focus groups, rather than polls, and to embed themselves in local communities. The question is not whether the president did his job well, it is whether voters believe they got what they deserved from the policies he (and his predecessor) enacted.

The Russia Sanctions: The Economic Response to Russia's Invasion of Ukraine
Christine Abely. Cambridge: Cambridge University Press, 2023.
£29.99. 216 pp.

Russia's full-scale invasion of Ukraine triggered an unprecedented wave of sanctions by the United States and European Union. Within hours, policymakers in the West began cutting off Russian banks, firms and individuals from the global financial system. They seized and stranded Russian assets – including central-bank reserves. They changed the terms under which Russian firms traded with the West. They reduced the purchase of Russian gas and oil. They pushed Western firms to divest from Russian markets. And they prevented key Russian politicians and oligarchs from travelling to Western countries. By the end of 2022, Western governments had levied ten rounds of sanctions against Russia, including secondary sanctions against firms or individuals who helped Russian firms maintain access to Western finance, technology and markets. Russia's war against Ukraine continued, nonetheless.

Sanctions were never meant to end the war. As Christine Abely explains, the most important aid provided by the US and EU on that front came in the form of military, financial and humanitarian assistance (pp. 2, 118). Indeed, only a few of the sanctions had significant short-term consequences, such as the seizing of assets, the removal of 'most-favoured-nation' trading status, and the restrictions on the trade in oil and gas. Meanwhile, some of the more important shorter-term consequences – such as the sudden spike in energy prices – were hardly a boon for the West. Many of the sanctions were symbolic, taking the war to Russian oligarchs by seizing their yachts and placing them on 'no-travel' lists.

The remaining sanctions would play out only over the longer term. This is the point that Abely underscores in her otherwise fast-paced account of events as they unfolded in 2022. The US and the EU placed 'unprecedented' sanctions on Russia as far back 2014, in response to Russia's annexation of Crimea and its support for armed separatists in the Donbas region. Those sanctions did not deter Russian President Vladimir Putin from his full-scale invasion; they put him on notice of what to expect. They also started a long, slow process of decoupling the Russian economy from its dependence on Western markets, investment, technology and finance. Russian banks began preparing to process their own payments both inside the country and with key institutions in foreign markets. Russian firms began exploring new opportunities either to replace Western imports or to find new export partners.

That decoupling was hardly complete when Russia launched its full-scale invasion of Ukraine, and the Russian government underestimated the scale of the Western response. With the new rounds of sanctions, however, the decoupling has accelerated. The Russian government is more aware of its vulnerabilities and has a better understanding of Western resolve. Russian firms have updated their planning apace. So have governments and firms elsewhere, particularly those vulnerable to secondary sanctions. Decoupling has not only accelerated, it has spread.

The economic consequences for Russia will be significant. That is the intent of the policy. Russian firms will lack the latest technology; they will have greater difficulty finding markets for their exports or sourcing quality imports for their supply chains or domestic clients; and they will face a higher cost of capital when trying to build up inventories or finance other investments. Over time, the Russian economy will be poorer, less productive and of lower quality than it would have been otherwise. This will chip away at the government's ability to wage costly military interventions. Of course, there will be important consequences for the global economy too. Western sanctions on Russia may be targeted, but their longer-term effects could prove to be comprehensive. Abely's timely book is not only a reminder of what has happened, but also a warning of what to expect.

Another Special Relationship? The United States and Japan

Robert Ward

I

The bilateral relationship between the United States and the United Kingdom is sometimes described as 'special'. A similar claim could be made about the relationship between the US and Japan, which have seemed peculiarly intertwined since the Second World War. Security challenges in the Asia-Pacific have made this relationship more strategically vital than it has ever been.

Japan's occupation by Allied forces – which in practice meant US forces – after Tokyo's catastrophic defeat in 1945 until the restoration of Japanese sovereignty in 1952 was without historical precedent.[1] The 'focused intensity' of the American occupation of Japan distinguished it from the Allied occupation of Germany, shared among France, the Soviet Union, the UK and the US.[2] In the five years after Japan's surrender, the US imposed a 'controlled revolution' on the country, implementing economic, social and political reforms.[3] It also imposed a new constitution, in which, uniquely, Japan 'renounce[d] war as a sovereign right'.[4] Promulgated in 1946 and replacing the Meiji Constitution of 1889, the new constitution was not universally welcomed: it has been described as un-Japanese, with 'language and concepts patched together from the Anglo-American political

Robert Ward is IISS Japan Chair and Director of Geo-economics and Strategy.

Survival | vol. 66 no. 3 | June–July 2024 | pp. 201–212   https://doi.org/10.1080/00396338.2024.2357493

tradition',[5] and Japanese nationalists have long chafed at the loss of sovereignty it implies. Nevertheless, it remains unchanged and is now the world's oldest unamended constitutional document.[6]

Having demilitarised Japan immediately after Tokyo's surrender, the US reversed course from the late 1940s as the communist threat in Asia rose. The 1950–53 Korean War reinforced Japan's strategic importance for the US as a strongly anti-communist bulwark in the region. Supplying steel and other goods for the conflict also provided a much-needed boost to Japan's war-battered economy. Coupled with what Eric Hobsbawm has described as the '"Great Leap Forward" of the capitalist world economy' in the 1950s and 1960s, this spurred an economic boom in Japan. By the late 1960s, Japan had become the world's second-largest economy.[7] The US–Japan security relationship, meanwhile, was cemented with the coming into force of the US–Japan Treaty of Mutual Cooperation and Security in 1952. Revised in 1960 against considerable political opposition within Japan and renewed without incident in 1970, this remains Japan's only formal security alliance and is the cornerstone of its security policy.[8]

Despite increasing US pressure for Japan to play a greater role in supporting Asian security, Yoshida Shigeru, Japan's prime minister in the late 1940s and early 1950s, recognised the importance for Japan's domestic stability of focusing on economic growth rather than rearmament. Indeed, the so-called Yoshida Doctrine, under which Japan relied militarily on the US, maintained a 'low posture' in global affairs and focused on economic growth, proved remarkably durable, lasting in its purest form for over 40 years. From the 1950s, however, the US went from pressing Japan for greater burden-sharing on security, to sniping at Japan's perceived 'free riding' when this was not forthcoming and, by the 1970s, to seeing Japan's rapidly growing economy as a threat even to US security interests.[9] During the first Gulf War in 1990–91, Japan was excoriated for limiting its response to a financial contribution.

II

Differences in the countries' political cycles and cultures have often aggravated bilateral tensions. Japan's parliamentary system has experienced prolonged periods of intense volatility, resulting in short-lived administrations. Although Japan's Liberal Democratic Party (LDP) has ruled for some 64 of the 69 years since it was created in 1955 through the merger of two conservative parties, it comprises powerful factions that have weakened the party's internal structures and left it prone to disequilibrium and crisis.[10] The two brief periods since 1955 in which the opposition took power, in 1993–94 and 2009–12, were also characterised by governmental instability. Thus, between 1955 and 2024, Japan had 31 prime ministers (all men).[11] The US, meanwhile, had only 13 presidents during the same period.

Many of the Japanese prime ministers who have taken office since 1955 have been politically weak, with power spread between the LDP's factions and the prime minister often spending his energies on mediating between them.[12] It was not until the political reforms of the 1990s – themselves triggered by public anger at a series of LDP scandals in the late 1980s and early 1990s that caused the party to lose power in 1993 – that a Japanese prime minister was given the 'clear legal right' to initiate policies in the cabinet.[13]

The lack of a clear focal point of Japanese power frustrated Henry Kissinger, national security advisor and then secretary of state (for a while, both at once) in the Nixon White House. Kissinger compared Japan's leaders unfavourably with those of China, criticising their 'decisions by consensus' and their 'anonymous style': 'a Japanese leader does not announce a decision; he evokes it'.[14] The limited English of many of Japan's post-1955 prime ministers, and even occasionally their inarticulacy in their native Japanese, also muddied communication.[15]

Kissinger's mistrust of Japanese diplomats to keep secrets, combined with misunderstandings between long-serving prime minister Sato Eisaku and Richard Nixon over Japan's commitments to regulate Japanese exports of textiles to the US, contributed to the two 'Nixon shocks' of 1971.[16] The first came in July with the public announcement that Kissinger had secretly visited China to pave the way for a visit by Nixon to Beijing to normalise US relations with China. Sato was given only minutes' notice before Nixon's broadcast.[17] This abrupt strategic shift upended Japan's regional geopolitical assumptions: from the onset of the Korean War, the United States' priority had been to contain China. Adding American insult to Japanese injury, Nixon would be visiting China as president before he had visited Japan, a key US ally in the region.[18] The second shock came in August, when the US suspended the dollar's convertibility to gold and slapped a 10% surcharge on imports to the US. Although Sato was able to achieve his long-held goal of ending American control over Okinawa in 1972, the Nixon shocks weakened his administration. His LDP faction split just days before a ceremony in Tokyo to mark the return of Okinawa to Japanese control.[19]

Nonetheless, since 1955 some relationships between Japanese prime ministers and US presidents were arguably comparable to that between Margaret Thatcher and Ronald Reagan in the 1980s, or Tony Blair and George W. Bush in the early 2000s. As with Thatcher and Blair, prime-ministerial longevity was a factor. Nakasone Yasuhiro served for 1,806 days in 1982–87, Koizumi Junichiro for 1,980 days in 2001–06 and Abe Shinzo for 3,188 days in 2006–07 and 2012–20.[20] All three enjoyed close relations with their corresponding US presidents: Reagan (Nakasone), Bush *fils* (Koizumi) and Donald Trump (Abe). Abe's second administration also overlapped with that of Barack Obama.

In his memoirs, published posthumously in 2023 – Abe was murdered in July 2022 while campaigning for the LDP – he recalled being inspired by Nakasone's habit of seeking meetings with Reagan to 'demonstrate the health of Japan–US relations'.[21] The closeness of the relationship was novel for both sides, accustomed as they were to greater formality. Abe replicated this with Trump to considerable effect and with great theatri-cality, breaking with diplomatic convention to visit Trump at his home in New York immediately after his election victory in 2016 with a gift of a gold-plated golf club for the golf-loving president-elect.[22] In his book, Abe contrasted the 15–30-minute phone calls he had with Obama with those he had with Trump, which could last for up to 90 minutes, sometimes with 70–80% of the conversation about golf.[23] Koizumi, for his part, had charmed Bush with his love of American Westerns and Elvis Presley.[24]

In addition to personal compatibility, ideological alignment could also bring the two sides together. LDP administrations have tended to have greater ideological affinity with Republican than with Democratic presidents, the close relationship between current Japanese Prime Minister Kishida Fumio and US President Joe Biden being a notable exception. Low points in the bilateral relationship came with Jimmy Carter's pledge to withdraw US troops from South Korea in the 1970s, which caused Japan to question the United States' broader commitment to regional security, and what Tokyo saw as Bill Clinton's 'Japan passing' in favour of China during visits to the Asia-Pacific.[25] Abe was concerned about a nascent US–China condominium squeezing Japanese interests after the 2013 Sunnylands summit between Obama and Chinese President Xi Jinping.[26] US–Japan relations had grown chilly during Obama's presidency and Japanese sensitivities were thus heightened.[27] Nevertheless, there were some notable diplomatic successes during the Obama administration, including Abe's historic speech to a joint session of the US Congress in 2015 to mark the 70th anniversary of the end of the Second World War; Obama's visit to Hiroshima in mid-2016, where he laid a wreath to commemorate the victims of the US atomic bombing of the city in 1945; and Abe's reciprocal visit at the end of 2016 to Pearl Harbor.

Nakasone agitated for Japan's 'autonomous defence'

Nakasone, Koizumi and Abe all challenged the Yoshida Doctrine, seeking greater agency for Japan within the US security alliance. Even before becoming prime minister, Nakasone had long been an agitator for Japan's 'autonomous defence' (*jishu bōei ron*).[28] As premier, his efforts to boost Japan's military capabilities, although ultimately falling short of his stated wishes, aligned well with Reagan's push to increase US defence spending and to persuade American allies to increase their own military spending.[29] In so doing, Nakasone broke the unofficial post-war taboo on discussing Japan's defence needs, paving the way for later changes made by Koizumi and Abe. Nakasone's efforts may also have partly offset rising trade tensions with the US in key areas such as semiconductors and cars.

Koizumi's support for Bush's 'war on terror' after the September 2001 attacks on the US was unprecedented for Japan and did much to promote the closeness of the Bush–Koizumi relationship. Koizumi used the increased powers of the prime minister to respond to the international security crisis, banishing memories of Japan's diplomatic failures in the first Gulf War. In November 2001 he enacted legislation to deploy the Japan Maritime Self-Defense Force to the Indian Ocean to provide logistical support for the US-led coalition's operations in Afghanistan. This was the first time Japan's military had been sent overseas during a conflict, albeit in a non-combat capacity, since the end of the Second World War. Further legislation enabled the dispatch in January 2004 of the Ground Self-Defense Force and Air Self-Defense Force to Iraq and Kuwait, again in non-combat roles – the first instances in which Japanese forces had been deployed internationally without a United Nations mandate. In 2003, the Koizumi administration decided to build a ballistic-missile-defence system, in effect committing Japan to strategic and technological alignment with the US on missile defence.

Abe's success – where many others had failed – in building a relationship with Trump during the former's second term allowed him to navigate Trump's diplomatic unpredictability and to recalibrate Japan's relations with China, which Abe had identified as a challenge for Japan as far back as 2006.[30] Singapore's founding father Lee Kuan Yew had noted that 'relations between Japan, the US and China are most stable when they take the form of an isosceles triangle. This means maintaining a triangular configuration in which US–Japan ties are closer than either Sino-Japanese relations or Sino-American relations.'[31] Abe understood this and was able to use Trump's hardline China policy as cover for strengthening Japan's position vis-à-vis China by enacting domestic economic and security reforms, which reinforced the US–Japan security alliance and built new networks.[32]

Abe was not always successful in his relations with Trump. The United States' withdrawal from the Trans-Pacific Partnership (TPP) in 2017 was a strategic blow to Japan, which viewed the bloc as an important tool for supporting the rules-based order in Asia. Although the Japan-led resurrection of the trading bloc in 2018 in the form of the Comprehensive and Progressive Agreement for Trans-Pacific Partnership (CPTPP) was a highlight of Abe's foreign policy in his second term, the US remains outside the bloc. Abe favoured a hard line against North Korea, and did not welcome

Trump's diplomatic courtship of North Korean leader Kim Jong-un, which resulted in three bilateral summits in 2018–19.[33] Even so, among Japan's G7 peers Abe was surely the most productive in managing the diplomatic turbulence of Trump's presidency and securing advantage for Japan.

III

The US and Japan are now experiencing heightened political uncertainty. In Japan, the neologism *moshitora*, or 'what if Trump wins?', has emerged, reflecting Japanese unease about the return of Trump's diplomatic roller-coaster.[34] Japan's strategic concerns include whether Trump, like Carter before him, might seek to remove US forces from South Korea. Such a move could fuel doubts in Seoul about the reliability of US extended deterrence, adding momentum to the debate about whether South Korea should have its own nuclear-weapons capability.[35] Should it develop one, all of Japan's nearest neighbours – China, the Koreas and Russia – would possess nuclear weapons. Relatedly, Tokyo fears the damage that a Trumpian 'America First' programme might do to the various strategic groupings of which the US and Japan are members, such as the US–Japan–South Korea and US–Japan–Philippines trilateral relationships that the Biden administration has sought to nurture. Other worries include the sustainability of recent US–Japan cooperation in the realm of economic security given Trump's domestic focus and pledge to impose a 10% tariff on all imports into the US.[36]

Kishida, who was Japan's foreign minister during the first seven months or so of Trump's administration, will draw some comfort from his own programme of defence reform. This includes raising Japanese defence spending to 2% of GDP by 2027–28, with the hope that this will assuage Trump's frequently stated desire for greater burden-sharing among US allies. Pressure from a Trump White House might in fact prove useful in accelerating Kishida's reforms.[37] But neither he nor any of the LDP favourites to succeed him as prime minister possesses the strategic charm that Abe was able to wield so effectively with Trump.

Tokyo's predicament has been aggravated by unrest among the LDP factions. In late 2023, a financial scandal broke involving the largest of the party's six factions, the right-leaning Seiwa Seisaku Kenkyūkai (Seiwakai), formerly Abe's faction, and that of key party powerbroker Nikai Toshihiro (the Shisuikai faction).[38] In breadth and importance, this scandal ranks alongside the insider-trading and corruption scandal that brought down prime minister Takeshita Noboru in 1989 and led to the LDP's fall from power in 1993. In a bid to quell public anger, Kishida announced in January 2024 that he was dissolving his own faction, the dovish Kōchikai, which prompted Seiwakai and Shisuikai to do the same.[39]

All this leaves Kishida both strengthened and weakened. The dissolution of Seiwakai and Nikai's decision not to seek re-election have removed two major constraints on Kishida's freedom of action and considerably enhanced the power of the party's central executive. Never before has an LDP prime minister eliminated his intra-party political adversaries in this way. Yet in doing so Kishida may have left the party structurally unsound. Much as the death of prime minister Obuchi Keizo in 2000 precipitated a power shift within the LDP in favour of the then-resurgent Seiwakai – four of the subsequent five LDP prime ministers hailed from this faction[40] – so the death of Abe in 2022 may be seen as marking another structural break in Japanese politics.

Kishida's April 2024 state visit to the US, during which he participated in the first-ever US–Japan–Philippines trilateral summit and delivered only the second address by a Japanese prime minister to a joint session of the US Congress, marked another high point in US–Japan relations. The Biden–Kishida relationship could now be said to rival those of Trump–Abe, Bush–Koizumi and Reagan–Nakasone. If Biden wins re-election in November, Japan will hope for a few more years of diplomatic stability to build on this success, notwithstanding the potentially high turnover of Japanese prime ministers as the LDP reorganises itself.

Even if Biden does win, questions will remain about the long-term direction of US diplomacy. Biden could still prove to be the last of the generation of US leaders espousing liberal internationalism. Kishida, meanwhile, faces an LDP leadership election in September amid sagging poll ratings, and lower- and upper-house elections are due by October 2024 and July 2025, respectively. The Biden–Kishida Joint Leaders'

Statement released on 10 April spoke of the 'unprecedented heights' reached by the US–Japan alliance since Biden took office.[41] This is a fair description. Yet China's increasingly coercive behaviour in the Asia-Pacific, along with the growing links between China and Russia and Russia and North Korea, mean that the strategic importance of the US–Japan relationship will only increase. Kishida's assertion in his speech to the US Congress that Japan had transformed itself from 'a reticent ally, recovering from the devastation of World War II, to a strong, committed ally, looking outward to the world' was a signal of Japan's desire to play a greater role in its partnership with the US. Detecting an 'undercurrent of self-doubt' about America's proper role in the world, Kishida described Japan as the 'United States' closest friend' and as 'ready to do what is necessary' to help defend 'freedom, democracy, and the rule of law'.[42] Clearly Japan sees its relationship with the United States as special, and the United States may well need it if it decides to continue upholding these values.

Notes

1   See John Dower, *Embracing Defeat: Japan in the Aftermath of World War II* (London: Penguin Books, 1999), p. 23.

2   *Ibid.*, p. 23.

3   Michael Schaller, *Altered States: The United States and Japan Since the Occupation* (Oxford: Oxford University Press, 1997), p. 7.

4   This language can be found in Article 9 of the Constitution of Japan, available at https://japan.kantei.go.jp/constitution_and_government_of_japan/constitution_e.html.

5   Kenneth B. Pyle, *The Making of Modern Japan* (Lexington, MA: D.C. Heath and Company, 1996), p. 219.

6   John Dower writes in his book, *Embracing Defeat*, that 'no modern nation has ever rested on a more alien constitution – or a more unique wedding of monarchism, democratic idealism, and pacifism; and few, if any, alien documents have ever been as thoroughly internalized and vigorously defended as this national charter would come to be'. Dower, *Embracing Defeat*, p. 347.

7   Eric Hobsbawm, *Age of Extremes: The Short Twentieth Century, 1914–1991* (London: Michael Joseph, 1994), p. 268.

8   Cabinet Secretariat of Japan, 'National Security Strategy of Japan', December 2022, p. 5.

9   Schaller, *Altered States*, p. 4.

10 For the most complete account of the LDP's factions that this author has read, see Nakakita Koji, *Jimintō 'Ikkyō' no Jitsuzō* [The true face of the LDP's dominance] (Tokyo: Chuko Shinsho, 2021), especially pp. 14–45. One feature of the party's factions historically has been their high degree of

institutionalisation, which has helped reinforce party discipline.

11 Data on the number of prime ministers and the lengths of their premierships is taken from Yawata Kazuo, *Nihon No Sōri Daijin Taizen* [Compendium of prime ministers of Japan] (Tokyo: President, 2022).

12 Bradley Richardson, *Japanese Democracy: Power, Coordination, and Performance* (New Haven, CT: Yale University Press, 1997), p. 100.

13 Aurelia George Mulgan, *The Abe Administration and the Rise of the Prime Ministerial Executive* (Abingdon: Routledge, 2018), p. 11.

14 Quoted in Schaller, *Altered States*, p. 211; and Walter LaFeber, *The Clash: US–Japanese Relations Throughout History* (New York: W. W. Norton & Company, 1997), p. 349.

15 Ohira Masayoshi, prime minister from 1978 until his death in 1980, was a good example of this: he was pilloried as the 'ah, ooh prime minister' (*ā ū saishō*) after his faltering speaking style. But Ohira, who served as foreign minister during Tanaka Kakuei's premiership in 1972–74, was also a key player in Japan's normalisation of relations with China. See Hattori Ryuji, *Nicchū Kokkō Seijōka, Tanaka Kakuei, Ōhira Masayoshi, Kanryōtachi no Chōsen* [The normalisation of Japan–China relations: the challenge for Tanaka Kakuei, Ohira Masayoshi and the bureaucrats] (Tokyo: Chuko Shinsho, 2012), p. 19.

16 According to documents released in 2003 and analysed by *Nikkei Business* in 2022, Kissinger said during a visit to China that while Japanese diplomats swear to keep a secret, they only mean they'll do so for 72 hours. See Haruaki Deguchi, 'Kage de Nihon wo Jōdan no Neta ni Shita Beikoku Kissinjā to Chūgoku' [The United States' Kissinger and China make jokes at Japan's expense behind the scenes], *Nikkei Business*, 18 November 2022, https://business.nikkei.com/atcl/gen/19/00516/110900003/.

17 See Schaller, *Altered States*, p. 228.

18 See Ryuji Hattori, *Eisaku Satō, Japanese Prime Minister, 1964–72: Okinawa, Foreign Relations, Domestic Politics and the Nobel Prize* (Abingdon: Routledge, 2020), p. 215.

19 *Ibid.*, p. 225.

20 Abe was also a grand-nephew of Sato and a grandson of Kishi Nobusuke, who was prime minister in 1957–60.

21 Abe Shinzo, *Abe Shinzō Kaiko Roku* [Abe Shinzo's memoirs] (Tokyo: Chuokoron Shinsha, 2023), p. 179.

22 Abe's 'golf diplomacy' throughout his relationship with Donald Trump echoed that of his grandfather in relation to Dwight Eisenhower. See 'Eisenhower Takes Kishi Out for Golf: Japanese–U.S. Ties Tested Over 18 Holes as President Employs a Little-used Diplomatic Technique on Premier', *New York Times*, 20 June 1957, https://timesmachine.nytimes.com/timesmachine/1957/06/20/issue.html.

23 Abe, *Abe Shinzō Kaiko Roku*, p. 180.

24 See Reiji Yoshida, 'Koizumi–Bush Friendship One for the Ages', *Japan Times*, 29 June 2006, https://www.japantimes.co.jp/news/2006/06/29/national/koizumi-bush-friendship-one-for-the-ages/; and Sheryl Gay Stolberg, 'Foreign Policy Tries a Little Shake, Rattle and Roll', *New York Times*, 30 June 2006, https://www.

nytimes.com/2006/06/30/world/
asia/30cnd-elvis.html.

25 On Japan's reaction to Carter's plan,
see Larry A. Niksch, 'U.S. Troop
Withdrawal from South Korea: Past
Shortcomings and Future Prospects',
Asian Survey, vol. 21, no. 3, March
1981, p. 330.

26 See White House, Office of the Press
Secretary, 'Remarks by President
Obama and President Xi Jinping of
the People's Republic of China After
Bilateral Meeting', 8 June 2013, https://
obamawhitehouse.archives.gov/
the-press-office/2013/06/08/remarks-
president-obama-and-president-xi-
jinping-peoples-republic-china-.

27 See, for example, Stephen Harner,
'After the Obama–Xi Summit:
Pressure on Japan to Concede on
Senkaku/Diaoyu?', *Forbes*, 19 June
2013, https://www.forbes.com/
sites/stephenharner/2013/06/19/
after-the-obama-xi-summit-pressure-
on-japan-to-concede-on-senkakudiaoy
u/?sh=7171cf291d1e.

28 Hattori Ryuji, *Nakasone Yasuhiro,
'Daitōryōteki Shushō' no Kiseki*
[Nakasone Yasuhiro: the trajectory of
a presidential prime minister] (Tokyo:
Chuko Shinsho, 2015), pp. 118–20.

29 For example, while Nakasone pushed
for higher Japanese defence spending
and in 1987 abolished the Japanese
government's self-imposed spending
limit of 1% of GNP, he was only able
to increase spending by a fraction
above that limit. Defence spending
fell back under 1% of GNP after he
left office. The limit was imposed in
1976 by Miki Takeo in the spirit of
the Yoshida Doctrine to ensure that
Japan's burgeoning economy did not

translate into outsized military power.
See Tanaka Akihiko, *Anzen Hoshō,
Sengo 50 Nen no Mosaku* [Security:
an exploration 50 years after the
end of the war] (Tokyo: Yomiuri
Shimbunsha, 1997), pp. 263–4. From
the 1950s to the mid-1960s, Japan's
defence spending had stood at
around 1.1–1.8% of GDP, trending
at under 1% from 1967 until the start
of Nakasone's administration, when
it started to rise. For data on Japan's
defence spending, see Akihiko, *Anzen
Hoshō, Sengo 50 Nen no Mosaku*, p. 301.

30 For Abe's views on China, see,
for example, his *Utsukushii Kuni E*
[Towards a beautiful country] (Tokyo:
Bunshun Shinsho, 2006), pp. 146–56.

31 Quoted by Funabashi Yoichi, 'Foreign
Policy Requires a Keen Sense of
Balance', *Japan Times*, 10 February
2017, https://www.japantimes.co.jp/
opinion/2017/02/10/commentary/
japan-commentary/foreign-policy-
requires-keen-sense-balance/.

32 A 2020 article in the *American Interest*
by a presumably high-level Japanese
official using the byline 'Y.A.' does
a good job setting out the Japanese
perspective. See Y.A., 'The Virtues of
a Confrontational China Strategy',
American Interest, 10 April 2020,
https://www.the-american-interest.
com/2020/04/10/the-virtues-of-a-
confrontational-china-strategy/.

33 Abe, *Abe Shinzō Kaiko Roku*, p. 292.

34 *Moshitora* is formed by combining
the Japanese word for 'if' (*moshi*) and
the first two characters of Trump's
name as rendered in Japanese (in
full, *To-ra-n-pu*). Variants include
hobotora ('nearly Trump') and *majitora*
('Trump, really?').

35 See Ramon Pacheco Pardo, 'South Korea Could Get Away with the Bomb', *Foreign Policy*, 16 March 2023, https://foreignpolicy.com/2023/03/16/south-korea-nuclear-weapons-military-defense-security-proliferation-npt/.

36 See Mike Dolan, 'Trump Tariff Plans Spur Talk of Inflation 2.0', Reuters, 1 March 2024, https://www.reuters.com/markets/us/trump-tariff-plans-spur-talk-inflation-20-mike-dolan-2024-03-01/.

37 *Gaiatsu* is a term used in Japan to describe foreign pressure that results in reforms that would otherwise be avoided.

38 Around 100 members of the Japanese Diet (parliament) belonged to Seiwakai.

39 Kōchikai had been the LDP's oldest faction.

40 They were Mori Yoshiro, Koizumi Junichiro, Abe Shinzo and Fukuda Yasuo.

41 White House, 'United States–Japan Joint Leaders' Statement', 10 April 2024, https://www.whitehouse.gov/briefing-room/statements-releases/2024/04/10/united-states-japan-joint-leaders-statement/.

42 'Full Text of Japanese Prime Minister Kishida's Speech to U.S. Congress', Nikkei Asia, 12 April 2024, https://asia.nikkei.com/Politics/International-relations/Full-text-of-Japanese-Prime-Minister-Kishida-s-speech-to-U.S.-Congress.

Printed in the United States
by Baker & Taylor Publisher Services